THE INSTITUTE FOR GOVERNMENT RESEARCH
OF
THE BROOKINGS INSTITUTION

STUDIES IN ADMINISTRATION No. 29
For a full list of publications see the end of the book.

THE BROOKINGS INSTITUTION

The Brookings Institution—Devoted to Public Service through Research and Training in the Social Sciences—was incorporated on December 8, 1927. Broadly stated, the Institution has two primary purposes: The first is to aid constructively in the development of sound national policies; and the second is to offer training of a super-graduate character to students of the social sciences. The Institution will maintain a series of co-operating institutes, equipped to carry out comprehensive and interrelated research projects.

The responsibility for the final determination of the Institution's policies and its program of work and for the administration of its endowment is vested in a self-perpetuating Board of Trustees. The Trustees have, however, defined their position with reference to the investigations conducted by the Institution in a by-law provision reading as follows: "The primary function of the Trustees is not to express their views upon the scientific investigations conducted by any division of the Institution, but only to make it possible for such scientific work to be done under the most favorable auspices." Major responsibility for "formulating general policies and co-ordinating the activities of the various divisions of the Institution" is vested in the President. The by-laws provide also that "there shall be an Advisory Council selected by the President from among the scientific staff of the Institution and representing the different divisions of the Institution."

ADMINISTRATIVE LEGISLATION
AND ADJUDICATION

ADMINISTRATIVE LEGISLATION AND ADJUDICATION

BY

FREDERICK F. BLACHLY

AND

MIRIAM E. OATMAN

WASHINGTON, D.C.

THE BROOKINGS INSTITUTION

1934

7

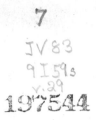

Printed in the United States of America
George Banta Publishing Company
Menasha, Wisconsin

DIRECTOR'S PREFACE

With the beginning of the twentieth century came the realization that the cumbersome methods of enacting and administering certain types of social legislation called for radical revision. Vexatious delays, involved and expensive litigation, and the artificiality of the established procedures frequently combined to defeat the very purposes of the law. For example, it was found that in formulating rules to safeguard the worker from industrial accidents the legislature not only lacked the technical knowledge of the safety engineer and other experts, but it lacked the requisite speed of action. New inventions coming in unending array called for new safeguards, if life and limb were to be secure. Before the consciousness of these needs had become articulate in the legislative mind still newer inventions had come, calling for legislative relief. The legislature, established as a large deliberative body, a cross-section of the public and not a professional group of public administrators, could not keep pace with the rapidity of industrial development.

Likewise in the field of administering employers' liability for industrial accidents, the accepted method of common law action in the courts was proving ineffective. The cost and delay of litigation frequently constituted a denial of justice. To meet this and related groups of problems, administrative commissions were established. To these commissions was delegated a combination of administrative, legislative, and judicial powers. For the time being this experiment met with popular success. The idea spread to other fields of government activity and innumerable commissions were established, with every conceivable distribution of powers. These commissions differed among themselves in every detail

vii

of organization, function, practice, and procedure. The methods of control represented different and conflicting points of view. Thus there settled over the framework of government a fog of bewildering confusion. In the federal government alone there are some sixty different administrative tribunals making judicial decisions affecting private rights. These do not proceed according to any single form, do not follow any uniform procedure, and do not fit in as integral parts of a coherent or intelligible system.

Perhaps even more confusing is the great number of authorities exercising sub-legislative powers. Some of their regulations impinge upon private rights and have the binding character of law. Others control public expenditures. Still others deal with the organization and distribution of administrative powers. There is no set procedure established. There is, save in a few instances, no provision for the publication of decrees. There is no official depository where one may ascertain the sum total of administrative rules and regulations that constitute a part of the law of the land. It would be impossible for any human being to be sure that he has access to all the rules and regulations upon any given subject. All of this confusion and uncertainty has obviously been accentuated by the new administrative agencies created to deal with the present emergency.

In the movement which led to the creation of these administrative devices, attention was so concentrated upon the evils of the old cumbersome system that little attention was given to certain generally accepted principles of government and administration. They were largely ignored in the haste and confusion of the new development. For the same administrative officers to be made legislators, judges, and administrators in the same case has tended to produce the bad results which have always followed the concentration of these powers in a single authority. That abuses have not been worse is a singular tribute to the unusual personnel generally found in the more important commissions.

The authors have attempted to analyze the whole situation in the federal government in the light of what they regard as valid principles of public administration. They have sought to determine how technical efficiency and speed in working out legislative detail and economy of time and effort in the administration of legal rules may be accomplished, while providing an intelligent method of control and a just and impartial system of administration. They find that certain principles seem to indicate rather clearly the avenues of escape from the present jungle of confusion.

This volume is the fruit of ten years of study in administration in America and abroad. Happily, the authors find that American experience affords the basic materials out of which an effective system of administration can be evolved. It is anticipated that this study ultimately will be extended into the same problems in state administration.

The authors are indebted to innumerable federal officials, many of whom are serving on administrative commissions and courts, for advice and counsel, and particularly to Professor John P. Comer, who read the manuscript and contributed many helpful suggestions.

The members of the committee appointed to co-operate with the authors in the preparation of this volume were Lewis Meriam, Laurence F. Schmeckebier, and the Director.

ARNOLD BENNETT HALL
Director

Institute for Government Research
    October 1934

CONTENTS

CONTENTS

DEVELOPMENT AND SIGNIFICANCE OF ADMINISTRATIVE LEGISLATION AND ADMINISTRATIVE ADJUDICATION

The twentieth century has witnessed a remarkable development in administrative legislation and administrative adjudication. More and more frequently, the authorities charged with the administration of the law are permitted or even required to issue general rules and regulations. Such action is administrative legislation, since the regulations thus established become, for all practical purposes, a component part of the law itself. More and more frequently, also, administrative authorities must decide questions affecting definite rights. When the action of the administration upon such a question gives rise to a controversy which is decided by an administrative authority acting in a judicial capacity, such a decision is really judicial in nature. Even though a rigid separation of powers is established in theory, the force of necessity has been too strong for it. The most orthodox doctrinaires have been driven to the recognition of what they call "quasi-legislative" and "quasi-judicial" functions, performed as a part of the administrative process. In the United States today, the regulations issued and the decisions made by administrative authorities are so numerous, so weighty, and so far-reaching that the daily life of every individual citizen is affected by them. Administrative legislation and administrative adjudication have become significant features in the work of government.

The reasons for this important development in public administration are both quantitative and qualitative. During the last generation the state has assumed many new functions, thus necessitating the making of countless rules and regulations and the rendering of numerous decisions. These functions, moreover, are so different from the traditional tasks of government that new methods of procedure have become imperative.

Under the compulsion of the changed conditions brought about largely by mechanical and technological development, the modern state has rapidly ceased to resemble the old political organization, whose chief functions were defense, the administration of justice, and the exercise of a rather narrow police power. "Today, the state acts also as doctor, nurse, teacher, insurance organizer, house builder, sanitary engineer, chemist, railway controller, supplier of gas, water and electricity, town planner, pensions distributor, provider of transport, hospital organizer, road-maker, and in a large number of other capacities."[1] More and more intimately the state regulates the day-by-day affairs of the community. It regulates banks, insurance companies, building and loan associations, investment companies, omnibus lines, electric light and power companies, telephone and telegraph companies, radio and wireless operations, water-power production, and many other enterprises and undertakings.

Under the stress of the crisis which has recently involved the economic system of the world, many states, including our own federal government, have been forced to assume a considerable degree of control over foreign competition, agricultural production and distribution, the

---

[1] *Committee on Ministers' Powers*, Vol. II, 1932, *Minutes of Evidence*, p. 52 (memorandum of W. A. Robson).

production and distribution of raw materials such as coal and oil, the management and development of forests, and other fundamentally important economic enterprises. To prevent the evils resulting from ruinous domestic competition, over-production, and under-consumption, Congress and the national administration have been compelled to control manufacturing by establishing (and as far as possible enforcing) maximum working hours, minimum rates of pay, exclusion of unfair practices, and so on. A similar type of control has been exercised over the distribution of goods and services.

The supplying of money and credit has become an important government enterprise. In addition to acting as the authority to control the currency, the government has been forced to act as a great credit agency, lending money, either directly or through subsidies, to banks, railroads, insurance companies, private business undertakings, and owners of homes and farms. Because of the extensive unemployment which has prevailed for several years, various units of government have been compelled to provide for temporary employment and poor relief on an unprecedented scale; also to construct public works and to undertake numerous enterprises directly offering employment to those who cannot secure it elsewhere.

This increase in government business has had profound effects upon administration. In the first place, it has resulted in placing upon the administrative branch of the government a great variety of functions hardly dreamed of only a few years ago. This added burden has necessitated the establishment of new authorities, the re-allocation of work, the changing of relationships among different authorities, the establishment of a large and variously equipped personnel, the development of new methods for its control, and the devising of new methods, rules, and procedures by which work is carried on.

A change of even greater significance is the increased proportion of administrative legislation involved in the rapid assumption of new functions by the state. The legislative body, overburdened with difficult problems of policy, is proportionately less able to consider matters of detail, which must therefore be left to the executive and administrative authorities. The specialized nature of certain undertakings sanctioned by the legislature, and the desire occasionally expressed by the administration to have a free hand in carrying out particular functions, contribute toward the rapidly developing importance of administrative legislation.

But this is not all. The vast increase of government business, particularly that of a regulatory or controlling type, compels the administration to make many decisions which are very like judicial decisions in nature. So great is their number, so technical is the knowledge required for making them, so intermingled may they be with the administrative process, so important is it that they be made rapidly, that the regular judicial courts are obviously not the proper authorities to make them. The work of rendering these decisions must be done by some sort of administrative authorities: either the active administration itself, or administrative tribunals.

The administration today is thus a great deal more than a mere machine for the application of law. To an increasing extent it has become a creator of law; in this sense and within the limits of their respective competences, the administrative departments and agencies resemble a group of special legislative bodies. The administration is the authority which, in an increasing number of instances, intervenes between the legislature and the ordinary citizen. The general rules and principles set forth in statutes must often be filled in, extended, and made more definite, before they can be applied in individual cases. In other words, the administration is called upon to render the law tangible to the citizen. In so doing it must exercise power which partakes of the nature of legislative power.

Today, also, the administrative process must necessarily pass beyond the mere enforcement of law, not only in respect to the creation of law, but also in respect to the determination of rights. In many instances, the determination of rights is an integral part of the administrative process; and the finding of facts by administrative bodies, as a part of their regular work, frequently involves the same kinds of procedures and processes as the finding of facts by a court. But above and beyond this, the administration often performs acts of an unmistakably judicial nature which are not a part of the ordinary routine work of carrying out various functions, but are special acts of administrative adjudication.

I. GROWTH OF ADMINISTRATIVE LEGISLATION AND ADMINISTRATIVE ADJUDICATION

Although the rapid growth of administrative legislation and administrative adjudication in the United States is common to both the state and the federal governments, several causes have made it particularly noticeable in the latter. The first cause which should be mentioned is the demonstrated inadequacy of state regulation of such matters as child labor, the purity of foods and drugs, lotteries, bankruptcies, and banking and corporation practices. State regulation has not been able to control these and similar situations that demanded national regulation. In the second place, the wealth of the country is so unevenly distributed that it is impossible for some of the poorer localities or states to carry out various functions now considered necessary, such as highways, poor relief, education, public health, and so on. In the third place, technologically, commercially, and industrially, the nation rather than the state is the effective unit. Business enterprise is national in scope, and public regulation must be the same. "American business is today dominated by its national characteristics—buying and selling without regard to state lines, transportation without regard to state lines; but above all, it is dominated by the fact that it looks toward and culminates in, in short, exists for the interstate market."[2] Since experience has shown that local regulation of activities national in scope can end in nothing but confusion and disaster, the alternative, national regulation, could hardly have been avoided.

There are many special activities which demand national regulation and national administration because their nature requires a unified system of control. Among such activities should be mentioned: control over radio and other means of communication, control over aviation, control over water power, prevention of floods, the organization of a system of national highways, and the prevention of contagious plant and animal diseases. Several kinds of work now undertaken by the national government, such as control over securities, control over stock exchanges, control over crop production, and the stabilization of business and industry, must, if done at all, be done on a national scale. The center of government activity today, particularly in respect to the grand regulatory and controlling functions, is the nation. It

[2] Edward S. Corwin, "Congress's Power to Prohibit Commerce a Crucial Constitutional Issue," *18 Cornell Law Quarterly* 502.

is in these regulatory activities that there is the maximum amount of government intervention by way of sub-legislative rules and regulations and by way of administrative adjudication.

A factor that has contributed to the development of administrative legislation and administrative adjudication in the federal government is the particular method by which the government has intervened in the economic life of the nation. Instead of attempting to own and manage the railroads, electric light and power plants and their distributing systems, radio, telegraph and telephone lines, and so on, as has been done in Germany and to a lesser extent in France; and instead of controlling various public utilities and special types of business by way of contractual concessions, as France has done, the United States has adopted the method of public regulation of private enterprise.

This choice of methods carries with it certain consequences. When the state owns economic enterprises, the problems regarding them are largely problems of internal management, plus various questions of policy. When it controls economic enterprises by contractual concessions, the regulations which it desires to impose may be contained in the terms of the contract, and may be enforced by the courts as if they were ordinary contractual agreements.

When, on the other hand, the state attempts to exercise a day-by-day regulation over private economic enterprise, it is confronted with very difficult administrative problems. Instead of agreeing on terms, or controlling the internal management of its own business, it is regulating and controlling a business which it does not own, the internal management of which is entrusted to private individuals, the fiscal relationships of which must meet the necessities of private profit as well as the requirements of public service.

For example, if a government owns the railways it may adopt a fiscal policy of operating under rates that will barely cover expenditures, or even of operating at a loss. It may make up such loss out of the general budget. On the other hand, it may seek to make a profit from the operations of its railroads. Either choice is purely a matter of fiscal policy. The rules and regulations that are established by the government for the operation of the railways are regulations of internal management. But when the government attempts to regulate private enterprises, some of the administrative rules and regulations will have the nature of legislation, and some of the decisions made by the administrative authority will have the nature of judicial decisions.

Another important factor is the extent to which intervention is attempted. When the federal government endeavors to regulate practically the whole economic life of the nation, through such agencies as the National Recovery Administration and the Agricultural Adjustment Administration, the amount of administrative legislation and administrative adjudication must necessarily be greatly increased. Each industrial or other economic code adopted by the administration (even though private agencies have done much in formulating it), is virtually an act of administrative legislation. The enforcement of these codes by the government will inevitably involve the making of a multitude of decisions of a quasi-judicial nature, either by such authorities as may be established to administer the far-reaching economic policies, or by special administrative tribunals. If, on the other hand, the enforcement of all codes were placed upon the shoulders of established trade associations or guilds, a much smaller number of quasi-judicial decisions would have to be made by the government authorities.[3]

Other factors of less general importance have added greatly to the amount of administrative legislation and administrative adjudication included in the work of our federal government. One of these is the practice of land grants. The task of selling and giving a continent to individuals has inevitably given rise to many controversies demanding administrative adjudication. The fact that certain lands have been found valuable not only for homestead purposes, farming, grazing, or timber, but also for petroleum, copper, silver, gold, and other minerals, has increased the necessary quantity of both administrative legislation and administrative adjudication. The recent policies of the United States concerning the admission, exclusion, and expulsion of aliens have compelled the authorities which execute these policies to engage in the work of administrative legislation to a certain extent, and in that of administrative adjudication to a very considerable extent. The various uses made by Congress of its power to regulate commerce between the states have added greatly to the legislative and judicial tasks of the administrative authorities.

II. EXTENT OF ADMINISTRATIVE LEGISLATION AND ADMINISTRATIVE ADJUDICATION

It is difficult for one not thoroughly acquainted with the work which the federal government is doing, and the methods by which it is accomplishing its ends, to

[3] We are not concerned here with questions of economic or social policy connected with the regulation of business, but merely with the effects of such regulation upon administrative legislation and administrative adjudication.

realize the extent of administrative legislation and adjudication at present. Some 50 or 60 federal administrative authorities of various kinds, as well as the hundreds of special code authorities, and the score or more of proprietary corporations, are exercising the power to make rules and regulations which intimately affect the rights, liberties, and property of individuals. Among the more important of these authorities, a few will be mentioned as examples: The President of the United States; the heads of the government departments; various boards, commissions, and other authorities, such as the Commissioner of Customs, the Commissioner of the General Land Office, the Commissioner of Indian Affairs, the Bureau of Animal Industry, the Bureau of Plant Industry, the Forest Service, the Bureau of Biological Survey, the Bureau of Agricultural Economics, the Bureau of Plant Quarantine, the Food and Drug Administration, the Aeronautics Branch of the Department of Commerce, the Bureau of Mines, the Commissioner of Immigration and Naturalization, the Civil Service Commission, the Interstate Commerce Commission, the Federal Reserve Board, the Federal Trade Commission, the Shipping Board, the United States Employees' Compensation Commission, the Federal Power Commission, the Federal Communications Commission, the Agricultural Adjustment Administration, the Administrator for Industrial Recovery and the various authorities under him, the Petroleum Administration, the Securities and Exchange Commission, and various other administrative authorities. Such federal proprietary corporations as the Reconstruction Finance Corporation, the Federal Deposit Insurance Corporation, and the Tennessee Valley Authority, may issue certain rules and regulations within their special competence.

In the great majority of instances, these same authorities are also exercising quasi-judicial powers. Furthermore, special provision for rendering administrative judicial decisions has been made through establishing reviewing authorities in various administrative services, and through organizing several administrative courts such as the United States Customs Court, the Court of Customs and Patent Appeals, the Board of Tax Appeals, and the quasi-judicial authorities connected with the National Recovery Administration.

It is impossible to secure accurate statistics regarding the number of sub-legislative acts which are issued by all such authorities each year; or to find out the number of administrative judicial decisions of various sorts which are made by them. Their published rules and regulations cover altogether about eight or ten times as many pages as the acts passed by Congress. Furthermore, some of the administrative regulations have a more immediate and direct effect upon various classes of individuals than do the general provisions of many formal legislative enactments. The decisions of the various authorities which exercise administrative judicial powers are several times as numerous as the recorded decisions of all the federal judicial courts.

III. THE SIGNIFICANCE OF ADMINISTRATIVE LEGISLATION AND ADMINISTRATIVE ADJUDICATION

Administrative legislation and administrative adjudication are important, not merely because of the wide range of personal rights and relationships which they touch and control today, but for several other reasons as well. These two processes are causing a profound transformation in our constitutional system, in our public law, in the organization of various government authorities, in the relationships among them, in methods of handling government business, in procedures, and in remedies against illegal government action. So far-reaching a transformation involves a serious conflict between old and long established principles and methods, and new and slightly tried principles and methods. The change has already shaken such apparently impregnable citadels as the principle of the separation of powers, the doctrine of constitutional limitations, the doctrine of due process of law, the old theory of the relationship between the individual and the law which is commonly called "the supremacy of the law," and the principle of the supremacy of the judiciary as the prime agency for the control of administration.

Upon our system of constitutional law, statutory law, and common law as the chief methods for controlling administration, there has been grafted a rapidly growing administrative law. The latter is formally bound by limitations set through the first-named types of law; but to an ever increasing extent it is breaking away from these limitations, and is developing its own principles, criteria, and methods.

The need in many fields of public administration for more detailed regulations than the legislature can give, and the insistent demand that administrative cases be settled rapidly, are having a remarkable effect upon our government organization. Special advisory authorities are set up to assist the administration in making determinations of policy and in formulating rules and regulations for carrying out the same. Various boards and commissions, endowed with a greater or less degree of independent authority, are being established to carry on particular functions. Special tribunals are being established to handle special types of administrative cases. In several government departments some sort of reviewing authority is being set up to examine and review administrative decisions which have given rise to controversies.

The relationships among various government authorities are undergoing significant changes because of the development of administrative legislation and administrative adjudication. Almost of necessity the administration has had to take an increasingly important place in directing and guiding legislative policy. The chief executive, the heads of departments, and other administrative agencies, instead of merely carrying out the laws, must also participate in their making. The necessities of government are so specific and so technical that these authorities must both assist in shaping the bills to be passed by Congress, and develop the statutory law by many detailed rules and regulations. As the administration has gained in power and influence, Congress has lost a certain amount of prestige because of its apparent inability to handle all of the complicated problems presented to it for consideration, and to work out a definite public policy amid the clamor and confusion caused by the special interests which seek to influence its acts. Yet Congress is acting wisely, in principle at least, by refusing to attempt the impossible, by accepting expert advice from the executive and administrative branches of the government, and by leaving many matters of detail to those who actually apply the law.

The relationship between the administration and the courts is likewise undergoing a process of transformation. The great number of the disputes arising between the individual and the administration as the latter carries out its multitudinous functions, would alone make it impossible for the regular courts, using their regular procedures, to control administration by adjudicating all such disputes. Both the legislature and the courts have found means of relieving the latter of much of this burden. Several administrative courts have been established to decide special kinds of cases. In many instances the legislature has made the decisions of administrative courts and other administrative adjudicating authorities final and conclusive in respect to questions of fact, and in certain instances it has even made them final and conclusive in respect to questions of law. The courts themselves have developed doctrines and criteria as to when they will or will not take jurisdiction over administrative acts; for instance, the doctrine of finality of administrative decisions; the doctrine of the right of the administrative authorities to interpret the law; and the doctrine that where only privileges are concerned, such as the use of the postal service, the securing of government land, or entrance into the United States by aliens, adjudicable rights are not ordinarily involved. By these criteria the courts have freed themselves from deciding many disputes involving administrative action. The Supreme Court, both by legislative action and by virtue of its own rules and criteria as to when it will take jurisdiction, has been freed from passing finally upon administrative cases in any very great numbers.

As administrative adjudication develops, old procedures and complicated rules of evidence seem inapplicable, and new procedures and rules are evolved. Again, since administrative disputes must be counted in hundreds of thousands, the jury system of determining upon facts must give place to a more rapid system. New scientific methods have made it possible to determine many kinds of facts by scientific instruments or methods with such accuracy and certainty as to make the action of a jury on facts of these types meaningless and absurd.

Remedies such as the certiorari, the mandamus, and the injunction are proving inapplicable for the control of the present-day government machine. Suits for damages against officers are proving of little defense to the individual in a state which not only exercises the police power but also carries on countless mechanical operations and exercises innumerable controls. It is more and more clearly apparent that there is a need for suits against the state itself, if the ends of justice are to be served.

One of the most significant things about this transformation of relationships is the fact that it has not been the result of any new social and political philosophy, or of any conscious attempt to create a new machinery for the handling of new problems, but that it has crept upon us almost unobserved. We have added new functions here and there as necessity seemed to demand; we have added new authorities from time to time. We have allowed the relationships among government authorities to make such adjustments and developments as they could, despite the fact that some of the innovations have been out of harmony with our philosophy of government and our constitutional system. We have done little in a formal way regarding rules of evidence; the rules are consequently very uncertain. We have made sporadic and generally unsatisfactory attempts to adapt to the new situation old methods of controlling administration by the use of extraordinary and common law remedies. We have not developed our public law systematically to meet the practical necessities of an increasing burden of public administration; but have rather hoped vaguely that the legislature with the aid of the courts could hold the new wine in the old bottles.

This haphazard development of the functions of administrative legislation and administrative adjudication within our governmental, constitutional, and legal system has led to unfortunate results. One of the most important of these is the general confusion of thought in respect to the handling of present-day problems. Interesting examples of this confusion are the numerous court decisions which, although ostensibly built upon the old constitutional and legal concepts, are compelled by the very pressure of circumstances to introduce new criteria and to recognize new sets of values, some of which —despite the solemn efforts to throw a decent veil of legal fictions and legal terminology about the painful truth—are fundamentally inconsistent with the older doctrines. Thus, since the doctrine of separation of powers forbids the executive or administrative authorities to legislate, although the necessities of practical administration require them to do so, various "distinctions without differences" are made, and the administration continues its work under the innocuous name of quasi-legislative activities. Since the same doctrine forbids such authorities to adjudicate, although they are compelled to do so, their work in this field is called a quasi-judicial function. Such evasions do not make for the clarity of thought that is demanded by the problems of the present day.

Another undoubted evil resulting from the present situation is the fact that there has been introduced into our constitutional and administrative law a complexity which is almost unbelievable. None but highly trained specialists can pretend to know what our public legal system really is; and even among the specialists there are not only doubts and hesitations, but serious disagreements.

Finally, our public law has become so uncertain that it is quite impossible to predict, with any reasonable degree of accuracy, whether specific legislative or sub-legislative action will or will not be declared constitutional. It is impossible even to predict whether a court will or will not take jurisdiction over certain types of administrative determinations. It is impossible to predict whether in a given case a given question will be called a question of fact or a question of law. No one can predict, from the facts or the nature of many cases, whether the court will or will not grant the remedies, such as injunction, mandamus, or certiorari, which have been requested as a means of obtaining relief against the administration.

IV. CONCLUSIONS

If our analysis of the present-day situation is correct, a sound system of administrative legislation and adjudication can be attained only by a proper integration of government functions with the constitutional and legal system, with the structure and organization of administrative agencies, and with the relationships of various authorities one to another. This integration must be accompanied by the establishment of suitable methods and procedures, and by adequate means of control. It is evident that mere repairs and adjustments of the present system, made as occasion arises, and in the manner that seems reasonable and wise in each given case, are wholly insufficient.

In order that the necessary functions of administrative legislation and administrative adjudication may be performed to the best advantage, far-reaching changes must be made in the government structure. A careful study of the principles involved and the experience already available will serve as a basis for working out a system of public law and government organization, methods, procedures, and controls, that will meet the present-day situation and pave the way for future developments. The experience of the United States with administrative legislation and administrative adjudication has been quite extensive and is accumulating at a rapid rate. The experience of other countries which have been confronted with similar problems should also be taken into consideration; for, although we cannot adopt any foreign system, we can learn many things of practical value from the experience of others.

A proper system of administrative legislation and administrative adjudication, operating under adequate controls, was never needed more than it is at present. These administrative processes are the two prime methods of making the adjustments required by a complex and changing social order in which it is necessary to plan socially, to harmonize conflicting interests, to make a multitude of economic innovations, and to control a huge government machine which regulates and directs the activities of citizens in countless ways. The remarkable development of these processes during recent years is a testimony to their value in a crisis.

But they are not mere emergency methods. They are important to the daily work of government. It is therefore essential that they should be set up and managed in the best possible way. Like other parts of the government machinery, they can do great good when correctly established and controlled, or great harm if abused. It is in the hope of securing and disseminating definite knowledge about these important processes, which may be of direct assistance in avoiding dangers and obtaining all the benefits to be expected from a properly organized system of administrative legislation and administrative adjudication, that the present study is undertaken.

CHAPTER II

THE NATURE AND SOURCES OF ADMINISTRATIVE LEGISLATION

Before entering into a consideration of the problems that arise in connection with the process of administrative legislation, it is necessary to discuss the nature of this process. In particular, it is necessary to distinguish between this function and related functions.

In a broad sense, legislation, or the making of rules for the guidance and control of society or for the carrying on of its enterprises, is a continuous process which includes every sort of enforceable rule, from fundamental or constitutional principles, through statutory law and common law, to orders and regulations made in the course of everyday administrative and judicial activities. In contemporary democratic states, the basic rules and regulations, which may be nothing more than a plan for organizing the government system, are presumably set forth in the constitution; the more specific yet generally applicable rules and regulations affecting the rights, liberty, and property of citizens are made by the legislature; the rules and regulations filling in the details of legislative acts, implementing legislative acts, and making necessary adjustments, are formulated by the executive and administrative authorities; the interpretation—which often means, to all intents, the development—of rules of law governing particular cases is made sometimes by the administration, and sometimes by the courts.

Thus, in actual practice today, the validity and the

significance of a rule or regulation, its applicability as law, cannot be determined by identifying the authority that has made it. Every kind of public authority—constituent, legislative, executive, administrative, and judicial—participates in the legislative process. The basic criterion by which legislative action can be recognized is, then, not its source, but its nature. In numerous instances, the true significance of a rule or regulation is not dependent upon the authority that issues it, but upon its meaning and importance in the general scheme of things. A rule or regulation which affects the rights, liberty, property, or conduct of citizens, which is made in correct form and through the proper methods, by an authority empowered to make it, and which can be enforced by some sort of judicial authority, is an act legislative in nature.

It is true that efforts are made to confine the work of legislation to the legislature, under the generally adopted systems of separation of powers. All that these efforts accomplish, however, is to give the legislature the exclusive right to make statutory law. Other types of legislation must continue to be made by other authorities if the functions of government are to be carried on. The executive and administrative authorities, especially, must do a great deal of work that is truly legislative.

Administrative legislation, which is often called sub-legislation, includes rules and regulations made by the executive, by heads of departments, by boards and commissions of various sorts, by administrative tribunals, and even, under certain conditions, by ordinary courts. The methods of exercising sub-legislative power which are employed by these authorities vary so greatly, according to circumstances, that perhaps no complete analysis is possible. Certain important classes of sub-legislation, however, can be distinguished.

I. SUB-LEGISLATION BASED ON DELEGATED POWER

There are several different types of sub-legislation based upon power delegated by the legislative authority to some executive or administrative agency. The practice of delegating power in this way is by no means new, as examination of the various types of sub-legislation will show.

A. The first kind of sub-legislation which should be considered is that which originates in a delegation to the executive of power to organize the government authorities. The extent to which the organization of public administration is a sub-legislative act depends primarily upon the political theory of a given country as to whether it is a legislative or an executive function. In European countries generally, it is considered as primarily executive in nature. Unless the legislature itself wishes to assume this function it is presumed to belong to the executive.

In the United States, on the other hand, it is considered as a legislative function; and, except for making minor adjustments in the administrative machinery, the executive has no inherent power of organization. During the present emergency, however, the President has been given extremely wide powers in organizing and reorganizing the government departments.[1] Under these powers, there have been numerous transfers of functions from one department to another; several consolidations have taken place; several government units have been abolished; and various divisions or bureaus have been created.

[1] Act of Mar. 3, 1933, 47 Stat. L. 1517.

By the National Industrial Recovery Act,[2] the President is "authorized to establish such agencies, to accept and utilize such voluntary and uncompensated services, to appoint, without regard to the provisions of the civil service, such officers and employees, and to utilize such federal officers and employees, and with the consent of the state, such state and local officers and employees, as he may find necessary, to prescribe their authorities, duties, responsibilities, and tenure, and, without regard to the Classification Act of 1923 . . . to fix the compensation of any officers and employees so appointed." In exercising this and other authorizations to organize government agencies, during the first year of his administration the President established a National Emergency Council, a Science Advisory Board under the National Research Council, a Central Statistical Board, a Federal Co-ordinator of Transportation, a Federal Emergency Administration of Public Works, an Executive Council, a Public Works Emergency Housing Corporation, and a Commodity Credit Corporation; and in addition he has created a Federal Civic Works Administration, a Federal Alcohol Control Administration,[3] and various other authorities. The National Industrial Recovery Administration, with all of its various ramifications, was established by executive authority. The President has thus exercised his delegated powers in determining the nature of the organization and the methods of administration of a great number of very important agencies.

B. A type of sub-legislation, which is closely related

[2] Act of June 16, 1933, 48 Stat. L. 195.
[3] The numbers of the executive orders which provided for these organizations are: 6433-A, 6238, 6225, 6196, 6252, 6202-A, 6470, 6340, 6420-B, and 6474.

to the foregoing, is based on a delegation of power to make rules and regulations affecting the legal rights of persons employed in the government services. This power, as stated above, may be exercised in connection with the power to organize such services; but it is often used quite independently. Examples of this type of sub-legislation are the rules, regulations, schedules, classifications, and so on, issued by the Civil Service Commission, the Personnel Classification Board, and the President of the United States when he exercises his special powers of control.

C. Another type of administrative legislation depends upon the delegation to the chief executive or to some other authority of power to make rules and regulations which affect the rights of citizens, through such methods as decrees, executive orders, public announcements, or proclamations. Recent examples of such acts are the declaration of a bank holiday;[4] the proclamation of processing taxes by the Secretary of Agriculture;[5] and the use of the regulatory powers bestowed on the President in respect to transactions in foreign exchange, transfer of credit, export, hoarding, melting, or earmarking of gold or silver coin or bullion or currency.[6] The Agricultural Adjustment Act[7] of 1933 provides that the Secretary of Agriculture may issue licenses permitting the commercial handling of any agricultural commodity or product thereof, or any competing commodity or product thereof; and that such licenses shall be "subject to such terms and conditions . . . as may be necessary to eliminate unfair practices or charges that prevent or tend to prevent the

---

[4] 73 Cong. 1 sess., Session Laws, Proclamation Section, p. 1.
[5] For instance, AAA Cotton Regulations, Series 2, Item 9.
[6] 73 Cong. 1 sess., Session Laws, Proclamation Section, p. 1.
[7] 48 Stat. L. 35.

effectuation of the declared policy and the restoration of normal economic conditions in the marketing of such commodities or products and the financing thereof."

D. The types of administrative regulation just described may overlap, but do not cover, the large and familiar category of instances in which the legislature expresses its will in a law couched in general terms, and leaves to the executive or administrative officers the task of filling in details. Sub-legislation of this kind takes place, for instance, when the Secretary of Agriculture, acting to carry out the will of Congress as expressed in law, makes detailed rules and regulations governing the use of the public forests, grazing lands, and mineral lands. How far Congress should go in laying down norms, standards, and methods by which the action of the administration will be controlled is still an open question. In the act creating the National Recovery Administration the purpose of the legislature is couched in such general terms as to permit the interpretation that the President has been given practically uncontrolled discretionary power to prescribe regulations for industry, to control the interstate transportation of oil, and to change tariff rates, the only limitation being that the purpose of his activity must be "to rehabilitate industry," "relieve unemployment," "eliminate unfair trade practices," and otherwise "provide for the general welfare."[8] The ideal legislative basis for detailed sub-legislation is not only a theoretical problem of constitutional law, but is likewise one of the most important practical problems connected with the whole process of administrative legislation.

E. Another type of administrative legislation based

[8] "Some Legal Aspects of the National Industrial Recovery Act," 47 *Harvard Law Review* 85.

on delegated power occurs when a law is passed whose enforcement depends upon the action or finding of an executive officer or administrative authority. The classical example of this type of sub-legislation is that provided for in an act of Congress passed in 1890,[9] which authorizes the President to exclude from importation into the United States products of foreign countries that unjustly discriminate against the importation therein of products of the United States. Regarding this provision, the Supreme Court said: "Although the legislature cannot delegate its powers to make a law, yet it can delegate a power to determine some fact or state of things upon which the law may depend."[10] Authorization of this same type of sub-legislation is found in the law providing for pay adjustments of federal employees, in accordance with the index figures of the cost of living, which are established by executive order after investigations by certain agencies of the government.[11]

An important field of administrative legislation is provided for in the Agricultural Adjustment Act of 1933.[12] This act permits the President, when the foreign commerce of the United States is adversely affected by reason of the depreciation of the value of the currency of any other government, or when action is necessary to regulate and maintain the parity of currency issues of the United States, or when an emergency requires the expansion of credit, or when an expansion of credit is necessary to secure by international agreement a stabilization at proper levels of the currencies of various governments, to conduct open market operations, establish by

[9] 26 Stat. L. 415, Sec. 4.
[10] *Field* v. *Clark*, 143 U. S. 649, 694, quoting Locke's Appeal, 72 Pa. St. 491.
[11] 48 Stat. L. 13, Sec. 3 (a) and (b).
[12] 48 Stat. L. 51, Sec. 43.

proclamation the fixed weight of the gold dollar and the silver dollar, and take various other financial measures.

F. A delegation of sub-legislative power is sometimes made in the form of a statutory authorization of certain executive or administrative authorities to establish certain standards, norms, or principles. A few examples of this are: The laws permitting the Secretary of the Treasury to establish standards of purity of tea;[13] requiring railways to keep their accounts in the manner prescribed by the Interstate Commerce Commission;[14] bestowing upon the Interstate Commerce Commission the power to determine the advisability of making a lower rate for a longer haul than for a shorter haul;[15] permitting the Federal Reserve Board to make rules and regulations under which national banks may act as trustees, executors, and so on;[16] permitting the Interstate Commerce Commission to determine what shall be standard equipment for safety of railways;[17] giving to the Shipping Board the power to determine the type, size, speed, and other characteristics of vessels used in ocean mail service;[18] and authorizing the American Railway Association and the Interstate Commerce Commission to designate the standard height and the maximum variation of drawbars for freight cars.[19]

G. Where executive or administrative officers are given the power to permit exemptions from the ordinary operation of the laws under certain conditions, there is manifestly a delegation of legislative power. Thus, under

[13] Tea Inspection Act of Mar. 2, 1897, 29 Stat. L. 604.
[14] 24 Stat. L. 386, Sec. 20; 41 Stat. L. 493, Sec. 435.
[15] 24 Stat. L. 380, Sec. 4; 36 Stat. L. 548, Sec. 8.
[16] 38 Stat. L. 262, Sec. 10 (k).
[17] 36 Stat. L. 298, Secs. 2 and 3.
[18] 45 Stat. L. 693, Sec. 403.
[19] 27 Stat. L. 531, Sec. 5.

a recent statute the Secretary of the Treasury was authorized to permit postponement of payment of processing
taxes for a period not exceeding 90 days.[20]

II. SUB-LEGISLATION BASED ON RE-DELEGATED POWER

Sometimes the President or other officer who is authorized to exercise certain powers of sub-legislation is
permitted to delegate said powers to subordinates. For
example, the Industrial Recovery Act of 1933[21] provides: "The President may delegate any of his functions
and powers under this title to such officers, agents, and
employees as he may designate or appoint, and may establish an industrial planning and research agency to aid
in carrying out his functions under this title." Section 8
(b) of the same act provides: "The President may, in
his discretion, in order to avoid conflicts in the administration of the Agricultural Adjustment Act and this title,
delegate any of his functions and powers under this title
with respect to trades, industries, or subdivisions thereof
which are engaged in the handling of any agricultural
commodity or product thereof, or of any competing commodity or product thereof to the Secretary of Agriculture."[22]

III. SPECIAL TYPES OF DELEGATION

A. One of the newer methods by which Congress has
delegated legislative functions is found in the Industrial
Recovery Act, wherein Congress delegates to the President the right of approving codes.[23] This is equivalent to
a wide delegation of sub-legislative power, since upon approval "the provisions of such code shall be the standards
of fair competition for such trade or industry or sub-

[20] 48 Stat. L. 41, Sec. 19 (b).
[21] 48 Stat. L. 195, Sec. 2 (b).
[22] 48 Stat. L. 199.
[23] 48 Stat. L. 196, Sec. 3 (a) and (b).

division thereof;" and violations of the codes are misdemeanors subject to penalties enforceable by the courts.[24] In other words, these codes become law when approved by the President, just as they might become law upon passage by the legislature.

B. Government departments or authorities may be given power to issue instructions for the carrying out of some government activity. Thus, the Commissioner of the Land Office, almost from the time when the office was established, has had wide powers of giving directions as to the proper construction of the land laws.[25]

To recapitulate: There are a considerable number of methods by which the legislature may delegate power to the executive and the administrative authorities in respect to secondary legislation. For example, it may make such delegation of power by permitting said authorities to establish the government organization, to issue rules and regulations that affect their own departments, government employees, or even third persons, to supplement laws or fill in details; by permitting a law to go into effect upon the establishment of some fact by an executive or administrative authority; by permitting the executive or administrative authorities to establish standards, norms, or principles of action, and to make exemptions from the operation of the laws under special circumstances; by permitting the executive further to subdelegate his powers; by permitting the executive, by accepting sub-legislative enactments, to give them the force of law; and by various other methods.

The legal significance of each of these methods cannot be discussed at this point. For the present, the thing

---

[24] The same, Sec. 3 (b), (c), and (f).

[25] See Henry L. McClintack, "The Administrative Determination of Public Land Controversies," 9 *Minn. Law Review* 420.

to be kept in mind is that the legislature uses varied methods, according to particular circumstances, for accomplishing its purpose of empowering the executive and administrative authorities to implement and supplement legislation. Undoubtedly they are all common-sense methods of handling the complex problem of making rules and regulations for society. Chief Justice Taft, who more than any other chief justice had occasion to understand from the viewpoint of the administrator the needs of present-day legislation and administration, laid a sound basis for such delegation when he said: "In determining what it [Congress] may do in seeking assistance from another branch, the extent and character of that assistance must be fixed according to common sense and the inherent necessities of the governmental coordination."[26]

IV. SUB-LEGISLATION AS AN INCIDENTAL FEATURE OF ADMINISTRATION

The making of rules and regulations does not cease when the law has been passed, and the executive and administrative authorities, acting under legislative delegation, have performed any or all of the functions discussed above. A little thought will show that even when the law itself and the rules and regulations made under it have been issued, unforeseen conditions and circumstances will arise and must be faced, however carefully the attempt has been made to lay a clear and definite basis for detailed administrative action. The extent to which this will occur depends largely upon two main factors: (1) How far the legislature has gone into detail; and (2) how well the law has been implemented by executive and administrative action of various sorts.

---

[26] In *Hampton, Jr., and Co.* v. *United States,* 276 U. S. 394, 406.

When a law is dealing with a large and complex problem, even if the attempt is made to cover all contingencies that may arise, it is impossible for the legislature to look ahead far enough to see what they will be. The same thing is true in a minor degree when the executive and administrative authorities have developed, supplemented, and filled in the law by rules, regulations, and orders. A certain minimum of incidental sub-legislation will still be needed. On the other hand, if a law merely sketches the outlines of a subject, and the executive and highest administrative authorities do little by way of regulation to fill in these outlines, naturally the administration, in enforcing the law, must make many interpretations and applications which are virtually acts of sub-legislation.

A special example of incidental sub-legislation is the formulation of policy as the secondary result, so to speak, of an administrative order. Thus, when the Federal Trade Commission ordered a business firm to cease and desist from circulating catalogues in which the statement appeared that all of its teas and coffees were imported directly from Japan or from the best plantations of the world—a statement which the Commission found to be false—this order virtually established the public policy that false and misleading advertising is prohibited.[27] Again, when a moving picture corporation changed the names of certain pictures and represented them as new pictures, a "cease and desist" order of the same Commission had the effect of announcing the general principle that it is an unfair practice to represent reconstructed or second-hand goods as new goods.[28]

[27] *Sears, Roebuck and Co.* v. *Fed. Trade Commission,* 1 F.T.C. 163.
[28] *Fox Film Corporation* v. *Fed. Trade Commission,* 6 F.T.C. 191.

V. JUDICIAL SUB-LEGISLATION

Closely related to administrative legislation, although performed by a different type of authority, is legislation by the courts, as a part of the process of law enforcement. Since judicial legislation is often but a substitute for administrative legislation, it may be considered briefly at this point.

"A process of judicial lawmaking has always gone on and still goes on," says Dean Pound,[29] "in all systems of law, no matter how completely in their juristic theory they limit the function of adjudication to the purely mechanical." This is due not only to the fact that the courts are called upon to interpret the law, but more particularly to the fact that the legislature could not possibly foresee the many different questions, and types of cases, that would arise under the law. Particularly if the legislature does not give to the administrative or executive authorities any specific powers of implementing the law and making it directly applicable to concrete cases, there are likely to be numerous gaps which must be filled in as the law is put into effect. In the ordinary course of administration, as we have seen, a part of the filling-in process will take place through administrative legislation. When this is insufficient to cover a special point which forms the basis of a lawsuit, or when individuals bring suit attacking the regulations or decisions of the administration, if the courts enunciate principles to cover the point in question, or if they decide against the administration and establish their own rules and regulations governing the subject, replacing those of the administration, evidently such action is judicial legislation.

[29] Roscoe Pound, *The Spirit of the Common Law*, p. 172.

Nor may the courts refuse to settle a case simply because there is no very clear and complete law or regulation governing the subject. They must to all intents and purposes legislate when no law exists, or when the legal basis for adjudication is extremely slight or vague. Further, in both England and the United States, the courts will apply the general principles of the common law when no statutory law or regulatory enactments seem to apply. So strong, indeed, is the control of the common law that, even if there is some statutory law or regulatory act which applies to the case at issue, the courts will often force it if possible into the framework of the common law. As a result of this bias, to a very appreciable extent the courts become the real lawmakers. Since they have the final duty of applying the law to concrete cases, and since their decisions are published and furnish precedents for further decisions, the legislative work done by the courts is truly significant.

Under the guise of preventing regulatory bodies from taking property without due process of law, or from interfering with economic liberty, the courts to a very large extent have legislated. Thus, the basic rules and regulations governing the valuation of public utilities were laid down by the Supreme Court in *Smyth* v. *Ames*[30] and many other cases. The making of rates is, theoretically, a legislative function delegated to the regulatory body by the legislature. The courts, whose duty it is to interpret and apply principles established by the legislative authority, in the decisions of concrete cases have often insisted that their own policies as to rate-making, rather than those of the utility commissions, should be followed by the regulatory body.

[30] 169 U.S. 469.

In providing for the regulation of business and industry under the Federal Trade Commission Act and the Clayton Act, it seems to have been the intent of Congress to empower the Federal Trade Commission to lay down principles and standards as to what constitutes unfair competition.[31] Through the process of judicial review, the courts themselves have taken over this power delegated to the Commission. In the Gratz Case[32] the court said: "The words 'unfair methods of competition' are not defined by the statute and their exact meaning is in dispute. It is for the courts, not the Commission, ultimately to determine as matter of law what they include."

The importance of the part taken by the courts in the legislative process evidently depends upon the factors that have been indicated above: (1) The extent to which the legislature itself lays down details for administrative action; (2) the extent to which the executive and administrative authorities are given the right to exercise the rule-making power in supplementing, filling in, and implementing legislative action; (3) the extent to which the courts fill and supplement the law through their decisions; (4) the extent to which common law principles are applied as limitations upon legislative and administrative acts; (5) the definition and application of constitutional provisions made by the courts.

Even when the law is quite definite, and when rules and regulations made under it are fairly clear and pre-

---

[31] The report of the Committee on Interstate Commerce of June 13, 1914, 63 Cong., 2 sess., No. 597, said: "The Committee gave careful consideration to the question as to whether it would attempt to define the many and variable unfair practices which prevail in commerce, and to forbid their continuance, or whether it would, by a general declaration condemning unfair practices, leave it to the Commission to determine what practices were unfair. It concluded that the latter course would be the better. . . ."

[32] 253 U.S. 421, 427.

cise, there is often an opportunity for its interpretation by a court if an individual demands the opinion of a judicial authority. In everyday life there are few persons who could agree to give the same interpretation to any written document, be it ever so simple; and judges and administrators are subject to the same rule.

Let us take a concrete example. Are artificial "Easter rabbits" to be admitted into the United States under paragraph 1513 of the Tariff Act of 1930, as "toys" or "toy containers;" or are they "articles . . . composed wholly or in chief value of earthy or mineral substances, not specially provided for?" The customs administration claimed that they were toys. The United States Customs Court took the view that they were not, saying: "It seems to us that the uncontradicted facts establish that the prime use of this merchandise is for decorative purposes and not for amusement. These rabbit figures when imported may have the characteristics of toys, and may in their imported form attract the attention of a young child. Yet such attraction may not be amusement and is not sufficient to render them toys. It is their chief use after importation which earmarks these articles. It is not a question of first impression, but the fact of chief use that classifies this merchandise."[33]

Here evidently was a question upon which there might well be absolute disagreement. If the court had taken the testimony of children and mothers and fathers, their answer might have been very different from that given by vendors of candy, whose testimony was considered conclusive. The court laid down the criterion of "fact of chief use" as determining the nature of the import.

[33] *F. W. Woolworth Co.* v. *United States.* Treasury Decisions, Vol. 62, p. 393.

But what is a chief use may be entirely a matter of opinion. In this case there was no application of technical knowledge, no application of legal criteria, no application of principles of law, no application of custom. There was merely the statement: "According to the intent of the law, artificial Easter rabbits of the kind in question are not toys." The only thing which made this statement judicial sub-legislation instead of administrative sub-legislation was the fact that the court had the last word.

If the legislature had wished, it could have gone into detail, providing that Easter rabbits should be classified as toys. If the legislature had wished, it could have required the Treasury, with the assistance of the Commissioner of Customs, to analyze in more detail what are to be considered as toys or toy containers, or to lay down further criteria as to what shall constitute such articles. Since the legislature did not do so, and the court had the last word on the matter, the court to all intents and purposes acted as a sub-legislative authority. Moreover, the fact that this decision will be used as a standard for deciding future cases is further evidence that it is sub-legislative in nature, since it establishes a classification.

Let us contrast this case with another, equally simple as to facts. Paragraph 1506 of the Tariff Act of 1922 authorizes the Collector of Customs to allow free entry to animals imported for breeding purposes, provided that a certificate of pure breeding is furnished him in respect to such animals by the Secretary of Agriculture. But it was decided that since the Secretary of Agriculture keeps no records of pedigreed rabbits, and therefore can issue no such certificates as are required by the statute, the claim of an importer for exemption from the customs duties on the ground that his rabbits are pedigreed, can have no validity.[34] Here there was no sub-legislation by either the administration or a court. No attempt was made to add to the law or even to interpret it in detail. There was merely the application of the law to a given set of facts. The exemption could be made only under certain conditions, and the necessary conditions did not exist.

It is unnecessary to elaborate the argument that judicial legislation does take place, and will continue to take place. Its value, even its necessity, where some unforeseen situation must be met, cannot be denied. But the courts should never assume the functions of the legislature, or the sub-legislative powers of the executive and administrative authorities. Judicial legislation should be restricted as far as possible, by both the foresight of the legislative and sub-legislative authorities, and the "self-denying attitude" of the courts themselves.

VI. DISCRETION

Earlier in this study it was shown that the extension of government functions and the increase in their complexity have made it impossible for the legislature to lay down specific rules for all subjects. There are a considerable number of subjects, also, concerning which no rule of law has been laid down, or should be laid down, by the courts. The legislature must therefore confer discretion upon either executive or administrative authorities to make rules and regulations for carrying out their own functions. Moreover, a certain amount of discretion, lessening from higher to lower administrative agents, must rest with those who are actively engaged in government work. No administrative system, however detailed may have been the statutory law, the judicial sub-legislation, or the superior rules and regulations gov-

[34] *Dr. George Senn* v. *United States*. Treasury Decisions, Vol. 62, p. 327.

erning its work, can function without recourse to the experience, the opinions, and the common sense of those who are operating it. An able critic has remarked that in connection with the regulatory functions, particularly: "What is wanted is not a rigid rule at all, but the intelligent and flexible discretion of a responsible directing mind."[35] Without going so far as this—for the present writers believe that there should be a great many "rigid rules" even in regulatory matters—it may be accepted as a principle that, in every phase of administration except the merely mechanical (such as the copying of documents, the keeping of records, and so on), more or less discretion must be used by the administrator.

From its very nature, discretion stands almost halfway between the legislative and the judicial process. In its most important form it may virtually amount to sublegislation, for it involves to a very large extent minor policy determination. Thus, the legislature may confer upon administrative authorities of lower rank than the executive the power to determine that rates shall be "reasonable," that services shall be "adequate," that methods used are "appropriate." It may authorize certain agencies to do what is "expedient," to see that buildings are "safe" and that food is "wholesome," and to take such action as may be "necessary" in a matter.[36] Unquestionably, the legislature itself could make the classifications, analyses, and standards which it has left in so many instances to the administration. Hence, when it decides to have them made by administrative officers, in a broad sense it authorizes administrative legislation.

Quite often the discretion of the administrative au-

---

[35] John Dickinson, *Administrative Justice and the Supremacy of Law*, p. 14.
[36] See Ernst Freund, *Administrative Powers over Persons and Property*, p. 71.

thority is exercised in weighing evidence as a basis for its decisions. For example, such questions as the expediency of a given action, the reasonableness of a certain rate schedule, or the wholesome qualities of a particular substance used in preparing canned foods, will be decided upon the weighing of several different types of evidence.

Since the executive and administrative authorities must of necessity exercise a considerable power of discretion, so that they virtually legislate, what limitations should be imposed upon the use of such discretion? By what authority should limitations be imposed? We have seen that the courts ostensibly decline to interfere with administrative discretion, yet often do so in deciding cases based upon an administrative decision or other administrative act. In thus wantonly assuming sub-legislative powers, the courts themselves become minor policy determining authorities, infringing upon the functions of either the legislature or the administration.[37] Evidently the legislature, or the superior executive or administrative authorities, must set the bounds of discretion. This problem will be discussed further in other connections.

VII. SUMMARY

The modern state must fulfil a vast number of important duties and functions. In addition to the long recognized functions of government, such as defense, the pres-

[37] "If the right of judicial review is not in some degree limited, the courts will have purely administrative duties imposed upon them and they will be encroaching upon the legislative power when they are forced to deal with regulatory matters. The judiciary does not exercise any supervisory authority over the legislative or executive branches of government. . . . When the supervisory power of the courts has been extended to matters of executive and legislative decision and discretion, the courts have been given a place of pre-eminence which our scheme of constitutional government never contemplated." C. W. Pound, "Constitutional Aspects of Administrative Law," in E. Freund, *Growth of American Administrative Law*, 1923, pp. 122-23.

ervation of internal order, and the dispensation of justice, it must undertake new tasks, forced upon it by new conditions. The state itself must manage certain enterprises; it must direct, regulate, and control, to a greater or less extent, a wide variety of others which are semi-public or even private; it must endeavor to adjust conflicts of interests, particularly economic interests, between bitterly opposed groups. In doing all these things, and many more, the state must act by means of laws, and rules and regulations made to carry out the laws.

Experience has demonstrated that no single agency can possibly make all the requisite laws, rules, and regulations. No legislature could find time to do so, even if it were not hampered by slow and cumbersome procedure, by lack of technical knowledge of the processes and methods involved in certain functions, and by sectional and partisan struggles. Moreover, in some instances the legislature feels that the formulation of policy should result from experimentation, or that policy should conform to changing conditions. Under these circumstances, it is more than probable that the legislature will share the function of rule-making with the executive and administrative authorities. In other words, it will provide for administrative legislation.

As each situation warrants, these authorities may be allowed to make plans of organization; to establish rules and regulations for those employed in the government service; to issue decrees with the force of law, affecting persons and property; to implement laws by building a complete body of detail upon the mere framework of principles supplied by the legislature; to determine the time, place, or circumstances under which laws go into operation; to establish standards, norms, or principles governing a particular activity; to allow certain exemptions from the ordinary operation of the law; to delegate powers of sub-legislation to other specified authorities; to formulate general rules of a sub-legislative nature, subject to executive or higher administrative approval; and sometimes even to determine matters of public policy through the issuance of orders or instructions of very wide significance.

Not all the sub-legislative power actually used is formally bestowed upon the executive and administrative authorities. Administrative legislation is an essential factor in the functioning of practically all government service, and must be exercised even though the legislature has not given it to the administration in express terms. No matter how carefully the provisions of a law may be drafted, it almost inevitably happens that as soon as they become effective, gaps and omissions appear which must be filled in by administrative action. Again, sub-legislation often occurs when an administrative authority is called upon to exercise wide discretion in certain matters.

Sometimes the courts perform sub-legislative functions, although they seldom admit doing so. Since the laws, rules, regulations, and decisions, however detailed, may still fail to provide a principle of law applicable to every administrative case, the courts occasionally sub-legislate in deciding cases under such circumstances. Again, the courts often feel it necessary to supplement the written laws and regulations by the principles of the common law. A great deal of judicial sub-legislation is due to the fact that the courts have taken upon themselves, without any legislative authorization, the function of determining certain types of public policy under the guise of interpreting the constitution and the laws, or of determining what is a matter of law or a rule of law. Although judicial sub-legislation cannot be avoided altogether, it should be restricted to the narrowest possible limits.

All this means that the legislative process, as we have said above, may be a continuous process starting from the most fundamental law and continuing down to the most minute regulation or rule. It may be performed by constituent bodies, legislative bodies, administrative bodies, administrative judicial bodies, and even judicial bodies. The scope and significance of any action legislative in nature which is performed by each type of authority depends upon several factors: The extent and method of legislative delegation; the different methods by which the legislature permits the administrative or executive authorities to implement the law; the extent to which the administration must fill in the law in order to make it directly applicable; the amount of control exercised by the courts over this process; the degree to which the administration is left free to interpret the law; the extent to which the courts, in settling cases before them, must fill in the omissions or gaps of the law; the extent to which courts make the statutory laws and regulations conform to their common law concepts; and the extent to which the courts, under the guise of interpreting the law, establish norms, rules, regulations, and classifications that are legislative or administrative in nature.

In a general way, when the executive and administrative branches of the government are in a strong position, as in England, Germany, and France, and within the past few years in the United States, much legislative activity will be carried on by the executive and administrative authorities. This is particularly true where there is a relationship of agency between the legislature and the executive and the administration; and where the doctrine of separation of powers is not applied in such a way as to prevent the legislature from delegating to the latter some measure of sub-legislative authority. Where the custom has become firmly established that the executive or higher administrative authorities shall implement in detail most legislative acts, so that few omissions exist, there is a decreasing possibility that the active administrative authorities carrying on detailed functions may exercise important sub-legislative power either by supplying omissions in the law or by interpreting it for application to concrete situations. Under such circumstances, also, the courts will do relatively little sub-legislative work, since the conditions which encourage judicial sub-legislation on a large scale are not present.

The exercise of sub-legislative power by several types of authorities who employ a variety of different methods suggests many questions, a few of which may be stated here. Is our present constitutional system flexible enough to provide for as wide a delegation of powers by the legislature as is necessary? What are the best methods by which sub-legislative powers may be conferred? To what types of authorities should powers legislative in nature be given? What should be the relationship between the legislature and the authorities that are exercising sub-legislative powers? What methods should be used to control the exercise of functions legislative in nature?

We shall not discuss here the advantages, the disadvantages, or the difficulties connected with the various types of sub-legislation. Nor are we interested at this point in constitutional questions regarding the respective powers of the different branches and agencies of government, or the relationships that should exist between them. Our present interest lies in the realization that all branches of government participate in the legislative process, and that administrative legislation is an indispensable daily part of the work of government.

CHAPTER III

ADVANTAGES AND DISADVANTAGES OF ADMINISTRATIVE LEGISLATION

That administrative legislation is inevitable and necessary, there can be no serious doubt. The work of the legislature must be supplemented by regulations issued by those whose function is to carry out the law. A clear recognition of this fact is indispensable to an understanding of the operations of government today.

To accept administrative legislation as an important factor in government work is not, however, equivalent to assuming that it has no faults, or that it is incapable of improvement. An unbiased inquiry into both its advantages and its faults and disadvantages, as at present organized, may be expected not only to emphasize its value and significance, but to suggest possibilities of making it more efficient and more satisfactory. It is the purpose of the present chapter to examine very briefly the chief advantages and disadvantages of administrative legislation.

I. THE ADVANTAGES OF ADMINISTRATIVE LEGISLATION

A. One of the outstanding advantages of sub-legislation by executive and administrative authorities is the fact that it economizes the time of the legislature, which can do its best work and perform its most useful services if it is spared a futile struggle with masses of detail that have little meaning except to persons intimately acquainted with the subject at hand. The legislature can best employ its time in working out large outlines of social policy, and in carrying out its important function of general rather than specific control over administration by the various methods at its disposal.

B. The availability of expert knowledge in the preparation of rules and regulations is another great advantage. Each department and each important specialized service can command the advice of its own experts in regard to any proposed measure of sub-legislation. Expert assistance from other sources can also be obtained, if needed; but it is the combined knowledge of the subject matter as such, and of the needs of practical administration, that makes a capable member of the higher administration so valuable in a sub-legislative capacity. It is true that he might, and often does, advise the legislature; but, as we have seen, time does not permit legislative examination into the details which make or mar a regulation from the standpoint of the active administrator. Hence it is in administrative legislation that the expert is most valuable, as well as most easily available.

C. The absence of party conflicts over details is a decided advantage. When such conflicts arise in connection with measures before the legislature, they generally result in compromise, failure to insert necessary provisions, or the insertion of objectionable provisions merely for party expediency. Under the same conditions, a bill is quite likely to be burdened with a multitude of irrelevant, useless, ill-worded amendments, often inconsistent with one another and with the main purpose of the bill, introduced by members who have little knowledge of the whole problem, and consequently little ability to make the rules and regulations conform to existing law and to other rules and regulations. When the legislature confines itself to making a clear, definite, well-outlined, and carefully defined statement of its will concerning a given policy, leaving the details for sub-legislative action by the appropriate administrative agency, the chances of such foolish and mischievous meddling are greatly lessened.

D. Administrative legislation avoids the inelasticity of legislative enactments, which may, by going too much into detail, include provisions that are impracticable and unworkable. This makes an awkward situation, since the administrative authorities are faced with the dilemma of either attempting the impossible and perhaps defeating thereby the central purpose of the legislature, or ignoring or evading a provision of the law and accomplishing said purpose by technically illegal means. Such a situation may be long drawn out. The legislature may be too busy with other important questions to take time for amending certain apparently trifling details of an earlier bill until a considerable period has elapsed and a great deal of pressure has been brought in favor of such amendment. In the meantime, there may have been difficulties involving action by the courts. All this can be avoided by leaving details to the administrative authorities, which are not only better able than the legislature to judge the practicability of detailed provisions in the first place, but are also able to make changes quickly and easily if experience or altered circumstances should lead to dissatisfaction with the original provisions.

E. The circumstances under which administrative regulations are prepared are conducive to proper drafting, since the subject matter can be studied with especial reference to the needs of active administration and can be arranged in a logical and intelligible manner, uncontrolled by the exigencies of parliamentary procedure.

F. The ability to fill in the details of legislative enactments in such a way that the details have the force and application of law results in completing, defining, and clarifying the law before cases are brought under it. Consequently it prevents the endless litigation which inevitably arises when serious omissions and ambiguities leave the meaning of the law uncertain.

II. THE DISADVANTAGES OF ADMINISTRATIVE LEGISLATION

A. There may be such a scattering of the sub-legislative function that the rules and regulations made independently by various executive and high administrative authorities will not be consistent with one another; that there will be no unity of policy; that there will even be conflicts of policy. The probability that this will happen is particularly great when many independent agencies organized to carry on special functions are endowed with broad powers of sub-legislation.

B. There may be secrecy in the making of sub-legislation, so that the people do not know just what is taking place until some administrative authority announces sub-legislative provisions which develop the outlines of the law in unanticipated and unpopular fashion.

C. Special groups and interests may exercise influence in secret ways and through underhand types of pressure, in order to persuade some administrator to include or omit certain provisions in the rules and regulations issued under specific statutes.

D. The general will, as contrasted with the will of special interests, may not be considered; it may even lack all certain and adequate means of expression.

E. In case those especially interested in sub-legislative policies are allowed to participate in the sub-legislative process (as for instance in the framing of industrial codes), the various interests concerned may not be equitably represented, or the particular viewpoints of certain groups may receive too much consideration and the viewpoints of other groups too little, as judged by any standard of social equity.

F. There is a possibility that the rules and regulations, particularly if they are of a large and general nature, will be made too exclusively from the viewpoint of a particular head of an administrative department, rather than from the viewpoint of society as a whole.

G. A danger of very real significance is that the legislature may practically surrender to the administration its own functions of determining general lines of policy, establishing standards to be followed by the sub-legislative authority, organizing the procedures that are to be followed, and providing for the proper remedies against untoward sub-legislative action. The disadvantages of such a situation are especially great in the United States, where the executive and administrative organization is separate and independent from the legislature, instead of being directly subordinate and responsible for its actions day by day, as in parliamentary countries. Because Congress controls the administration in a general way only, it ought to be particularly careful not to bestow upon the administration powers and functions which should be exercised by the legislature alone.

Although the courts in this country are reluctant to interfere with acts involving the use of executive or administrative discretion, nevertheless the absence of adequate standards set by the legislature must inevitably lead to conflicts between the administrative authority that is attempting sub-legislation, and the courts. For example, Section 5 of the Federal Trade Commission Act provides that: "Unfair methods of competition are hereby declared unlawful." It fails to define the meaning of "unfair" as used in the law, to establish any criteria by which to judge the fairness or unfairness of a method, or to empower the Commission to establish such criteria in the form of general rules and regulations. When the Commission, in deciding specific cases, laid down standards as to "unfair methods of competition" based on new and developing economic practices, over and above the specific acts recognized as "unfair competition" under the common law, the courts stepped in and negated the Commission's standards. This intervention not only prevented the fulfilment of the wishes of the legislature in establishing the Commission, but transferred to the courts the function of laying down general lines of social policy, which the legislature itself should have drawn clearly enough for the Commission to follow.

Much the same thing has happened over and over again to the Interstate Commerce Commission. The latter, however, has repeatedly asked Congress to repair its omissions. As Blaisdell says:

The history of the Interstate Commerce Commission, which is probably the most important federal commission for industrial control, has been a struggle marked by empowering acts of Congress, followed by a series of court decisions limiting the powers of the Commission, followed in turn by further acts of Congress strengthening the Commission. . . . Its power was gained only after half a century of conflict with the courts, during which it has again and again been necessary for Congress to intervene on the side of the Commission.[1]

Conflicts of this kind, leading to assumption by the courts of powers that should be shared by the legislature and the administration, could be avoided in large part by a clear expression of legislative will and intent in the statute laying down the general policy, or by an express

---

[1] T. C. Blaisdell, *The Federal Trade Commission*, pp. 306 ff.

authorization of the appropriate authority to issue rules and regulations defining or applying certain expressions used in the law. This would give to the courts, or to the administrative courts which the writers hope to see established, definite standards for deciding whether acts of sub-legislation, as well as other administrative acts, did or did not conform with the provisions of the law. At present our courts are often confronted with the dilemma of refusing to exercise any check upon the administrative authority, or else themselves taking over the function of establishing standards, principles, and so on, to atone for the omissions of the legislature.

H. There is a special disadvantage attaching to our present system of establishing regulatory bodies which exercise sub-legislative, administrative, and judicial powers, under some measure of control by the ordinary courts. This is the fact that many of the most important rules and regulations governing the functions bestowed upon such bodies are not made in the proper way. Although the same criticism may be made occasionally in respect to other authorities, it applies with particular force to the regulatory commissions.

As a matter of principle, sub-legislative rules and regulations should develop and apply the meaning of the law as a whole. They should be issued after a mature consideration of all relevant factors, and so far as is humanly possible, prior to the taking of any definite action in a particular case. They should be made in prescribed form, and according to a prescribed procedure which includes adequate investigation, due deliberation, and the hearing of interested parties. Unfortunately, they are often made in a very different fashion, as a part of decisions in particular cases, rendered by either the regulatory authority or the courts.

Thus, the rules for the valuation of public utilities that have largely governed and controlled both administrative authorities and courts for the past 40 years were laid down by the United States Supreme Court in the famous decision of *Smyth* v. *Ames*. Such rules should certainly be established on the basis of clearly expressed legislative principles, by sub-legislative action taken as the result of hearings, research, expert advice of economists and political scientists, and careful deliberation. Instead, a battle involving vast questions of public welfare, political economy, social policy, and planning, was fought out in a court room by lawyers. The decision was made according to narrowly construed constitutional and legal principles which failed to include several important principles of administrative law and public policy. This is but one of many examples that might be cited to show the seriousness of the disadvantage now under discussion.

Several undesirable results follow from the making of rules and regulations of general significance during the decision of particular cases, whether the decisions are rendered by the administration or by the courts.

1. This practice causes great uncertainty as to what the rules and regulations may be or are. No one knows in advance what rules or regulations may be laid down in a particular case affecting his rights. He cannot tell, until after he has obtained a decision of the administrative body plus a decision of a court, whether his acts of various kinds are illegal or legal. He must act at his peril. This has been one of the greatest difficulties in applying the Sherman Anti-Trust Act. Since definite standards defining what constitutes monopoly in restraint of trade were not laid down in the act, companies were often forced to go ahead with their arrangements without

knowing whether these were legal or illegal until a suit had been brought for violation of the provisions of the law, and the courts had finally decided the case.

2. The rules and regulations are not worked out under the proper circumstances when they are developed as portions of a specific decision. They are too likely to be made either under the sway of partisan eloquence, or in the dry atmosphere of well-established and narrowly applied legal concepts. This is wrong because the very nature of sub-legislation demands consideration and discussion of all factors involved, economic and political as well as legal. To decide questions of public policy, in a judicial contest regarding the legality of a specific action, almost inevitably means that such questions will be settled according to the particular legal points brought out in the briefs of opposing counsel, rather than according to all relevant considerations. They will be settled largely from the viewpoint of the claims made by particular litigants, rather than from the viewpoint of the needs of society.

3. A related danger is that, in case a decision embodying rules and regulations is appealed, the appellate court, while theoretically deciding only points of law, will actually decide large questions of social policy.

4. If the courts, rather than the legislature or responsible administrative authorities, must lay down principles affecting social policy during the decision of particular cases, the courts of necessity become political agencies rather than judicial authorities. Members of such bodies then will be chosen according to their economic and political beliefs, rather than because of the capacities that make them able judges—a result which is deplorable from every point of view.

Although it is impossible to prevent a certain amount

of judicial legislation, especially in new fields of social control, yet in public and administrative law, quite as much as in private law, there should be a serious effort to decrease the amount progressively. As rapidly as possible, in view of developed experience, rules and regulations should be made so that all parties concerned will know their rights under the law, and will not need to learn them from the decision of a particular case. There can be no proper process of law when individuals are unable to know what the law is, until brought into court.

5. Another danger that has developed within the past few years is that of considering nothing as "law" except the final word of the court.[2] This is due to the facts already discussed, that legislative enactments have not been definite enough to apply directly to the cases that arise; and that rules and regulations, instead of being made prior to the taking of administrative decision or the taking of court action, are made during the settlement of a particular controversy. If the legislative bodies and the agencies to which sub-legislative power is entrusted perform their work with proper care, so that their meaning is unmistakably clear, the last word will normally be theirs.

III. SUMMARY

Administrative legislation has become a necessary part of the functioning of the complex modern state. There can be little question as to its great advantages, in case it is properly organized and controlled. Unless it is so organized and controlled, however, several dangers and difficulties are sure to arise, which may largely counter-

[2] See Karl N. Llewellyn, "A Realistic Jurisprudence, the Next Step," *30 Columbia Law Review* 431 ff.; Jerome Frank, *Law and the Modern Mind*; J. C. Gray, *Nature and Sources of the Law*, Chap. V.

balance the advantages that should accompany its proper use.

Its principal advantages are: Economy of the time of the legislature; availability of expert knowledge; absence of partisan conflicts concerning details; flexibility; possibility of correct drafting; completion and clarification of the statutory law, and consequent avoidance of unnecessary litigation.

Its principal disadvantages, under the system now existing in our federal government, are: Possibilities of inharmonious and inconsistent sub-legislation; of secrecy; of improper influences; of failure to consider the general will; of lack of balance among conflicting interests; of too narrow a viewpoint; of lack of an adequate statutory basis, ending in the assumption by the courts of important and inappropriate sub-legislative powers; and of incidental sub-legislation by either the courts or the administrative authorities, particularly the great regulatory commissions, in the process of deciding particular cases.

The most interesting thing about these advantages and disadvantages, when thus set forth side by side, is the fact that the advantages are general, permanent, and inherent in the function of administrative legislation in any government system organized with reasonable care; whereas the disadvantages are almost all dependent upon special conditions and lack of careful organization. This means that due attention to the government structure will eliminate, or at the least minimize, the disadvantages of administrative legislation, while all its advantages will remain.

CHAPTER IV

METHODS OF CONTROLLING
ADMINISTRATIVE LEGISLATION

There are five principal methods by which the advantages of administrative legislation may be safeguarded: The proper exercise of the legislative power by the legislature; the delegation of powers of sub-legislation to appropriate authorities; the organization of the relationship between the legislature and the sub-legislative authority so that the legislature can control the latter; control through existing courts of law or administrative courts; and the employment of certain technical devices. These methods will be discussed in the order in which they were named.

I. THE PROPER EXERCISE OF ITS POWERS BY THE LEGISLATURE

In order that both administrative legislation and administrative adjudication may be carried on in a correct and satisfactory manner, it is necessary that the legislature itself shall lay down the basic principles, standards, and criteria under which the authorities entrusted with powers of sub-legislation are required to act. It should either explain these beyond any possible doubt, or specifically authorize the sub-legislative authorities to do so. Otherwise, it is impossible for such authorities to act with certainty, and it is equally impossible for any type of judicial authority to control their acts properly.

Many of the difficulties which have beset the work of the Federal Trade Commission, as we have seen, have been due to lack of clear legal standards.[1] The expres-

[1] See T. C. Blaisdell, *The Federal Trade Commission*, pp. 290 ff.

54

sions employed by the law, such as "maintaining competition," "lessening of competition or a tendency to monopoly," "unfair methods of competition," and so on, are not sufficiently definite to show exactly what policies Congress wished to have enforced by the Commission. Was it the function of the Commission to apply such tests as dishonesty, coercion, and fraud; or was it to apply such standards as would preserve small business units, equalize bargaining power, prevent monopoly prices, prevent discrimination between customers, and protect the consumers' interests? Did Congress intend that the expression, "unfair methods of competition," should mean merely those "unfair methods" recognized by the courts under the common law, or was the Commission itself to develop new standards? Congress did not say. Nor did it give to the Commission power to complete and develop the law and to issue regulations defining the various phrases employed in the statute. The inevitable result of its silence was to throw all these great questions of public policy into the courts for ultimate decision.

Another example of the need for standards appears in the history of the regulation of public utilities. Neither Congress nor the state legislatures have established adequate standards, rules, or principles regarding the most significant problems in the regulation of public utilities of various sorts. Consequently, there has been complete confusion in regulation. The criteria laid down by the courts, particularly in *Smyth* v. *Ames*, have been far from satisfactory.[2] Why has it been necessary for the

---

[2] In *Southwestern Bell Telephone Co.* v. *Mo. Public Service Commission*, (262 U.S. 276, 292.) Justice Brandeis, in a dissenting opinion, said: "The experience of the last twenty-five years since that case was decided has demonstrated that the rule there enunciated is delusive. In the attempt to apply it insuperable obstacles have been encountered. It has

courts to lay down rules and standards? Largely because the legislatures had failed to answer such important questions of public policy as the following:

A. What may be capitalized? May the capital value include franchise rights, good-will, water rights, other competitive advantages, promotion costs, going value, early losses, and so on?

B. How shall utility land be valued? Shall appreciation be allowed on land taken by eminent domain or on land given by the state? If appreciation is allowed, is the land to be valued according to its value for utility purposes, its replacement cost, or according to the value of surrounding property?

C. Shall capital prudently invested be taken as a basis for fixing the value of a public utility, or shall reproduction cost be allowed?

D. In case proper accounts have not been kept in the past, how shall the value of the property be determined?

E. What is a fair rate of return?

These, and many other questions which have led to conflicts between the regulatory authorities and the courts, and which have caused an endless amount of confusion, should have been answered by the legislatures, if not at the moment of establishing regulation over public utilities, at least as soon as experience had demonstrated that such questions were arising day by day. They are clearly questions of public policy which should have been settled by legislative action.

It may possibly be contended that the courts would have had to settle these questions sooner or later, because of the fact that they involve constitutional law problems, particularly under the fifth and the fourteenth amend-

---

failed to afford adequate protection either to capital or to the public. It leaves open the door to grave injustice."

ments to the federal Constitution. It is doubtful, however, whether the courts would have interfered if the legislatures had established well thought out and logical standards. Certainly their interference would have been minimized.

In case the legislative body cannot work out proper standards immediately when facing new and complicated situations, because it does not have the requisite detailed knowledge, several courses are open to it. It may establish some agency composed of those best capable of planning, to assist it in formulating policies prior to preparing the law. This would help to eliminate the difficulties that result from the formulation of rules, regulations, and standards during the administrative or the judicial process. Again, the legislature may request, or accept, the assistance of the executive and higher administrative authorities in preparing bills which may be enacted into law. The principle that the executive authorities, especially the Cabinet, should play a major part in shaping policy and initiating legislation is expressly recognized in almost every modern government outside of the United States. Although in theory this principle is not accepted here, in practice it is becoming a function of the President, after consultation with expert advisers, cabinet members and departmental specialists, to decide upon certain policies which he desires to see adopted, to have these policies set forth in bills, and to sponsor the initiation of the bills in Congress. Sometimes the bills are prepared and sponsored by government departments or agencies, acting on their own initiative (normally with the tacit consent of the President), or at the request of the President, or at the request of Congress.

Occasionally the legislature is unwilling to develop its policies, or to accept advice or assistance in doing so,

until administrative experience is available. Such hesita-
tion, however plausible the reasons therefor may seem,
is always the cause of trouble and confusion. Consequently, the legislature, even when it is entering a new field,
should make its intent as clear and unmistakable as conditions permit; and should follow its initial action as soon
as possible with more complete legislation based on the
information which has been accumulated as the result
of administrative experience and judicial decisions. It
can be helped in such supplementary work by the authority which administers the matter in question. An excellent example of this possibility is found in the relationship between Congress and the Interstate Commerce
Commission, of which Scharfman says:

> From the beginning, in its annual reports to Congress, it has
> not only been rendering regular accounts of its stewardship,
> but, in accordance with its statutory duty, recommending such
> changes in the terms and conditions of this stewardship as in
> its informed judgment were deemed necessary or desirable. Few
> aspects of the regulative process have escaped its critical con-
> sideration, in the light of practical administrative experience,
> and few of the significant legislative enactments of the past
> four decades have emerged without the imprint of its potent
> influence. . . . One can readily recall, for example, the con-
> spicuous part played by the Commission in the establishment of
> mandatory rate-making authority; in the resuscitation of the
> long-and-short-haul clause; in the assertion of the rate suspen-
> sion power; in the initiation of the valuation project; in the
> relaxation of the principle of enforced competition; in the ex-
> tension of control to security issues and to the safety and ade-
> quacy of the transportation service; in the provision for co-
> operative arrangements between the federal and state authorities;
> in the attainment of the divisional organization of the Com-
> mission; in the elimination of procedural difficulties in the en-
> forcement of the Comission's orders in the courts.[3]

[3] I. L. Scharfman, *The Interstate Commerce Commission*, Vol. I, pp.
290-91.

II. DELEGATION OF SUB-LEGISLATIVE POWERS TO THE PROPER AUTHORITIES

The second chief method of safeguarding administrative legislation is by having the legislature delegate powers of sub-legislation to a proper authority. The question may well be asked, what is a proper authority? The reply to this question evidently depends upon the nature of the sub-legislation, which may vary greatly according to the subject matter, according to circumstances, according to the objects to be attained, or the functions to be performed, or the possibility of controlling different authorities to a greater or less degree.

At times such delegation may involve merely filling in the details of a law. At other times it may involve the establishment of norms and standards by the executive or administrative authorities, that in actual material content are more important than the law itself, even when the legislature has acted carefully and thoroughly.

In case a correct delegation of sub-legislative powers is established, it is possible for the legislature to relieve itself of work that it cannot do well and that detracts from its own fundamental purposes, which, as we have seen, are the setting up of basic policies, standards, and norms, and the exercise of general control over the administration. Proper delegation enables the legislature to leave a mass of details to the administrative authorities. On this matter the present writers agree heartily with Lord Thring,[4] who remarks:

The adoption of the system of confining the attention of Parliament to material provisions only, and leaving details to be settled departmentally, is probably the only mode in which parliamentary government can, as respects legislative functions, be satisfactorily carried on. The province of Parliament is to decide material questions affecting the public interest, and the

[4] *Practical Legislation* (1877 ed.), p. 12.

more procedure and subordinate matters can be withdrawn from their cognizance, the greater will be the time afforded for the consideration of the more serious questions involved in legislation.

As we have seen above, circumstances may sometimes be such as to make it necessary for the legislature to leave much more than details to the administrative or executive agency upon which it bestows sub-legislative authority. In case of emergency, or in case the subject to be regulated is new, complex, and experimental in nature, the legislative basis for action may be exceedingly narrow, and the executive or administrative rules and regulations may be far-reaching and important. It may be virtually a fiction to say that there is an adequate statutory basis.

Thus, the National Industrial Recovery Act[5] of June 16, 1933, affords but a slight legislative basis for the huge structure of regulation that has been built up by the President and the National Recovery Administration. The Congress, in providing for codes of fair competition, and requiring that each of these should "be the standard of fair competition for such trade or industry or subdivision thereof," virtually delegated to the President complete regulatory power over industry. This was done, to all intents and purposes, by the very simple statement that:

The President may, as a condition of his approval of any such code, impose such conditions (including requirements for the making of reports and the keeping of accounts) for the protection of consumers, competitors, employees, and others, and in furtherance of the public interest, and may provide such exceptions to and exemptions from the provisions of such code, as the President in his discretion deems necessary to effectuate the policy herein declared.[6]

[5] 48 Stat. L. 195.
[6] The same, Sec. 3 (a).

It is true that trade and industry were to participate in the making of the codes, as well as labor interests and consumers. The final form of each code and its sanction, however, were left to the President. Under these powers, regulations have been enacted governing matters that have heretofore been subjects for constitutional or statutory law. Thus, the codes virtually eliminate child labor, a matter which has been agitated for years in the form of a proposed constitutional amendment. The codes set minimum wages, establish hours of employment, establish conditions of work, and decide many questions that were formerly regarded as purely legislative matters.

The National Industrial Recovery Act is an excellent example of the rule that the extent to which sub-legislative functions are delegated must depend upon the requirements of the given situation. This is in reality an application of the fundamental principle that powers must be adequate for the functions to be performed. Yet it must never be forgotten that under our system of government the legislature should do the fundamental work of establishing basic principles.

What authorities in our federal government should possess important powers of administrative legislation? There are four main authorities to which sub-legislative powers may be delegated: the chief executive, the heads of departments, *ad hoc* authorities established to carry on special functions, and *ad hoc* authorities established to make rules and regulations. All of these have been used at different times and for different purposes. From the experience of various countries, can any criteria be deduced as to what type is best? Are there certain factors that would seem to indicate the use of one type of authority as generally better than the use of other types? Does the nature of the function to be performed largely deter-

mine the type? Does the nature of the sub-legislative
enactments themselves determine the type of authority
that should issue them? Does one type of authority permit better control over such enactments than another
type?

Unquestionably the type of sub-legislation needed
must have a predominant influence upon the decision
as to the proper authority. Where the rules and regulations are of a familar type, such as building regulations,
the classification of employments and employees, or sanitary requirements, it may be entirely possible for an *ad
hoc* authority to formulate such rules and regulations.
Experience is such that there is no need for the trial and
error method; nor is there the need for obtaining further
knowledge as the result of settling concrete cases.

There are other types of rules and regulations of a
very different nature. One of these types is that of merely developing in detail the provisions of a law. The law
may be quite clear and definite in its terms, but the
legislature may consider it inexpedient to provide in detail for all the contingencies that may arise thereunder.
For instance, Congress is unwilling or unable to say in
respect to the public lands, that one particular acreage
is mineral land, that a given range shall be a sheep range
and the next a cattle range, or that certain lands are oil
lands. It does not wish to decide such matters of detail
as: What shall be the ingredients of sausage? What is a
fair freight rate on cement, iron ore, or steel rails?
Should a kind of refined butter manufactured from salt,
glucose, and imported low-grade or "grease" butter be
classified and taxed as adulterated butter? Evidently in
matters of this sort the filling-in of the details of a law
to make it applicable to concrete cases is a function of
the department or agency concerned. Although it is

proper whenever possible to lay down general regulations in advance, such a number of different situations may arise, especially as regards classification, that quite often an administrative ruling must be made in respect to a concrete case. It seldom happens that large questions of public policy must be solved in connection with this type of detailed work, especially if the legislature has done its duty.

Another type of sub-legislation includes acts affecting the administrative services themselves. Such acts apply to individuals in the public service, as regards their relationship to the government. Acts of this type include the organization of government departments, the allocation of functions to different departments, the consolidation of government agencies, the preparation of civil service rules and regulations, the classification of government employees, the establishing of procedures, and so on. In case the legislature itself does not wish to perform these activities, on whom should they be laid? The most general answer that has been given to this problem is, to vest power in the chief of state, who acts of course with the co-operation of the different departments concerned. This is the answer which has been adopted in the United States. In parliamentary governments, the organization of the administration and the drawing up of the most important rules and regulations governing the internal relationships of government departments are considered functions of the Cabinet. The organization of minor activities, and the issuing of rules and directions governing the internal workings of a particular department, are normally left to the head of each department.

In relatively few cases are such types of sub-legislation given over to an *ad hoc* authority. They are considered as technical administrative matters to be handled by the appropriate executive and administrative authorities. Several important problems of control over sub-legislative acts of this type may arise, however, when the rights of public servants are affected. How far shall such rules and regulations, especially civil service rules and regulations, have the effect of law? Shall administrative acts under them be controlled by judicial means, or only by administrative means? The answer to such questions should be contained in a civil service law. In other words, here as elsewhere the principle should hold, that important matters of policy should, as far as possible, be settled by law rather than by sub-legislative action.

By far the most important type of sub-legislation, from the viewpoint of control, is that concerned with the regulatory functions of the government which affect private citizens and private business. These may involve the establishment of new social policies, the harmonizing of many conflicting interests, and the setting up of norms and standards that affect society as a whole. Sub-legislation regarding the control or regulation of business and industry, public utilities, the production of raw materials, immigration, agriculture, aviation, radio broadcasting, and water power (to name a few matters almost at random) would come within this category. In most instances of this kind, the subject is relatively new, the amount of social policy involved in the regulation is great, the problems are complex in the extreme, and the interests concerned are large and diversified. It may well be, for reasons already discussed, that the legislature has been unable or unwilling to establish a broad legal basis for further regulation. The problem immediately presents itself: To what kind of authority shall the power of sub-legislation be given?

In practice, certain typical solutions to this problem are generally employed. Sub-legislative power may be given to the chief executive, to individual ministers or the Cabinet as a whole, or to some kind of executive council. The first solution named is employed quite frequently.

Important powers of sub-legislation, as well as administrative and quasi-judicial powers, are often bestowed upon *ad hoc* authorities which are more or less independent of the permanent administration. In many instances these authorities are not given specific powers to lay down rules and regulations in advance of other action, as a basis for the administrative or quasi-judicial functions which they are called upon to perform; but rather, rules and regulations are developed pragmatically as the agencies endeavor to administer the law. The general theory under which such authorities are organized seems to be that in respect to the newer regulatory and controlling functions the legislature is not able to lay down anything but the merest sketch of policy; that policy must develop through the process of trial and error; that Congress cannot well legislate for future unknown conditions; that the special authority established for the purpose of carrying out the activity will, through the settlement of cases as they actually arise, develop standards and methods of control, and learn what problems are confronting it. In an experimental and pragmatic way it will "feel itself into the subject," and will from time to time make the various adjustments necessary. Rules and regulations will develop, much as the common law has done, through decisions made in specific cases.

In the United States, most authorities of the nature just described are independent of the large executive departments, and are not under the direct control of the legislature. It is felt that since their functions are in part quasi-judicial in nature, they should not be controlled by political influences. Often they are made bi-partisan, and the terms of their members overlap the term of the President, in order that their actions may not be too much controlled by party considerations.

This general theory has been accepted and applied in the United States in establishing such bodies as the Interstate Commerce Commission, the Federal Trade Commission, the Communications Commission, the Securities and Exchange Commission, the Employees' Compensation Commission; and in England in establishing such bodies as the Railway and Canal Commissioners, the Railway Rate Tribunal, the National Health Insurance Tribunals, the Electricity Control Board, and the Agricultural Wages Committee.

The executive authority always possesses a considerable power of sub-legislation, either formal or real. Thus, in France the President nominally issues most of the sub-legislative regulations; yet actually they are prepared by the Cabinet as a whole or by the ministers concerned, who countersign them and are responsible to the legislative body for them. Although they bear the name of the chief of state, they are really the acts of the true executive authority, the Cabinet. Certainly the subordinate administrative authorities do much of the actual labor of preparing regulations, and the advice of the Council of State is often required; but the political responsibility is borne by the Cabinet. Under the Weimar Constitution, a very similar situation existed in Germany. In the United States, when the President issues acts of sub-legislation, such acts need not be countersigned by Cabinet members, and the latter need not answer to the legislature for them. As a matter of practice, even here, most of the sub-legislative acts of the President are prepared by the heads of the administrative departments or other agencies in the government; but the President accepts a degree of personal responsibility for them which is impossible in parliamentary countries.

There are many considerations in favor of entrusting sub-legislative power at least nominally to the head of state. This is particularly true in respect to subjects that involve large questions of public policy. The chief executive authority by his very position commands the attention of the people. His every speech, writing, order, or executive action receives the immediate attention of the news distributing agencies, so that each one is made known to the public immediately. In parliamentary countries, he is the figurehead representing national unity and national policy. In the United States, not only does he represent the people, but despite his constitutional position he has become an important policy determining authority, because of his powers of patronage, his ability to command attention, his ability to secure able advice, and his control over the Cabinet.

Moreover, the centralization of the rule-making functions in the chief executive authority makes it possible to co-ordinate sub-legislation instead of having it widely scattered among various authorities. Another advantage of giving the sub-legislative function to the executive authority is the fact that the latter is by its very nature a general authority, which can consider administration as a whole, and is not biased or distracted by the need of applying special policies to concrete cases.

In the United States, the issuing of rules and regulations by the President or even by members of the Cabinet prevents the courts from interfering with sub-legislation to the same extent as they could if the regulations had been issued by special *ad hoc* authorities. In respect to the President, both theory and practice make the courts reluctant to intervene. From the theoretical viewpoint, the President is co-ordinate with the courts. In practice, the courts themselves have refused as a rule to pass upon his acts, both on the ground of separation of powers, and on the ground that the President is exercising discretionary governmental powers that cannot be interfered with by judicial actions. They have held repeatedly that the mandamus and the injunction will not lie against his acts. Nor can his acts be reviewed by certiorari. Although this attitude of the courts need not be maintained absolutely, especially when the President is exercising sub-legislative powers clearly and specifically delegated to him by act of Congress, judicial interference with Presidential action cannot be expected under ordinary circumstances.

The claim is sometimes made that the practice of sub-legislation by the executive authority may combine the advantages of making rules and regulations in advance, with the advantages obtained from a gradual development of necessary sub-legislation by the trial and error method. The different agencies subordinate to the executive authority often have a wide enough and detailed enough experience with the subject to be controlled, or with closely related subjects, to assist the executive in laying down with some degree of accuracy the general rules and regulations that are to be followed. As the authorities empowered to carry on the administrative work or to make the judicial decisions become more familiar with the subject, they can place their information at the disposal of the executive authority, so that more accurate or more detailed regulations can be made.

To the objection that the executive authority may not have the time or the knowledge to formulate such rules and regulations, it may be replied that there is always the possibility of establishing new agencies to assist in this work, or of distributing it among subordinate agencies, even though the regulations when completed are issued and signed by the executive. Moreover, although the actual work of sub-legislation may be greatly subdivided, it is always possible for the central authority to co-ordinate it in such a way as to make it fit into the general lines of policy, which would perhaps be quite impossible were many independent agencies charged with minor policy determination.

The question may well be raised as to the conditions under which the sub-legislative function should be given to the head of state, to the Cabinet as a whole, to a single member of the Cabinet, or to the head of state and the Cabinet together. The answer to this question must depend largely upon the nature of the government organization and upon the significance of the sub-legislative powers delegated. When the head of state can act only through the Cabinet, as in England, France, and Germany, it would seem to make little practical difference whether power were delegated to the Cabinet as a cabinet, or to the head of state. Yet it may make a good deal of difference politically. The British device of "orders in council" is meant to avoid even the appearance of uncontrolled legislation by the sovereign. Where, as in the United States, the President is the direct controller of the Cabinet, the members of which are responsible to him rather than to the legislature, it would seem that for all important matters the sub-legislative function should be delegated to him. In any event, where large questions of policy are involved the power of sub-legislation should not be delegated to a single member of the Cabinet. Even though a department head may have the largest part in formulating a given sub-legislative policy, where an important matter is concerned he should not act merely in his own name and on his own authority. Minor rules and regulations that concern primarily his own department, however, may properly be issued by him.

III. CONTROL THROUGH THE ESTABLISHMENT OF THE PROPER RELATIONSHIP BETWEEN THE LEGISLATURE AND THE AUTHORITY EXERCISING SUB-LEGISLATIVE POWERS

The type of control which the legislature may exercise over the sub-legislative authority varies according to the nature of the authority. The legislature has a free hand in establishing *ad hoc* authorities; it can determine their organization, their functions, their relationships to other authorities, and the methods by which they are to be controlled. From the organizational viewpoint, then, it would appear that there is adequate control over them. A closer examination, however, may lead to a different judgment. Control through organization is static, rather than dynamic. It is a control over the general functioning of the authorities concerned, rather than a control over their specific functioning. In case the general lines of policy laid down by an *ad hoc* sub-legislative authority are not in harmony with the will of the legislature, it is true that the latter can change the authority, change its powers, its organization, the extent of its functioning, and so on. Nevertheless, the legislature seldom has a satisfactory method of checking or controlling specific sub-legislative acts or of keeping them in harmony with the legislative policy. It may entrust this function to the courts. It may seek to retain direct control by requiring that all sub-legislation shall receive its approval; but this means over-burdening the legislature and hampering the administration to an impractical extent.

When the function of sub-legislation is given to a constitutional authority co-equal to the legislative authority, such as the President of the United States, many of the lines of control that are available in respect to the *ad hoc* authority do not exist. The Constitution itself largely organizes the Presidency. Many of the President's relationships to other authorities are the result of constitutional provisions, of custom, or of court decisions. The legislature may control the President's acts to a certain extent by bestowing new functions upon him, withdrawing functions that it has previously given him, changing organizations that it has provided, reducing the budgets of his assisting authorities, and so on. It is not able, however, to exercise control over individual sub-legislative acts in any very direct and effective way; nor, as we have seen, can it depend upon the courts to keep the President narrowly within the authority that it has delegated to him in respect to sub-legislation. In a minor degree, the same things are true of delegation of sub-legislative powers to the heads of departments.

Theoretically, the objections to giving large sub-legislative powers to an authority which is not subject to legislative control are largely eliminated when the real executive authority, the Cabinet, is responsible to the legislature, as in a parliamentary form of government. Here Parliament can exercise a day-by-day control by holding the ministers or the Cabinet members responsible for their acts. In case the executive policy as expressed by sub-legislative enactments does not conform to the intent of the legislature in delegating powers, the legislature can readily rid itself of the Cabinet or of its individual members, for the Cabinet is the agent of the legislature and not its co-equal. In actual practice, parliamentary control over individual acts may be rather slight, owing to the number of such acts, their technical nature, and the inability of members of the legislative body to make any very careful examination of each one. There is always the possibility, however, in case of serious conflict, for the legislature to step in and exercise a complete control.

IV. CONTROL BY COURTS OR ADMINISTRATIVE COURTS

Judicial control over sub-legislation may take several different forms. The three most general forms are: Control over the laws delegating the power of sub-legislation; control over the rules and regulations issued by a sub-legislative authority; and control over specific acts or decisions which have the effect of establishing general rules and regulations. These will be discussed as between the courts and the other branches of government in the United States.

A. Control over the laws delegating the power of sub-legislation is not possible where the legislature is the supreme legislative authority and its acts cannot be declared unconstitutional by the courts. It is, however, one of the prime methods of· judicial control in the United States, where the courts take upon themselves the function of passing upon the constitutionality of legislative acts, and declaring null and void such acts as they consider unconstitutional.

The courts may find in the Constitution several grounds for declaring null and void a legislative enactment which delegates sub-legislative power. In practice, a person objecting to an act of sub-legislation under such an enactment usually attacks the enactment itself as contrary to the doctrine of separation of powers or the constitutional division of powers between the federal government and the states, as giving to the President or other authority powers which according to the Constitution cannot be thus delegated, or as contrary to due process of law. If the court agrees with the complainant, it will declare the act of Congress in question null and void.

The doctrine of separation of powers starts with the assumption that the Constitution is the "supreme law of the land," by which the sovereign people have delegated to the several government agencies all the powers which they possess. No redistribution of powers can be made by the agencies themselves. This can be done only by the process of amending the Constitution. Since the Constitution has given to Congress "all legislative powers herein granted," it follows (according to the principle of agency that a delegate may not re-delegate his powers) that Congress cannot re-delegate legislative powers.[7]

Though such is the theory, the imperative need for sub-legislation by the President, the heads of departments, and various administrative authorities has caused the Supreme Court and other courts to depart quite widely from this theory. The courts have evaded the difficulty by calling the delegated powers quasi-legislative, and by holding that since the line which separates legislation and administration is not a distinct line, the legislature can exercise considerable discretion in giving

[7] See James Hart, "Ordinance Making Powers of the President," *Johns Hopkins University Studies*, Vol. 43, Chap. VI; J. P. Comer, *Legislative Functions of National Administrative Authorities*, Chap. VI.

over the quasi-legislative or regulatory power to other authorities.

Despite this liberal attitude of the courts, despite the facts that in the past the Supreme Court has never held unconstitutional a delegation of discretionary power to the President, and that it has been very tolerant regarding delegations of power to the heads of the executive departments and even to *ad hoc* authorities, it must be recognized that under our system the question as to what part Congress shall play in the determination of public policy, and what part the executive and administrative authorities shall play, is actually one in which the last word lies with the courts rather than the legislature.

A serious objection to the possibility of control by the courts over sub-legislation, by annulling as unconstitutional any law delegating rule-making power, is the fact that the courts may have to face—and in the opinion of many able jurists, have faced—the dilemma of declaring unconstitutional in time of emergency a law upon whose validity vast policies undertaken by the government rest; or else of temporarily disregarding the theory of separation of powers. Either choice encourages general disrespect for both the Constitution and the courts.

B. Control over the rules and regulations issued by a sub-legislative authority must be provided if the authority is to remain within the bounds of legality in its formulation of sub-legislation. The necessary control in regard to such matters as questions of jurisdiction, questions of abuse or misuse of power, questions of violation of the forms and rules of procedure, disregard of standards laid down by the legislature, and impairment of rights validly established, must evidently be judicial in nature. The rules and regulations must be compared with the law, lest the sub-legislative authorities should pass beyond the limits set by the law giving them power to act. Even if an authority is acting within its power in sub-legislating, it may abuse that power by favoring certain interests at the expense of others, or making rules and regulations for improper motives and designs—for instance, in order to remove certain classes of officers from the public service, or in order to obtain personal financial advantage.

In many cases the legislature lays down rules and procedures that must be followed in exercising the sub-legislative power, such as notice, hearing, giving information to the special interests concerned, providing for the hearing of objections, participation in the sub-legislative process by special groups or associations, the presence of a quorum, and the like. In some instances, when an inferior administrative authority is laying down rules and regulations it is acting not only under the standards set by the legislature in respect to forms and procedures, but also under the general rules and regulations issued by a superior administrative authority. Under all the above circumstances, if individual rights are to be protected, it is necessary that some authority judicial in nature shall test the conformity of the administrative action with the laws or the superior rules and regulations safeguarding forms and procedure.

Violations of rules of law may take place under many conditions. A few of these may be mentioned as examples. If an administrative authority adds to the rules which it is empowered to make, the sanction of fines and penalties for which the law authorizing the rule-making does not provide, such addition is a violation of a rule of law. If the administrative authority charged with the sub-legislative function misinterprets the law under which it is acting; if the sub-legislative authority makes rules and regulations that violate acquired rights or impair the contractual obligations that have been undertaken by the government; if the rules and regulations are in conflict with any valid constitutional or legal provisions, a rule of law is violated.

In all such instances, some sort of judicial control is needed. The sub-legislative act must be compared with some law, contract, court decision, or other act superior to or controlling the sub-legislative act. Such comparison is a function judicial in nature, which cannot be performed properly by the administrative authority that issues the regulations to be examined. Moreover, if sub-legislative acts are to remain within the bounds of legality, they must be controlled irrespective of the authority that issues them, be it the President, a Cabinet member, or a board or commission.

Control by a superior administrative or executive authority is not desirable for many reasons. When the President issues regulations, there is no superior authority which can control them. Even when a superior authority exists, it is a part of the machine that is carrying out the active administration, and its impartiality is therefore open to question. Moreover, special training in law is necessary for the proper type of control. There should be a judicial atmosphere about the proceeding. Finally, there is no proper process of law when a party to a cause decides the cause. When some administrative authority claims the right to act and claims that it has acted in conformity with its powers, while opposed to it there is some individual who claims otherwise, the controversy is in its essence a case which ought to be decided by an impartial judicial authority.

Although control over the legality of administrative acts is a judicial function, it does not of necessity follow that this function should be given to the ordinary courts. It may be entirely possible to establish a special judicial authority that can exercise the controlling function even better than the ordinary courts. At this point, however, it is not necessary to discuss what form such an authority should take.

C. Control is needed over specific acts or decisions which have the effect of establishing general rules and regulations. In many instances, what amounts to sub-legislation results not from the establishment of rules and regulations in definite form prior to the taking of administrative action, but from the decision of concrete problems as they arise. This method of rule-making may grow out of several circumstances.

1. Sub-legislation may be the result of an order addressed to a specific person or corporation. Thus, the Federal Trade Commission is not given by law any general rule-making power; but it has the right to file a complaint with a view to making a thorough investigation of actions tending toward unfair competition; and if need be it may issue an order restraining such actions. But the order itself may in effect lay down large lines of social policy. For example, if after filing a complaint and making an investigation the Commission issues an order preventing a particular company from issuing "tying-in contracts," to all intents and purposes it establishes the principle that such contracts are a method of unfair competition. If it should take the same action in several instances, and its orders were not overruled, an important question of public policy as to control over business would be answered, and in effect sub-legislation would have resulted from specific orders.

2. Sub-legislation through concrete decisions may grow out of acts based on fact-finding. If a tariff law pro-

vides that the tariff on certain articles shall be such as to equalize the cost of production in the United States with that in foreign countries; sets up a commission to examine into the facts of production costs for the articles in question, here and abroad; and authorizes the President, in view of the information obtained by the commission, to set a rate that will equalize the cost of production; then, when the President sets the rate, his act is sub-legislation resulting from fact-finding.

3. Sub-legislation may result from an administrative decision in a particular administrative controversy. When the Interstate Commerce Commission reaches a decision after the original hearing of a rate case in which testimony is taken, witnesses appear, and documents are introduced, the reasons on which the decision is based are equivalent to sub-legislation. For example, in the Shreveport Case,[8] the Commission laid down the important principle that an interstate carrier may not discriminate against interstate commerce although an order of a state commission may permit it to do so.

4. Sub-legislation may result from the administrative interpretation of the provisions of a law in connection with a specific problem. Thus, Section 313 of the Tariff Act of 1930 provides: "Upon the exportation of articles manufactured or produced in the United States with the use of imported merchandise, the full amount of the duties paid upon the merchandise so used shall be refunded as drawback, less one per centum of such duties. . . ." A manufacturer imports watch cases and watch movements which he assembles as complete watches, and then attempts to export the watches under this law. The Collector of Customs makes a decision refusing a drawback, and the case is appealed to the administrative

[8] 23 I.C.C. 31.

decision of the Secretary of the Treasury. According to the interpretation placed upon the act by the Secretary of the Treasury, the action taken by the manufacturer in respect to the movements and cases was merely a subterfuge to evade the payment of duties, such action was contrary to the spirit of the tariff act, and the work performed in assembling the watches did not serve the purpose for which the drawback was intended. This interpretation is really sub-legislation, to the effect that the mere assembling of parts already completed does not constitute manufacture or production.

The extent to which sub-legislation results from the interpretation of statutes by the administrative authorities depends chiefly upon two factors: first, the amount of detail in the laws governing such authorities; second, the minuteness with which some superior administrative authority has laid down rules and regulations supplementary to the law. In case the legislature has failed to go into the detail necessary to make a given law directly applicable to concrete cases as they arise, and in case supplementary rules and regulations have not been made by a superior administrative or executive authority, the authority which actually is handling the particular cases may do a great deal of real sub-legislation.

Other factors that should be mentioned are the use of administrative supervision and the freedom with which administrative appeal is permitted. In case the lower officer can ask the advice of an administrative superior, or in case the injured individual can bring an appeal before a higher administrative authority (as by appealing from a customs collector to the Secretary of the Treasury), such possibilities may be nearly equivalent to the establishment of rules and regulations by the higher authority. It must be noted, however, that the decisions of the superior may be in form interpretations of the law, and not regulations issued in advance of administrative action in detailed cases.

The problems which arise in respect to judicial control over the decisions of regulatory authorities which establish rules and regulations incidentally, as it were, are very delicate and difficult. In England and the United States, especially, it is not easy to decide in a general way, whether and when the courts should take jurisdiction of controversies regarding the acts of such authorities. In specific instances, the courts decide the question of jurisdiction according to their view of the nature of a particular act. If any given decision made by the administrative authorities is regarded by the courts as judicial in nature, a different theory of review is applied than if the decision is regarded as administrative or legislative in nature.

Little by little our courts have laid down a complicated set of criteria as to when an act is to fall into one or another category. By the application of these criteria they determine not only whether or not they will take jurisdiction, but also the type and extent of any review which may be allowed. Since these criteria, as we shall see later,[9] are uncertain and often out of touch with present-day realities, the inevitable result is confusion in our administrative law, and a pitiable uncertainty as to what the court will do in a particular case.

When rather important sub-legislative powers are given to an authority that may exercise them at the same time that it is making a decision in a particular instance, a most difficult problem of organization is involved. If the decisions that are to be made will turn on questions

[9] Chap. IX.

of policy, evidently the authority should be organized as a policy determining authority. If, on the other hand, many acts of the authority are really judicial in nature, every effort should be made to guarantee that such acts shall be independent of political control.

The difficulties that follow the bestowal of sub-legislative functions upon authorities which also exercise administrative judicial functions can be lessened by two main methods. The first is the delegation of almost complete control over the power of sub-legislation to either the President or the Cabinet members, so that any subordinate administrative authority will have a very narrow margin of sub-legislative power. This method is employed quite often in our federal government. Thus, Section 484 of the Tariff Act of 1930 provides that certified invoices shall be filed for the importation of specific kinds of merchandise into the United States, but that exemptions from this requirement may be made by the Secretary of the Treasury. Under this law, the Secretary of the Treasury has established several classes of goods which may be imported without consular invoices. This sub-legislative act by the high executive officer leaves a minimum of opportunity for any subordinate to issue rules and regulations in the same field.

The second method, which is far more radical, consists of the separation of the active administrative functions from the quasi-judicial functions. This solution will be discussed later.

V. TECHNICAL METHODS OF CONTROL

Several technical methods have been used in various countries for the control of the sub-legislative process. These in general are: submission of the sub-legislative enactments to the legislature, which retains the power to annul, approve, or amend; a requirement that the rules be approved by some authority other than the one which makes them; a requirement that the advice of some council be obtained in the preparation and formulation of sub-legislative enactments; the establishment of special forms of procedure to be followed in the formulation of sub-legislative enactments; the establishment of definite classes of sub-legislative enactments; and the standardization of forms of publication. These various technical methods will be discussed briefly.

A. Control over sub-legislative action through requiring that it be laid before the legislative body has been used to a large extent in England. Although there is no general statute which requires regulations to be laid before Parliament, in many cases the delegating statute itself so requires.[10] A provision that regulations shall be laid before Parliament may take any one of various forms, such as: laying with no further directions; laying for a specified time; laying with provision that the regulation shall not operate beyond a certain fixed period; laying with provision that the regulation is not to operate until it has been approved by resolution.[11] Sometimes there is an added requirement, that the intention to issue regulations shall be made known, and the tentative draft of such regulations shall be obtainable on application.

Although there is something to be said for this system if properly operated, it displays several weaknesses as it is used at present. "It is impossible to discover any rational justification for the existence of so many different forms of laying, or on what principle Parliament acts in deciding which should be adopted in any particular

[10] See *Report of Committee on Ministers' Powers*, 1932, p. 41.
[11] The same, pp. 41-42.

enactment."[12] Again, the mass of necessary rules and regulations makes it impossible for Parliament to give the requisite time and attention to each, yet the "successful working of the device depends upon the amount of time which members of Parliament can spare to scrutinize every paper which is laid before the House."[13] There is the danger that in times of emergency, the very times when sub-legislative powers are exercised most freely and with the most far-reaching effects, laying regulations before Parliament may seriously hinder the actions of the executive and administrative authorities; yet failure to do so may mean giving those authorities too free a hand. This difficulty might be obviated by requiring Parliament to take action on such measures immediately, rather than merely allowing them to be before it for a given number of days. Such a requirement, however, might have the disadvantage of "shifting back into Parliament a discussion of things which Parliament had, with its eyes open, divested itself of."[14] On the whole, this method seems advisable in respect to special and important questions only, concerning which the legislature desires to retain a good deal of control.

B. Approval of rules by some authority or agency other than the one which makes them is a fairly common method of control. Thus, the customs rules and regulations in the United States are made by the Commissioner of Customs and approved by the Secretary of the Treasury. In Germany, the Weimar Constitution required the consent of the Reichsrat to ordinances regulating the construction, management, and traffic of railways; in various

---

[12] The same, p. 42.
[13] Cecil T. Carr, *Delegated Legislation*, p. 39.
[14] *Report of Committee on Ministers' Powers*, Vol. II, *Minutes of Evidence*, Sec. 3666, p. 272 (Testimony of Sir Cyril Hurcomb).

other instances some special advisory agency was required to assent to the issuance of certain types of ordinances.[15]

Several advantages may be claimed for this method. Particularly in case the general sub-legislative power is vested in one authority, it is important that any subordinate regulations shall be in harmony with those issued by the general authority. By requiring its approval, there can be a harmonizing of action not possible otherwise. In case several units or divisions within a government department may all issue rules and regulations, it may be necessary that they shall all conform to the departmental policy. In some instances it may be necessary that particular regional or sectional interests be guarded, so that some sort of authority representing these interests should be asked to give its consent or approval to sub-legislative acts. It is for this reason, more than any other, that the Reichsrat, which was to represent the German states as such, was given by many laws the power to approve certain sub-legislative acts affecting the states.

Again, the authority to which the sub-legislation is submitted may have a wider grasp of the whole field than the authority which actually draws up the measure. By its advice and criticism it may prevent mistakes and improve the regulations. It is generally safe to assume that an authority which is not faced with the immediate necessities of administration is likely to have a less biased view than the authority which is carrying on active administration, so that its criticism may prevent the difficulties arising from a too narrow, too departmentalized, too specialized view of the subject.

There are several possible shortcomings, however, in this form of control. The approving authority may not

[15] See F. F. Blachly and Miriam E. Oatman, *The Government and Administration of Germany*, pp. 136, 610.

have enough technical knowledge to pass adequately upon the sub-legislative act. It may not be so organized as to be able to check up on the act with any degree of expertness. It may be too busy to give the matter proper attention, and the approval may consequently become a mere formality: a situation which often arises when bureau regulations must be approved by heads of departments. In case this method of control is used, it is necessary that the function of approving sub-legislative acts shall be performed by some authority which has technical training, time, and staff facilities such as to enable it to make an adequate investigation of all relevant questions.

C. Securing the advice of some expert council or other advisory body is a method used to some extent everywhere, but notably in France. For control over regulations of public administration, which are the most important class of sub-legislative acts in France, the Council of State is employed. Regulations of public administration may be issued only after they have been discussed by the Council of State, which is both an expert advisory body on legislative and administrative matters, and the highest administrative court in France. There is general agreement that because of its wide experience with all kinds of administrative questions, its large and highly trained personnel, and its constant contact with law and regulations, this body is especially able to advise upon any kind of sub-legislation. Various other kinds of sub-legislative acts beside the important type just named are in fact submitted to it. There is no doubt that the advice of the Council of State, and the assistance which the Council gives in the drafting of sub-legislative enactments, have been significant factors in keeping such enactments within the sphere laid down by the legislature, preventing conflicts between different sub-legislative enactments, and assuring that the rules and regulations shall be written in a clear and simple style.

In many instances, laws delegating the power of sub-legislation especially provide for procedures by which the advice of expert boards, commissions, or other advisory bodies shall be given in the formulation of rules and regulations. This is excellent as far as it goes, but it fails to meet the difficulty that expert bodies may understand the technical and factual aspects of a matter and may be in harmony with the policy of a law, without possessing the knowledge and skill necessary for keeping sub-legislative enactments within the boundaries set by the law, and especially for keeping them within the limits of other constitutional and statutory provisions. For this reason an advisory and drafting body which possesses a complete knowledge of all relevant law and jurisprudence, and which can easily obtain the advice of expert individuals and organizations in particular fields, is certainly the better choice.

D. The establishment of special forms of procedure to be followed in the formulation of sub-legislative enactments may include specific provision for: notice that regulations on a given subject are to be drafted; hearings at which interested parties may appear and be heard; filing of objections against a particular regulation; participation of certain interested groups or associations in the drafting of rules and regulations; complaints against any feature of a sub-legislative act before it goes into operation.[16] In a significant sense, such procedure provides for some of the safeguards that ordinarily result from legislative action. Procedural requirements such as those just mentioned are particularly applicable when

[16] See J. P. Comer, *Legislative Functions of National Administrative Authorities*, Chaps. VII and VIII.

the rules and regulations which are to be made are so far-reaching and important as codes of fair competition, codes of business ethics, and the like.

E. The establishment of definite classes of sub-legislative enactments is a very useful method of control. Nothing helps more to solve the legal difficulties which may result from sub-legislation than a proper legislative classification of sub-legislative enactments according to the authority which issues them, their sphere of application, their juridical significance, the procedures that must be followed in their enforcement, and the grounds on which they may be attacked.

Thus, when the sub-legislative power is somewhat scattered, a distinction should be made between regulatory acts issued by the President or chief of state, and those issued by the head of a department or the head of a subordinate administrative agency. This device will be unnecessary, of course, if all regulations are issued in the name of the chief of state. A distinction should be made among regulatory acts, as to whether they are mere instructions to control detailed actions within government departments, or whether they affect the rights of civil servants or the rights of the public. It should be made clear under what legal authorization each sub-legislative regulation is issued. Rules and regulations should be classified, as far as possible, according to whether they are supplementary measures, interpreting and filling in the details of a special law and providing for its execution; or whether they are "police" or "emergency" measures, with a different legal basis from that of a mere executory order. It is important to set up the procedures that must be followed in respect to securing individual rights under these different kinds of sub-legislative actions. In some instances, an appeal to a higher administrative authority is sufficient; in others, the individual should have a right of action before a court or an administrative court.[17]

F. Standard forms and methods of publication are a very useful device for controlling sub-legislation. Obviously, the publication of rules and regulations is important not only for the information and direction of those who must apply them, but also as a method of enabling those concerned to know their rights and duties, and of allaying the discontent and suspicion which will inevitably arise if there is any cause to think that the government is acting secretly in respect to matters which affect the public directly. The form of the publication should vary considerably with the nature of the rules and regulations, and the extent of their applicability; but all important sub-legislation should be made accessible in an official gazette, and even the most unimportant regulations should be listed in series and by a descriptive title in the gazette. There should be many official depositories open to the public, where every rule and regulation would be accessible to any interested person. When regulations are of particular interest to certain special groups, such as cotton manufacturers, apple growers, or railroads, they should be published in trade journals as well as in some official publication.

VI. SUMMARY AND CONCLUSIONS

If our analysis is correct, the legislature must inevitably give over more and more power of sub-legislation to the executive and administrative authorities. It cannot be doubted that there are many advantages from such delegation. Side by side with these advantages,

---

[17] See James Hart, *Ordinance Making Power of the President*, Chap. V; Blachly and Oatman, *Government and Administration of Germany*, Chap. XIX.

however, there are many dangers. These can be overcome only by the competent exercise of its power by the legislature itself; by delegating sub-legislative power to the proper authorities; by the establishment of correct relationships between the legislature and the sub-legislative authorities; by adequate control over sub-legislation, exercised by some kind of judicial authority; and by the employment of certain technical methods of control.

It is the opinion of the present writers that federal administrative legislation in the United States should be regulated by having Congress pass a law requiring that:

A. All general rules and regulations, issued by every administrative agency, shall be prepared in a specified form which shall include a reference to the legal basis on which each one depends, and shall be published and made accessible in ways specified in the law.

B. All shall be issued in the name of the President of the United States. There is no reason why the signature of the Cabinet officer or administrative chief primarily interested in each regulatory act should not appear also, if Congress so wishes.

C. All rules and regulations shall be prepared for promulgation by a bureau of the President or similar agency, which shall take care that each document is in correct form, that it appears to have a legal basis and to comply with all rules of law which may apply to it in every way, and that it does not conflict with other sub-legislative regulations. The first of these tasks is simple; the second is more difficult; the third is quite complicated. True, each set of rules or regulations should provide that any others previously issued under the same section of the same law, and so on, shall be superseded in so far as they may conflict with the new regulations;

but this does not provide for the very frequent and very awkward contingency, that sub-legislation prepared by various departments and agencies touching the same question may be inharmonious and contradictory. The bureau should have no right to alter regulations under such conditions; but it should have the right to ask all persons concerned to reconsider the situation and to take such action as might seem best in order to eliminate the contradictions. If no agreement could be reached among the executives, the President should decide the matter.

D. All rules, regulations, orders, classifications, or other acts of sub-legislation issued by the President of the United States, acting on the authority of power bestowed by Congress, should be subject to review by the Supreme Court of the United States on questions of constitutionality, and review by administrative courts (which would be set up by another act of Congress) on other questions of law. This would not interfere in the least with the constitutional powers of the President. It would merely safeguard the delegation by Congress of sub-legislative power.

CHAPTER V

THE NATURE AND SOURCES OF ADMINIS-
TRATIVE ADJUDICATION

It is obvious that administrative authorities must make innumerable decisions in carrying out the many and varied functions of government. Some of these pertain only to the internal policies and management of the services themselves; some relate to a particular method of action; many affect the government employees, as, for example, those concerning the appointment, the suspension, or the dismissal of officers. Of all the decisions which must be made, the most important for the present study are those which involve the relationships between the government and individual citizens, partnerships, and corporations, since it is chiefly in respect to these that administrative adjudication takes place.

The expression "administrative adjudication" as employed in this book means the investigation and settling of a dispute, on the basis of fact and law, by an administrative agency which may or may not be organized to act solely as an administrative court. All cases subject to such adjudication have the following characteristics: The dispute is in substance an attack upon some decision (or possibly some overt act) of the administration, made by the individual whose interests are affected; the individual and the administration are to all intents opposing parties; the decision which states the results of the investigation will be enforced like a judicial decision, unless appeal is permitted to some other authority, either administrative or judicial.

It must be admitted at once that this theoretical description cannot be applied to all the acts which should be included in the general category of administrative adjudication, particularly in England and the United States, where until very recently it was heresy to suggest that any agency except the judicial courts could adjudicate. By keeping it in mind, however, as a standard pattern, we shall be able both to understand and to evaluate some of the interesting forms which administrative adjudication has assumed in this country.

The questions naturally arise, how does administrative adjudication differ from administration, and how does it differ from ordinary adjudication? An attempt will be made to reply to each of these questions in turn, after an examination into circumstances and methods which may enable us to develop an inductive answer.

I. COMPARISON OF ADMINISTRATION WITH ADMINISTRATIVE ADJUDICATION

Ordinary administration, as we remarked above, continually involves the making of decisions. These decisions, again, may involve investigations into law and fact, which are exactly similar to the investigations that would be made if a question were to be decided by a process of administrative adjudication. When a given investigation has resulted in a decision, the administration takes appropriate action. If no question is raised at any stage of this procedure, the work of ordinary administration is completed in respect to the given matter. If, on the other hand, a person whose rights are affected questions the power of the administration to act in the matter, the legality of its procedure, the accuracy of its fact-finding, or the validity of its interpretation or application of law or fact, this question may give rise to a new investigation which, though differing very little in content, and perhaps in form, from the ordinary work of administration, has the nature and effect of adjudication.

Since no single description can cover the very great range of procedures and acts that must be recognized as in fact administrative adjudication, and since not only lawyers and political scientists, but the very courts themselves, disagree violently as to the nature of this function, our only recourse is to examine some ordinary and typical situations, which may be regarded as fair examples.

A. Let us consider first a very common circumstance. The individual is called upon to perform some duty toward the government, such as the payment of taxes or customs; and the administration must see that this duty is performed. The administration has already determined that it has authority to act. It has established, by such administrative procedures as it considers necessary (or such as are prescribed by law or by superior regulations), certain facts upon which its action will be based. To these facts it has applied the law governing its present field of action. It has thus reached a decision as to the amount which the individual must pay into the public treasury, and has notified him accordingly. In the normal administrative process, in the great majority of instances, the individual accepts without question the jurisdiction of the administrative authority, the facts that have been established, and the application of the law, rules, and regulations to the facts; in other words, he accepts the decision. It is clear that here is no process of administrative adjudication, but merely the normal process of administration. Anything more than an administrative process appears only when the individual with whom the authority is dealing denies its jurisdiction; when he disputes its fact-finding; or when he questions its interpretation of law and rules and regulations.

B. In the next situation which we shall examine, the circumstances are not quite so simple. The administration, deciding that it has jurisdiction, upon its own initiative, usually with a certain fact basis tentatively established by investigation or otherwise, takes some overt action against the individual. It cannot, however, make a final decision in the matter until certain procedures have been accomplished upon which its final decision is to be based.

For example, the immigration authorities, after an administrative investigation of a suspicious case, may cause the arrest of a person whom they believe to have entered the United States illegally. They may not, however, make a decision to deport him until some procedure has definitely established the fact of illegal entry. The procedure actually employed in attempting to establish this fact is one of administrative adjudication. Here the government becomes one party, and the individual charged with having illegally entered the United States becomes the opposing party. The dispute between the government and the individual can be settled only by some procedure comparable to a judicial procedure; namely, a hearing, the presentation of facts, the calling of witnesses, the weighing of all the evidence, and finally a decision establishing the status of the person concerned.

A comparable situation arises when the Federal Trade Commission, after investigation by its own staff, examination by an examining attorney, and a decision by the Board of Review, recommends the issue of a formal complaint against a certain practice of a certain "person, partnership, or corporation" as constituting an unfair method of competition. This complaint contains notice of a hearing, at which the recipient may appear and "show cause why an order should not be entered by the Commission requiring such person, partnership, or corporation to cease and desist from the violation of the law so charged in said complaint."[1] The result of the hearing may be either that the complaint is dropped, or that the Commission issues an order requiring the person, partnership, or corporation in question, to "cease and desist" from using the method of competition described in the complaint. Evidently the first investigations made by the Commission, which may involve no further action, or may on the other hand serve as the basis of the formal complaint, are administrative acts. The hearing, however, is a process of administrative adjudication.

C. In a third type of administrative activity, the individual is asking the government for some sort of privilege or favor, and the administration must determine whether or not such request shall be granted. Thus, the Federal Communications Commission may be requested to grant a radio license; the Secretary of Commerce may be requested to give certificates of various sorts in respect to aviation; the Patent Office may be asked to issue a patent; the Postmaster General may be asked to permit the mailing of certain matter as "second class." Normally, if the petitioner meets the requirements for the privilege, as set forth in the law and in superior rules and regulations, the request is granted. There has been only an administrative process so far, even though the administrative authority has had to determine its jurisdiction in the matter, to interpret statutes, rules, and reg-

---

[1] 15 U.S.C.A., Sec. 45.

ulations, to make an investigation covering certain relevant facts, and to reach a decision either granting or refusing the request.

In substance, the administrative authority has done many of the same things that might be done by a court during a judicial investigation. For instance, the patent examiners not only apply scientific knowledge and technical principles to the applications for patents that come before them, but also interpret and apply statutes, Patent Office rules of practice, the decisions of various courts, and especially the decisions of the Court of Customs and Patent Appeals. If, as the result of such study and search, the primary examiner determines that the applicant is entitled to a patent, the application is granted upon the payment of the required fee.

So far, despite the legal research involved, there is no basis for saying that the action of the examiner is anything but administrative in nature. The same is true if the primary examiner rejects the application and the individual accepts his decision. If, however, the examiner rejects the application, and the applicant disputes the rejection, the basis is established for a case. The applicant may appeal from an adverse decision, first to the examiner in chief and next to the Board of Appeals; and again, from an adverse decision by this Board, to the United States Court of Customs and Patent Appeals. An option is given in this last instance of filing a bill in equity which may be adjudicated in a regular judicial court. The first step in patent appeals is thus necessarily administrative adjudication; the last may or may not be ordinary adjudication.[2]

D. Another typical situation arises when the Comptroller General is passing upon a claim brought by an

[2] 35 U.S.C.A., Secs. 57-63, and supplements.

individual against the government. Although the Comptroller General may have to audit accounts, refer to laws, rules, regulations, and court decisions, and take several other steps such as a court would take in order to determine upon the validity of each claim, he is thus far performing only an administrative function. If some particular decision which he has made is unsatisfactory to the individual whose interests are affected thereby, the latter may ask for a rehearing of the case by the Comptroller General. At this rehearing, evidence is submitted, witnesses are called, and the controversy is decided. This second decision is an example of administrative adjudication.

A kind of administrative action which closely resembles that just described, takes place when an administrative authority is called upon to settle claims by employees against the United States government under the Employees' Compensation Act.[3] The United States Employees' Compensation Commission considers the claim, as well as the report furnished by the immediate superior of the claimant; and carries out such investigations as it deems necessary. It makes a finding of facts, and an award for or against the payment of such compensation as the law provides. "In the absence of fraud or mistake in mathematical calculation, the finding of facts in, and the decision of the Commission upon, the merits of any claim presented under or authorized by this chapter if supported by competent evidence shall not be subject to review by any other administrative or accounting officer, employee, or agent of the United States."[4] It is clear that the work of the Commission is administrative rather than quasi-judicial in nature, since the payment of com-

---

[3] Act of Sept. 7, 1916, 39 Stat. L. 742.
[4] The same.

pensation is regarded as an act of pure grace. The individual injured has no right to sue the government. Although the action may appear quasi-judicial or even judicial in nature, it is prevented from being so by the fact that the government does not allow itself to be sued, but merely determines through its agents what it will do for the individual injured in the service.[5]

E. When the government is settling administratively disputes between private individuals concerning property rights, for instance between employers and employees under the Longshoremen's and Harbor Workers' Compensation Act,[6] the function is administrative adjudication, and not administration pure and simple. In this instance, the law itself definitely establishes the rights of those injured.

The procedure in respect to claims is much like a judicial hearing, with the employer and the claimant presenting evidence before a deputy commissioner appointed by the United States Employees' Compensation Commission. The deputy commissioner issues an order either rejecting the claim or making an award; and unless proceedings for the suspension or setting aside of such order are instituted within 30 days, it becomes final. If either of the parties believes that the order was not in accordance with law, injunction proceedings in the Federal District Court may be brought against the deputy commissioner who issued it, with the object of having the order suspended, or set aside in whole or in part. This procedure indicates that the deputy commissioner is acting, to all intents and purposes, as a court of first instance, in deciding cases under a law which

[5] See *Dahn* v. *Davis*, 258 U.S. 421; *Silva* v. *United States*, 292 Fed. 464.
[6] 44 Stat. L. 1424, c. 509, Mar. 4, 1927.

bestows certain definite rights upon individuals injured under conditions specified in the statute.

The typical situations which have just been examined do not correspond in every respect with the theoretical definition of administrative adjudication that was used as our point of departure. It is to be hoped, nevertheless, that they have served both to clarify that definition, and to illustrate the differences between administration proper and administrative adjudication, which we shall now proceed to summarize.

An administrative agency carries out its regular functions by means of certain fairly well defined methods. As a preliminary to action, either consciously or unconsciously it must determine whether it has jurisdiction in the matter. It must establish facts by various kinds of methods. In many instances it may hold hearings, summon witnesses, produce experts, and proceed by definite rules and regulations. It must interpret law, rules, regulations, court decisions, and decisions of administrative bodies and tribunals. It may draw inferences from facts, and it may make decisions. In performing many of these acts it may be doing almost exactly the same kind of work that is done by a court in trying a case; yet the whole process, as described so far, is merely one of administration.

When does the work of the agency lose its normal character of simple administration, and assume that of administrative adjudication? Evidently we cannot use the nature of a particular action as the criterion that determines whether the administration is acting in an administrative capacity or an administrative judicial capacity. Investigations into fact and law, and the making of decisions based on the findings, are actions common to both rôles. So long as those affected by the work of an administrative agency do not dispute the decisions which it reaches, or object to the acts which it performs in the normal course of its functioning, all these operations must be considered as belonging to the category of simple administrative duties.

When, however, an interested person objects that some administrative act, finding, or decision invades his legal rights in any way, it becomes necessary for an investigation to be made and a decision rendered, on the points of controversy. If the investigation and decision are made by an administrative agency or tribunal of any kind, from the Commissioner of Immigration to the Court of Customs and Patent Appeals, this function is administrative adjudication. As to fact and law, the investigation may cover exactly the same ground on which the original decision or act of the administration was based; but it now has the special purpose of deciding a controverted question of right. In most instances the administration will defend its position, so that the controversy will take the form of a dispute between opposing parties.

II. COMPARISON OF ORDINARY ADJUDICATION WITH ADMINISTRATIVE ADJUDICATION

In attempts made by various writers to distinguish between administrative adjudication and ordinary adjudication, several different criteria have been used. These take the form of distinctions as to: the subject matter of the dispute; the nature of the authority making the decisions; the nature of the action to be taken after finding facts and applying law; and the finality or lack of finality of the action.

A. In France and Germany, generally speaking, the distinction between ordinary adjudication and administrative adjudication consists largely in the nature of the subject matter handled. If the adjudication has to do with cases involving administrative acts (except for a few special matters such as contracts) it is administrative adjudication and is handled by administrative courts. In a broad way, a line is drawn between public law and private law. The administrative judicial authorities handle the cases involving public law, while the ordinary courts handle all cases involving private law. The criterion as to the nature of the subject matter is used also to a certain extent in the United States, where it is held that power to decide questions legislative or executive in nature may not be vested in the regular constitutional courts exercising the judicial power of the United States, but may be vested in so-called "legislative courts," or administrative tribunals.[7]

B. One may also make a distinction as to the nature of the authority which renders the decision. If the authority is primarily an administrative agency carrying on active administration as well as settling cases that may arise regarding its own activities, its decisions in respect to these cases are examples of administrative adjudication. When an authority does not carry on administrative functions of any nature, but, like the Court of Customs and Patent Appeals, or the Board of Tax Appeals, merely decides cases, it may still be established by law as an administrative court, to deal with certain classes of suits based on administrative acts. The Council of State in France is an administrative court which finally decides administrative controversies in every field. The nature of the authority to which the work of administrative adjudication is entrusted is evidently not

---

[7] Ex parte *Bakelite Corporation*, 279 U.S. 438.

to be described in a single formula; nevertheless, this type of authority is distinct and separate from the regular judicial court system.

C. A distinction between administrative adjudication and ordinary adjudication, based on the nature of the action to be taken after fact-finding and applying the law to the facts, was made in Great Britain in 1932 by the Committee on Ministers' Powers,[8] as follows:

A true judicial decision presupposes an existing dispute between two or more parties, and then involves four requisites:

(1) The presentation (not necessarily oral) of their case by the parties to the dispute; (2) if the dispute between them is a question of fact, the ascertainment of the fact by means of evidence adduced by the parties to the dispute and often with the assistance of argument by or on behalf of the parties on the evidence; (3) if the dispute between them is a question of law, the submission of legal argument by the parties; and (4) a decision which disposes of the whole matter by a finding of facts in dispute and an application of the law of the land to the facts so found, including where required a ruling upon any disputed question of law.

A quasi-judicial decision equally presupposes an existing dispute between two or more parties and involves (1) and (2), but does not necessarily involve (3), and never involves (4).

The place of (4) is in fact taken by administrative action, the character of which is determined by the Minister's free choice.

The Supreme Court of the United States makes a somewhat similar distinction between adjudication and administrative adjudication. In the case of *Federal Radio Commission* v. *General Electric Company et al.*,[9] in respect to a petition to review a decision of the Board of Tax Appeals, the court said:

[8] Vol. I, pp. 73-74.
[9] 281 U.S. 464, 469.

Such a petition (a) brings before the reviewing court the United States or its representative on the one hand and the interested taxpayer on the other, (b) presents for consideration either the right of the United States to the payment of the tax claimed to be due from the taxpayer or his right to have refunded to him money which he has paid to satisfy a tax claimed to have been erroneously charged against him, and (c) calls for a judicial and binding determination of the matter so presented—all of which makes the proceeding a case or controversy within the scope of the judicial power as defined in the judiciary article.

It must be observed that these distinctions would not apply in Germany or in France, where the judgments of the administrative courts, concerning matters that fall within their jurisdiction, do establish facts, apply the law of the land, and interpret this law when necessary. These judgments are "judicial and binding," although made by administrative courts. Hence the criteria just cited, as set forth in England and the United States, are not universally valid.

D. The Supreme Court of the United States, as we have just seen, appears to make the finality or binding effect of a decision one of the distinctions between administrative adjudication and ordinary adjudication. Under the law of the United States, a constitutional court exercising judicial powers cannot have its determinations subject to revision by executive officers or tribunals;[10] but the decisions of the latter, where questions of law, and particularly of constitutionality, are

---

[10] *Hayburn's Case*, 2 Dal. 409. This case was based upon a statute which attempted to confer upon the circuit courts jurisdiction to hear claims for veterans' pensions, but gave the Secretary of War power to withhold a pension if he had "cause to suspect imposition or mistake." I Stat. L. 243. See also Ex parte *Bakelite Corporation*, 279 U.S. 438; *Gordon* v. *United States*, 2 Wall. 561; *Federal Radio Commission* v. *General Electric Co.*, 281 U.S. 464.

concerned, may be reviewed by the judicial courts. This contrast obviously depends upon a particular situation within a given country, and does not demonstrate any inherent difference between administrative adjudication and ordinary adjudication.

The distinctions between administrative and ordinary adjudication made by the Supreme Court of the United States are based almost exclusively upon the distinction between the "constitutional courts" provided for by Article III, Section 1, of the Constitution, and the so-called "legislative courts" which Congress has established from time to time to carry on certain functions;[11] hence they cannot be considered as having any general application.

The only distinctions of primary importance and fundamental validity between administrative adjudication and ordinary adjudication, in the opinion of the writers, depend upon the nature of the acts adjudicated and the nature of the authority that is adjudicating. There may be other differences between the two types of adjudication, especially since administrative adjudication tends toward a simpler and less formal procedure, with less attention to precedent, than ordinary judicial adjudication employs; but such differences are of secondary importance. If acts are administrative in nature, and if they are adjudicated either by agencies which carry on administrative duties or by administrative tribunals, the function thus performed is administrative adjudication.

III. SUMMARY AND CONCLUSIONS

The work of government necessarily includes the making of countless decisions. Many of these have a di-

[11] Wilbur Griffith Katz, "Federal Legislative Courts," *43 Harvard Law Review* 894; "The Distinction Between Legislative and Constitutional Courts," *43 Yale Law Journal* 316.

rect and immediate effect upon individual rights. When such decisions are questioned or challenged by the person or persons affected, any one of three situations may arise:

A. Administrative review of a given decision may take place, and the decision may be modified, rescinded, or ratified. This action may be performed by the same agency which made the decision, or by its administrative superior. The distinguishing characteristics of administrative review are its simplicity and its non-controversial nature. The administration merely considers the question whether its decision was mistaken or faulty, and takes action accordingly.

B. Some cases based on decisions of the administration may be taken to the ordinary judicial courts. These must be such as the courts consider justiciable controversies. They may, according to their nature, the law, and the court decisions, go to the ordinary courts immediately (as when an individual claims with what appears to be *prima facie* incontrovertible reason that a given administrative decision deprives him of property without due process of law), or go on appeal from some administrative tribunal.

C. Administrative adjudication may take place. The individual may bring a case or a suit which is defended by the administration, or the administration may sue the individual who refuses to be guided by its decision or to obey its orders—as, for example, to pay the income taxes assessed against him. Such a suit may be decided by a special administrative court, or by an active administrator or administrative agency. Ordinarily, the individual and the government agency which made the original decision will be in the position of opposing parties; there will be notice, hearing, evidence, written briefs, and perhaps oral pleading—in other words, there will be a controversy which is adjudicated by an administrative tribunal. This tribunal may or may not be a separate agency outside the active administration. Some controversies may go in second instance, and a few even in third instance, to higher administrative tribunals.

Of the three possible ways of handling an administrative controversy which have just been described, it is the third which interests us at present. This is due to several factors, all of which are discussed elsewhere in this study; but it is due most of all to the very great and rapidly increasing number of such controversies. Neither the uncertainties and informalities of mere administrative action, nor the slow, costly, and inappropriate formalities of ordinary judicial action, can deal satisfactorily with the hundreds of thousands of administrative cases which must be decided each year. Neither the administration nor the courts can be organized for this task.

CHAPTER VI

THE FORMS OF ADMINISTRATIVE ADJUDICATION

In France, Germany, and various other countries where administrative adjudication is recognized as an important function of government, the forms and procedures by means of which this function is exercised are carefully worked out and systematized. In England and the United States, where no definite system of administrative adjudication has been worked out, but where the practice has grown up in a haphazard way as a result of attempts to solve specific problems of government, a great variety of forms have developed, many of which are neither simple, logical, nor effective. This is true for both original and appellate administrative adjudication.

I. ORIGINAL ADMINISTRATIVE ADJUDICATION

Original administrative adjudication in the United States takes half a dozen or more separate and distinct forms. It must be acknowledged that these forms sometimes overlap, or shade into one another by scarcely perceptible degrees. For the sake of clearness, however, several examples of well differentiated forms will be discussed below in the following order: Advisory administrative adjudication, with the power of final decision vested in the head of a department or other authority; administrative adjudication as a condition precedent to the performance of an administrative act; administrative adjudication as a part of the carrying on of regular functions by an administrative officer; administrative adjudication combined with a legislative administrative process; regular suits brought against administrative decisions; administrative adjudication in connection with licensing activities; administrative adjudication in connection with the settlement of claims.

A. Advisory administrative adjudication, with the power of final decision vested in the head of a department or other authority, is exercised by many divisions of the government. Cases arise from time to time which seem to require something more than a mere administrative decision. There may be a conflict between the interests of the affected person (against whom administrative action is about to be taken), and the views of the authority which proposes to take the administrative action. Furthermore, in many instances complicated questions of fact and law are involved. Several special authorities have been established, either by law, by executive order, or by administrative regulation, with the duty of investigating such cases. These authorities are generally called boards of appeal, or boards of review. This type of nomenclature is very misleading, since it implies appellate rather than original administrative adjudication; hence care should be taken to understand the true function of such boards. They do not decide the cases that come before them in any final manner; but after a careful examination they render an opinion. This opinion may or may not be followed by the head of the department or other authority with which they are connected.

Among such agencies several will be mentioned as examples. The former Board of Appeals in the Land Department gave "full consideration of all facts and equities in the cases" brought before it, and acted in an advisory capacity to the Secretary of the Interior, who made the final decision in the matter.[1] Within the Department of Commerce, a review board has been established to examine protested efficiency ratings. The Board of Appeals and Review in the Civil Service Commission passes upon all matters pending before the Commission. It reviews the records and considers the merits of appeals from ratings in all examinations (including character investigations); appeals against decisions to exclude persons from examination on account of unsuitability; appeals against actions taken in cases of transfer, reinstatement, promotion, or retirement; and appeals in connection with allocation.[2] Its decisions, although usually accepted by the Commission, are merely advisory. An important advisory agency is the Bureau of Formal Cases in the Interstate Commerce Commission. The Board of Review in the Federal Trade Commission reviews the reports of examining attorneys, and as a result of its investigation makes recommendations to the Commission.[3] The Board of Review in the Labor Department at Washington acts in an advisory capacity to the Secretary of Labor, who, through his assistant secretaries, makes the final decision in expulsion and exclusion cases.[4]

B. Administrative adjudication is sometimes made a condition precedent to the performance of an administrative act. In respect to unfair practices in import trade, the Tariff Commission makes investigations for the purpose of assisting the President of the United States in performing administrative duties. The findings of the

[1] Edward C. Finney, Board of Appeals, Department of the Interior, *American Political Science Review*, Vol. 10, pp. 290-95. This Board seems to have been created simply by an appropriation act. See 38 U.S. Stat. L. 488.
[2] *Current Organization Charts of U. S. Administrative Agencies*, No. 133.
[3] *Annual Report of the Federal Trade Commission.* 1928-29, p. 18.
[4] W. C. Van Vleck, *The Administrative Control of Aliens*, pp. 78, 147.

Commission, if supported by evidence, are conclusive; except that a rehearing may be granted by the Commission, and except that an appeal, on questions of law only, may be taken to the United States Court of Customs and Patent Appeals by the importer or consignee. The court may order additional evidence to be taken by the Commission. The Commission may modify its findings as to facts, or make new findings, by reason of additional evidence properly supported. These additional findings are conclusive in respect to facts, but an appeal may be taken as aforesaid, to the Court of Customs and Patent Appeals, on questions of law only. The judgment of this court is final. On the basis of the findings and records sent to him by the Commission, the President decides whether or not to exclude the importation of certain articles.[5]

C. Administrative adjudication is often a part of the regular functions of an administrative officer. In several instances the head of one of the executive departments exercises certain powers of administrative adjudication as a part of his ordinary duties. Thus, the Postmaster General passes upon such questions as: Whether a particular serial publication is a periodical; whether certain printed matter is obscene; whether the sale by post of certain articles or securities is using the mails to defraud.[6]

Another example of administrative adjudication in connection with the carrying out of regular administrative functions is found in connection with the work of the Land Department. The Land Department (including the Secretary of the Interior, the Commissioner of the General Land Office, and subordinate authorities) has the duty of administering the public lands of the United

[5] 19 U.S.C.A., Supp., Sec. 1337.
[6] 26 Stat. L. 466. 39 U.S.C.A., Supp., Secs. 259 and 732.

States. As a part of this general administrative work, it
must necessarily make many decisions of a quasi-judicial
and even judicial nature. The courts recognize the Land
Department authorities as a special tribunal, with judicial powers to hear and determine claims to public lands,
and power to execute judgments by conveyance of lands
to the proper parties.[7]

D. Administrative adjudication may be combined
with a legislative administrative process. Several important administrative agencies in our federal government
combine, at least occasionally, the function of administrative adjudication with that of administrative legislation. This combination of functions is especially likely
to occur as a part of the work of regulatory agencies. It
is almost inevitable when the legislature has established
only general and vague standards for the administrative
authorities, and has failed to require such authorities
to make supplementary rules and regulations in advance
of taking administrative action. Under these conditions
the regulatory authorities generally feel that they ought
to proceed by a sort of trial-and-error method, combin-
ing the sub-legislative and administrative aspects of regulation with the processes of fact-finding, holding judicial
hearings, and issuing decisions or orders based upon the
results of the hearings.

Thus, the Federal Trade Commission, which has the
duty of preventing persons and corporations engaged in
interstate commerce from using unfair methods of competition, has received almost no guidance from the legislature as to what constitutes unfair methods of competition. It makes investigations as to competitive practices,

[7] *United States* v. *Winona and St. P. R.R. Co.*, 67 Fed. 949, affirmed
in 165 U.S. 463; *New Dunderberg Min. Co.* v. *Old*, 79 Fed. 598;
Snyder v. *Sickles*, 98 U.S. 203, 211.

and if it believes that a certain practice is an unfair method it notifies the interested party and holds a hearing. If, as a result of the hearing, the Commission decides that the practice in question is an unfair method of competition, a cease and desist order is issued. A similar combination of functions is found in the work of the Interstate Commerce Commission. This authority often exercises both administrative-legislative and administrative-judicial powers when it is making a decision with respect to rates.

E. Regular suits may be brought against administrative decisions. The bringing of suits against administrative decisions is a standard form of administrative adjudication in France and Germany, and to a lesser extent in the United States. In both France and Germany, there are regular methods of appealing to the administrative tribunals, generally for the setting aside, or possibly the amendment, of an administrative act that has already been accomplished. In both countries, although certain of the active administrative authorities decide administrative cases in first or even in second instance, the specially organized administrative courts are tribunals whose almost exclusive duty is to decide administrative cases. In very few instances do the administrative tribunals carry on extensive administrative functions. It is true that the Council of State in France has certain advisory functions in connection with presidential decrees. Moreover, in several of the German states the lowest administrative tribunal has been an active administrative authority.[8] But in general, administrative courts do not perform duties of active administration.

Much of the original administrative adjudication in

[8] See F. F. Blachly and Miriam E. Oatman, *The Government and Administration of Germany*, p. 461.

the federal government of the United States is also carried out through the medium of regular suits brought in specialized administrative courts which exercise no administrative or legislative functions, but merely hear complaints against the final decisions of executive or administrative authorities. This is true in respect to customs appeals, tax appeals, patent appeals, and claims against the federal government. Cases in these fields are heard, respectively, by the United States Customs Court, the Board of Tax Appeals, the Board of Appeals in the Patent Office, and the Court of Claims.[9]

F. Administrative adjudication is sometimes exercised in connection with licensing activities. In connection with the granting and revocation of various kinds of licenses, there are several federal authorities which act in an administrative judicial capacity. For example, the Federal Communications Commission is given authority to revoke licenses of radio broadcasting stations, subject to certain contingencies. No revocation order, however, takes effect until due notice has been given to the parties interested, who may demand a hearing. Upon the conclusion of the hearing the Commission may affirm, modify, or cancel the order of revocation.[10]

Another instance of administrative adjudication in connection with licensing activities is found in the procedure of issuance, suspension, or revocation of aircraft and airman certificates by the Secretary of Commerce. Within 20 days after notice has been given that a certificate is denied, or that a certificate previously issued is suspended or revoked, the applicant for or holder of the certificate may file a request for a public hearing, which is arranged by the Secretary of Commerce. Either the Secre-

[9] The Court of Claims also performs certain advisory duties.
[10] 44 Stat. L. 1169.

tary, or any officer or employee of the Department of Commerce designated for this purpose, may hold such a hearing. The powers of the presiding officer include the right to administer oaths, examine witnesses, and issue subpoenas for the attendance and testimony of witnesses or for the production of books, papers, documents, and so forth. All evidence taken at the hearing is recorded and forwarded to the Secretary of Commerce for decision. This decision, if in accordance with law, is final.[11]

G. Administrative adjudication may occur in connection with the settlement of claims. In the settlement and adjustment of claims of the government or against the government, by the General Accounting Office, two distinct processes may be involved: the auditing of the claim, which is a mere administrative process; and the settlement of the claim, which if undisputed is also an administrative process, but which in case of dispute may give rise to an administrative judicial process. Let us consider a concrete instance. The Wilson-Martin Company applied for a review of a settlement which disallowed a claim for meat alleged to have been delivered to Camp Dix. The disallowance was based upon the lack of evidence of receipt at the camp. At the rehearing, the company submitted in support of its claim, a photostatic copy of an American Railway Express delivery receipt signed "Q.M.C. Det. Mike Hapstak." On comparison of the signature of said Hapstak with the signature on the receipt, they were found to be identical. The Comptroller General held that this evidence that the meat sold to the government was delivered to an enlisted man in the army, duly authorized to receive it, entitled the

[11] 44 Stat. L. 569 as amended by 45 Stat. L. 1404; 49 U.S.C.A., Supp., Sec. 173.

vendor to payment.[12] Examination of the Decisions of
the Comptroller General will show many such instances,
where a claim which has been disallowed upon audit is
brought before the Comptroller General as an administrative adjudicative authority.

In such an instance the government, through the administrative process of auditing the claim, has made a
decision which is disputed by the individual affected
thereby. Hence the Comptroller General must settle a
controversy which bears the distinguishing features of
an administrative judicial case: Opposing parties (the
government and the claimant); a question of rights,
which is also a complaint against an administrative act;
decision based on legal principles, made by an administrative authority.

II. APPELLATE ADMINISTRATIVE ADJUDICATION

Appeals from administrative judicial decisions do not
generally go, in the United States, to appellate administrative agencies. Many of these appeals go to the regular judicial courts, on points of law or pleas in equity,
and occasionally even on the facts. In some instances,
however, they go to appellate administrative authorities.
Sometimes there is a choice of appellate jurisdictions.

The forms of administrative adjudication in respect
to appeals are much less varied than the forms in respect
to original cases. As a rule, appellate administrative authorities are bodies organized as tribunals. In at least
one instance, appeal lies from an administrative judicial
authority to a higher administrative officer.

A. Appeals may be made to administrative courts.
Perhaps the clearest example of an appellate authority,

---

[12] *Decisions of the Comptroller General of the United States,* Vol. 4,
October 1924, p. 417.

which from the viewpoint of this study is certainly an administrative court, is the Court of Customs and Patent Appeals. This court hears appeals from the decisions of the United States Customs Court, and from the Board of Appeals which passes in second or third instance on patent and trademark cases.[13] By the Tariff Act of 1922, this court was also authorized to review the findings of the Tariff Commission in respect to complaints of unfair practices in the importation of merchandise.[14]

The Court of Appeals of the District of Columbia is a regular judicial court, but Congress has occasionally required it to act also as an appellate administrative tribunal. Thus, the Radio Act of 1927[15] bestowed on the Court of Appeals of the District of Columbia the power to "hear, review, and determine" appeals from the decisions of the Federal Radio Commission. The hearing was to be based "upon the record made before the Commission;" and the court was authorized to "alter or revise the decision appealed from and enter such judgment as it may deem just." The United States Supreme Court held that the nature of this grant of power made the Court of Appeals of the District of Columbia " 'a superior and revising agency' in the administrative field,"[16] so far as radio cases were concerned.

A more recent act of Congress, however, has limited appeals from the decisions of the Federal Radio Commission to this court. Appeals can now be brought only on "questions of law." The same act provided that "the

[13] For customs, see 28 U.S.C.A., Supp., Sec. 308. For patents, see 35 U.S.C.A., Supp., Sec. 59a; 28 U.S.C.A., Supp., Sec. 309a; 35 U.S.C.A., Supp., Sec. 63. For trade marks, see 15 U.S.C.A., Sec. 89; 15 U.S.C.A., Supp., Sec. 89.
[14] 42 Stat. L. 944, Sec. 316; 19 U.S.C.A., Sec. 176.
[15] 44 Stat. L. 1169.
[16] *Radio Commission* v. *General Electric Co.*, 281 U.S. 464, 467; *Radio Commission* v. *Nelson Bros.*, 289 U.S. 266.

findings of fact by the Commission, if supported by substantial evidence, shall be conclusive unless it shall clearly appear that the findings of the Commission are arbitrary or capricious." These provisions, as interpreted by
the United States Supreme Court, deprive the Court of
Appeals of the District of Columbia of its status as an
appellate administrative judicial authority for radio
cases, and leave it in the position of a regular judicial
reviewing authority for radio cases which raise questions
of law.[17]

The Court of Appeals of the District of Columbia also
had an appellate administrative jurisdiction in respect to
trademark proceedings from 1905[18] until 1929, when
this jurisdiction was transferred to the Court of Customs
and Patent Appeals.[19]

The Supreme Court of the District of Columbia has
appellate administrative jurisdiction over appeals from
decisions made by the Public Utility Commission of the
District of Columbia.[20] The United States Supreme
Court interprets this jurisdiction as a review of "legislative discretion," in the following remarkable statement:
"We cannot escape the conclusion that Congress intended
that the court shall revise the legislative discretion of the
Commission by considering the evidence and full record
of the case and entering the order it deems the Commission ought to have made."[21] Comparison with the
work of administrative tribunals in both the United

[17] 47 U.S.C.A., Supp., Sec. 96; *Radio Commission* v. *Nelson Bros.*, 289
U.S. 266. The new law incorporating the Radio Commission into the
Federal Communications Commission did not change the situation just
described.

[18] Act of Feb. 20, 1905, 33 Stat. L. 727. See *Postum Cereal Co.* v.
California Fig Nut Co., 272 U.S. 693, 698.

[19] Act of Mar. 2, 1929, 45 Stat. L. 1475.

[20] Act of Mar. 4, 1913, 37 Stat. L. 988, Chap. 150, Sec. 8, par. 64.

[21] *Keller* v. *Potomac Elec. Co.*, 261 U.S. 428, 442.

States and other countries, however, compels the authors of this study to maintain that administrative adjudication is an element in the work performed by the Commission in issuing its original orders after a hearing involving law and fact, and is certainly the function performed by the Supreme Court of the District of Columbia in reviewing the cases on appeal.

The examples just given show that the regular courts of the District of Columbia may be, and from time to time have been, vested by Congress with appellate administrative jurisdiction. The establishment of the Court of Customs and Patent Appeals shows that Congress may, if it so desires, bestow appellate administrative jurisdiction upon administrative tribunals which perform neither administrative functions nor ordinary judicial functions.

B. In at least one instance, appeal lies from an administrative judicial authority to a higher administrative authority. Administrative judicial decisions in immigration exclusion cases are made by boards of special inquiry. Any decision of such a board is final, unless appeal is taken to the Secretary of Labor, whose action on the appeal concludes the matter.[22]

III. SUMMARY AND CONCLUSIONS

Administrative adjudication in connection with the work of the United States government takes many different forms. The variety of forms is particularly noticeable in respect to original administrative adjudication. The purpose and the finality of administrative decisions also vary a great deal. Some of these decisions are merely advisory in purpose, and may be set aside or totally disregarded by the authorities in whom the power of final action is vested. Some decisions control the action of the

[22] Van Vleck, *Administrative Control of Aliens*, pp. 49, 246-50.

administrative authorities, unless a higher tribunal or agency, administrative-judicial or judicial, may review them on questions of law, questions of fact, or both.

Appellate administrative jurisdiction may be given to administrative tribunals, to the courts of the District of Columbia (which are under the control of Congress), or to a high administrative officer. The forms may involve either a hearing, or a decision based on the records.

In neither original nor appellate administrative adjudication is there any general method or system. This very important function is either allowed to grow up in a haphazard fashion out of the necessities of administration, or is provided for in some law as casually as Mr. Weller's name was spelled—"according to the taste and fancy of the writer." No ordinary citizen, unversed in the intricacies of the special law governing the matter which interests him, can possibly find his way through the maze of forms and procedures, varying from department to department and even from bureau to bureau, which characterize administrative adjudication in the United States. A clear recognition of the significance of this great function, and a serious effort to have it carried out by means of simple, adequate, and consistent forms, are fundamental requisites of progress.

CHAPTER VII

TYPES OF ADMINISTRATIVE ADJUDICAT-
ING AUTHORITIES

Closely related to the subject of types of administrative adjudication is that of types of adjudicative agencies. Any attempt to classify such agencies in our federal government, or even to list them, is beset with difficulties. Though about 60 government authorities settle disputes of various natures, several of them must be excluded from any list of administrative tribunals. For example, some of these agencies, although they perform most of the processes of adjudication, are in the last analysis merely advisory in nature. Some are fundamentally mediating, conciliatory, or adjusting authorities. Others make decisions regarding claims and disputes, but cannot be said to adjudicate because the controversies which they handle do not involve questions of recognized legal rights, but are held to be matters for administrative adjustment, or matters pertaining to favors granted by the government. Finally, there are one or two authorities whose status is uncertain for some technical reason. Despite the fact that these authorities do not possess the status of administrative tribunals, it is necessary to mention them and to outline their functions, since in several instances slight changes in set-up, powers, and relationships would transform them into adjudicating authorities. The question whether such changes would be desirable will be discussed later.

I. PRESENT-DAY ADMINISTRATIVE TRIBUNALS

We have seen in the chapter on the nature of administrative adjudication, that the cases decided by this type of adjudication arise out of or in connection with administrative action, and normally involve a contest between parties in respect to rights. Any genuine administrative tribunal, no matter how organized, no matter what its procedures may be, must be dealing with cases of this nature. It cannot be merely administering, merely advising, merely mediating or conciliating, or merely settling disputes as to the granting of gifts or favors.

The application of this criterion shows that there are approximately 50 administrative tribunals in the federal government. Although they might be classified in various ways, the classification which appears best adapted to the purposes of the present study is based upon the nature of the primary functions performed by them. This is due to the fact that, generally speaking, their organization, their relationships to other agencies, the method of appointment and the tenure of their members, their procedures, the methods by which they make decisions, the methods of executing their decisions, the methods of controlling their decisions, and even the publication of their decisions, all depend to a large extent upon the type of administrative authority to which they belong.

The use of primary function as a basis of classification indicates that there are, beside the types which we exclude from our list of genuine tribunals, nine primarily different types as follows: independent administrative courts, special administrative courts within departments or agencies, regulatory authorities, executive authorities, administrative authorities, regular courts exercising the functions of administrative tribunals, fact-finding authorities, licensing authorities, and the Comptroller General.

Neither this classification, nor any other, can avoid certain difficulties, the chief of which is the fact that in many instances the duties and functions of the adjudicatory authorities are so complex as to make clear lines of demarcation impossible. This classification must therefore be regarded simply as a scheme adopted for working purposes. The various types included therein will be discussed in the order in which they were named.

A. Primarily Independent Administrative Courts

The tribunals which fall within the category of independent administrative courts are: The United States Customs Court, the United States Court of Customs and Patent Appeals, the Board of Tax Appeals, and the Court of Claims. These courts are organized very much as ordinary judicial courts are. With few exceptions, they display the following features: Their members are called judges; the appointment of members is to all intents permanent, since it is not for a fixed term, but "during good behavior;" the independence of the courts is protected by their separation from other agencies of government, and by the removal of their members from political influences. The procedures in these courts resemble procedures in ordinary judicial courts.

The independent administrative tribunals neither exercise direct sub-legislative powers nor perform administrative functions. They merely settle, in first, second, or third instance, as the case may be, disputes that arise regarding the acts or decisions of administrative authorities. The chief reason for regarding them as administrative courts rather than special judicial courts is the fact that their jurisdiction is limited to administrative disputes. They do not decide controversies resulting from the relationships of private individuals to one another, but solely cases in which some act of public administration is involved. In the great majority of instances the government is a party to these suits.[1]

Because of the special interest attaching to the independent administrative courts, as recognized agencies of administrative adjudication, a brief description of each will be given at this point.

1. *The United States Customs Court* is the first instance in "almost every possible legal controversy which may arise between the importing taxpayer and his government concerning the rate or amount of duty paid."[2] Its judges hold office during good behavior.[3] It is organized into three divisions, each of which hears special groups of cases.[4] Its procedure is much like that of an ordinary court. It has power to punish for contempt. It enforces its decisions through the collector of customs. "The court's judgment order shall be the collector's mandate and shall constitute his authority for the reliquidation of an entry, if such be the order of the court."[5] In other words, the decision is enforced through an administrative method. Its re-appraisement decisions are published in the re-appraisement circular unless they involve a question of law, in which case they are published as Treasury decisions. Its other decisions (not including those stipulated to follow a test case) are published in full as Treasury decisions.[6]

---

[1] There are a few exceptions to this rule. For example, the authorities which settle disputes as to patents may decide infringement cases to which only private individuals are parties.

[2] George Stewart Brown, "The United States Customs Court," *American Bar Association Journal*, June and July 1933; and "Judicial Review in Customs Taxation," *The Lawyer and Banker and Central Law Journal*, 1933.

[3] 19 U.S.C.A., Sec. 1518.

[4] Rules of the U. S. Customs Court, 1930, Rule 50.

[5] The same, Rule 29.

[6] The same, Rule 32; U.S.C.A., Title 19, Sec. 1519.

2. *The Court of Customs and Patent Appeals,* as its name indicates, is an appellate administrative court. Unlike the Customs Court and the Board of Tax Appeals, its jurisdiction is not confined to one class of cases, but it is the appellate authority for several types of cases. It hears appeals from the decisions in customs cases made by the United States Customs Court,[7] appeals from the decisions of the Board of Appeals in the Patent Office,[8] appeals from the findings of the Tariff Commission on complaints of unfair practice in the importation of merchandise,[9] and appeals from trade-mark decisions made by the Commissioner of Patents.[10]

There has been much uncertainty regarding the nature of this court; that is, uncertainty whether it should be recognized as a so-called "constitutional court" which can settle "cases and controversies," or whether it is merely a so-called "legislative court," dealing primarily with administrative matters. The Supreme Court has finally decided that it is the latter.[11] The grounds for holding it to be a legislative court seem to be: that since any of the actions performed by the authorities from which appeals lie to it might be settled by executive, legislative, or administrative action, they cannot truly be cases and controversies under Article III of the Constitution.[12]

The five members of this court are appointed by the President, to serve during good behavior.[13] All the members of the court at present are trained in law. The court

[7] 36 Stat. L. 105-08.
[8] 44 Stat. L. 1336, Sec. 8, and 45 Stat. L. 1476.
[9] 46 Stat. L. 703.
[10] 15 U.S.C.A. 89; 15 U.S.C.A., Supp., 89; 45 Stat. L. 1475.
[11] Ex parte *Bakelite Corporation,* 279 U.S. 438.
[12] See footnote 27, p. 128, for citations to articles dealing with the subject of constitutional and legislative courts.
[13] 28 U.S.C.A. 301, and 28 U.S.C.A. 301(b).

sits *en banc,* and any three members constitute a quorum and may make a decision. All appeals are heard in Washington. In customs matters, the court remands cases back to the United States Customs Court for such further proceedings as are deemed proper to be taken in pursuance of the appellate court's decision.[14]

Appeals in respect to customs are brought both in respect to law and facts.[15] Appeals from the Tariff Commission in respect to unfair practices in importation are brought in respect to questions of law alone.[16] Cases concerning patents and trade marks may be appealed on both law and fact. It is interesting to observe that in customs cases the Court of Customs and Patent Appeals has exclusive appellate authority, whereas in patent cases, based on the refusal of a patent by the Commissioner, an appeal may be brought before the ordinary courts as well as before the Court of Customs and Patent Appeals. Final decisions by the latter court are subject only to review by certiorari by the Supreme Court.

In so far as the Court of Customs and Patent Appeals has jurisdiction it may affirm, modify, or reverse the action of the lower administrative tribunal by means of "such orders as may seem to it proper in the premises, which shall be executed accordingly."[17] The last few words, "shall be executed accordingly," are quite vague. They fail to indicate what authority shall execute the decisions of the court in respect to various classes of cases. As a matter of practice, decisions on appeals from the Commissioner of Patents or the Board of Appeals in the Patent Office are enforced by the Commissioner of

[14] Rules of the U.S. Court of Customs and Patent Appeals, 1931, Rule 22.

[15] Judicial Code, Sec. 198; 28 U.S.C.A. 310.

[16] 46 Stat. L. 704.

[17] Judicial Code, Sec. 194.

Patents. Decisions on appeals from the Tariff Commission are enforced by the Tariff Commission. Decisions on appeals coming from the United States Customs Court are sent for enforcement to that court, which issues to the Collector of Customs an enforcement order either giving the exact decision of the Court of Customs and Patent Appeals, or following it in some detail.[18] In the last analysis, the enforcement method is obviously administrative in all instances.

3. *The Board of Tax Appeals* was established as "an independent agency of the executive branch of the government."[19] It is not an agency of the Treasury Department or a division under the Commissioner of Internal Revenue, but an independent administrative judicial agency.[20] In the case of the *Old Colony Trust Co.* v. *Commissioner*,[21] Chief Justice Taft said: "The Board of Tax Appeals is not a court. It is an executive or administrative board, upon the decision of which the parties are given an opportunity to base a petition for review to the courts after the administrative inquiry of the Board has been decided." This dictum of the Supreme Court would appear to classify the Board too narrowly as an active administrative body rather than as an administrative court. That it is in reality the latter is indicated by the fact that a law of 1926[22] made its decisions final, although either party has a right to a review by the judicial courts. One can well agree with a recent writer in the *Harvard Law Review*,[23] who says that the Board "has become a court in everything but name."

[18] Information furnished by Mr. Arthur B. Shelton, clerk of court.
[19] Revenue Act of 1924, Sec. 900.
[20] *American Woolen Co.* v. *White*, 56 Fed. (2) 716; *Blair* v. *Osterlein Machine Co.*, 220 U.S. 220.
[21] 279 U.S. 716.
[22] 44 Stat. L. 109, 110.
[23] *45 Harvard Law Review* 1223.

The 16 members of the Board of Tax Appeals are not called judges, nor do they have an appointment during good behavior, but only a twelve-year term of office which is "staggered." The membership of the Board is grouped into 16 divisions for the hearing of cases. Hearings are held not only in Washington but in other cities throughout the United States, where the members of the Board go on circuit.

Although no such qualification is required by statute, practically everyone who is appointed to membership on the Board has had legal training and experience. Connected with the Board is an assisting staff of nearly 30 members, consisting of lawyers, auditors, and accountants.

Procedure before the Board of Tax Appeals is much like that before an ordinary court. The rules of evidence follow those of the courts of equity in the District of Columbia. In practice, evidence is admitted very largely upon its merits. Because of its limited jurisdiction,[24] the Board has become a highly expert technical authority on tax matters. Appeals from its decisions lie to the Circuit Courts of Appeals and to the Court of Appeals of the District of Columbia, and by certiorari to the Supreme Court of the United States. The decisions of the Board are enforced by the Commissioner of Internal Revenue, or, in other words, by an administrative process.

From its organization in July 1924 to February 1933, a total of 69,635 cases were appealed from the decisions of the Commissioner of Internal Revenue to the Board, which took action on 52,906. Only a small percentage

---

[24] The Board has jurisdiction to re-determine deficiencies in income and estates taxes determined by the Commissioner. 44 Stat. L. Chap. 27, Secs. 904, 274, and 308; Revenue Act of 1928, Sec. 272. It may increase or decrease a deficiency, or even find that there is no deficiency but rather an overpayment. Revenue Act of 1928, Secs. 272 (e) and 332 (d).

of the decisions made by the Board have been appealed
to the courts, and only about one per cent have been
reversed.[25]

4. *The Court of Claims* is primarily a judicial body
for the settling of claims against the United States. At
times it acts in an advisory capacity to Congress and to
the executive departments[26] in respect to claims pending
before them. As with the Court of Customs and Patent
Appeals, there has been a great deal of controversy regarding the nature of the Court of Claims. The Supreme
Court has from time to time taken inconsistent positions
on the question of whether this tribunal is a constitutional or a legislative court. It has finally decided that
since all matters over which the court has jurisdiction are
equally susceptible to legislative or executive determination, they are matters in respect to which there is no
constitutional right to a judicial remedy; therefore, such
cases cannot be given to a constitutional court, but must,
if given at all, be given to a legislative court.[27] Consequently it now maintains that the Court of Claims is of
the latter type.

The Court of Claims is composed of five members
appointed by the President, who hold office during good
behavior.[28] All the members of the court at present are
lawyers. The court is assisted by five commissioners.

The Court of Claims has general jurisdiction[29] over

[25] J. Emmett Sebree, "The United States Board of Tax Appeals," 7
Temple Law Quarterly 436.

[26] See 28 U.S.C.A., Secs. 250, 251, and 254.

[27] *Williams* v. *United States*, 289 U.S. 553. See also Wilbur G. Katz,
"Federal Legislative Courts," *43 Harvard Law Review* 894; and "The
Distinction Between Legislative and Constitutional Courts," *43 Yale
Law Journal* 316ff., for a criticism of the distinction between legislative
courts and constitutional courts.

[28] 28 U.S.C.A., Sec. 241.

[29] 36 Stat. L. 135.

"all claims founded upon the Constitution of the United States or any law of Congress, except for pensions, or upon any regulation of an executive department, or upon any contract, express or implied, with the government of the United States, or for damages, liquidated or unliquidated, in cases not sounding in tort, in respect of which claims the party would be entitled to redress against the United States, either in a court of law, equity or admiralty, if the United States were suable," except claims growing out of the Civil War and commonly known as war claims, and certain rejected claims. It has jurisdiction over claims which may be referred to it by the head of any executive department, involving controversial questions of fact and law; and over claims of disbursing officers of the United States for relief from responsibility for the loss of government funds and property by capture or otherwise, where there has been no negligence. By the Dent Act of March 2, 1919,[30] it was given jurisdiction over certain classes of war claims.

Whenever any bill is pending before either house of Congress providing for a claim against the United States, whether legal or equitable, or for a grant, a gift, or a bounty to any person, the house in which the bill is pending may refer it to the Court of Claims for an investigation and determination upon the facts. In case it does not itself have jurisdiction over the case it reports back its findings to Congress. In this respect the Court of Claims acts as an investigatory or administrative body. If, however, it appears to the satisfaction of the court that the subject matter of the bill is such that it has jurisdiction, it may give a judgment in the matter.[31]

The court sits only at Washington. The five judges

[30] 40 Stat. L. 1272.
[31] Judicial Code, Sec. 151.

sit together for the hearing of cases, and the concurrence of three of them is necessary for a decision in any case. The claims are prosecuted in the court by an action commenced by the filing of a petition. The procedure is much like that of an ordinary court. A final judgment of the court against the claimant forever bars any further claim or demand against the United States arising out of the controversy.[32]

Control over the decisions of the Court of Claims may be exercised in two different ways. The Court of Claims may certify to the Supreme Court any definite and distinct questions of law, concerning which instructions are desired for the proper disposition of the case; or the Supreme Court, upon the petition of either party, may require by certiorari that the case be certified to it for its review and determination.[33] No other review is allowed.

B. Special Administrative Tribunals Within the Government Departments

There are several administrative tribunals in various government departments or organizations. The most important of these are the examiners in chief and the Board of Appeals in the Patent Office; the Board of Appeals and the Insurance Claims Council in the Veterans' Administration; the individual deputy commissioners in the Employees' Compensation Commission; and the Board of Review in the Public Works Administration.

In most instances, the statutes and regulations which govern administrative tribunals of the type now under discussion are inadequate; since they fail to provide clearly and fully for organization, powers, duties, relation-

[32] The same, Sec. 179.
[33] 43 Stat. L. 939, Sec. 3.

ships, procedures, methods of control, and other important matters affecting these agencies.

These special tribunals have a few common characteristics, but differ appreciably in respect to other significant factors. The characteristics in which they resemble one another are: (1) They are all integral parts of some government unit; a feature which distinguishes them from the special independent tribunals that stand outside of the administrative organizations. (2) As a rule, their members are also members of the respective administrative bodies within which the special tribunals are organized; although in certain instances, such as the Board of Appeals in the Veterans' Administration, some members are chosen from the outside. The members of such bodies have neither a fixed term of office nor a permanent tenure depending upon good behavior, but are subject to administrative appointments and changes. (3) These members are not called judges, but board members or commissioners, as the case may be. (4) It is not necessary that the members of such authorities shall be lawyers, although the possession of "competent legal knowledge" is required of the members of the Board of Appeals of the Patent Office, and some of the members of the Board of Appeals in the Veterans' Administration must be lawyers. (5) Despite their lack of formal judicial status, the members do work which is really judicial in nature. They do not merely give opinions or advice, but actually decide conflicts in respect to administrative acts that have already taken place. (6) These tribunals, as such, neither exercise the rule-making power nor perform administrative work. It is true that in a few instances, individual members, when not sitting in a judicial capacity, may carry on administrative functions. For example, the Board of Appeals of the Patent Office is composed of the Commissioner of Patents, the assistant commissioners, and the examiners in chief, all of whom perform administrative duties when not sitting with the Board.

In respect to other important factors, the tribunals within the government departments or agencies display great variations. Thus, the Board of Appeals in the Patent Office, and the tribunals consisting of deputy commissioners in the Employees' Compensation Commission, are organized by acts of Congress. The Board of Appeals in the Veterans' Administration is organized under statutory authorization, by executive orders of the President of the United States. The Insurance Claims Council, in the Veterans' Administration, is organized by an administrative order. The Board of Labor Review, in the Public Works Administration, is organized by a regulation of the administration itself, supplemented by contracts in which the government and its various co-contractants agree to submit their differences to the Board.

The size of these tribunals is another point of dissimilarity. For example, in the United States Employees' Compensation Commission, a single deputy commissioner in each district constitutes a tribunal charged with the settling of cases under the Longshoremen's and Harbor Workers' Compensation Act; the 30 associate members of the Board of Appeals in the Veterans' Administration, sit in sections of three; and there are three members of the Board of Labor Review in the Public Works Administration.

Methods of appointment are likewise varied. The members of the Board of Appeals in the Veterans' Administration are appointed by the Administrator of Veterans' Affairs, with the approval of the President of the United States; but members of the Board of Appeals in the Patent Office are appointed by the President of the United States with the advice and consent of the Senate. The deputy commissioners who enforce the provisions of the Longshoremen's and Harbor Workers' Compensation Act are appointed by the Workmen's Compensation Commission, some of them from the members "of any board, commission, or other agency of a state."

C. Primarily Regulatory Authorities

The chief tribunals whose fundamental work is that of regulation are: The Interstate Commerce Commission, the Federal Trade Commission, the Federal Communications Commission, the Federal Power Commission, the Federal Reserve Board, the Securities and Exchange Commission, the United States Shipping Board, and the Petroleum Administrative Board.

In most instances these authorities are established by law rather than by executive order or any other method. They are all organized as collegial bodies, that is, as groups of several persons equal in rank and power, and working co-operatively. No agency in this class consists of, or is controlled by, a single administrator. These tribunals are not subdivisions of government departments or agencies, nor are they integrated with government departments, but are organized on an independent basis. They are not under the direct administrative supervision or control of the President, as are the department heads. They are not supervised by the administrative departments. Consequently they are free from administrative controls of every sort, and are responsible only for observing the law.

The greatest difference between these bodies and the

special administrative courts consists in the fact that the regulatory authorities as a rule are exercising all three powers of government: sub-legislative, administrative, and quasi-judicial. Most of them possess rather wide powers of sub-legislation, which they exercise either directly in making rules and regulations, or indirectly, in creating regulatory situations through administrative judicial decisions. Their administrative function consists in carrying out the necessary work of regulating and controlling the activities over which they respectively have jurisdiction. All these regulatory authorities exercise the power of administrative adjudication: sometimes by settling cases which come before them in connection with their own functioning, as is done by the Interstate Commerce Commission, the Federal Trade Commission, and the Shipping Board; and sometimes by deciding disputes regarding the granting, suspension, or revocation of licenses, as is done by the Federal Communications Commission.

The members of the regulatory authorities are not called judges and do not have a secure tenure of office. They are appointed by the President of the United States, and are apparently subject to removal by him at any time.[34] Their normal terms of office, however, are long and "staggered." In practice the members are more secure than in theory, for wanton removal by the President would be a political blunder which is not likely to occur.

Despite the common characteristics just mentioned, the regulatory agencies are not organized according to any one given pattern, but have grown up as necessity has seemed to dictate. This is true in respect to their terms

[34] See *Myers* v. *United States,* 272 U.S. 52.

of office, the methods by which they make their decisions, their rules of evidence, the nature and finality of their decisions, the means of executing their decisions, and the possibilities of appeal.

1. *The Interstate Commerce Commission* exercises a very broad authority over corporations engaged in the transportation of persons and property between the states. It has power to require rates to be just and reasonable; to prohibit unjust discrimination and undue or unreasonable preferences or advantages in transportation rates or facilities; to require carriers to establish through routes and joint rates; to permit the pooling of freights of different and competing railroads; to require the publication of rates, rules, and regulations applying to interstate traffic; to regulate the use, control, supply, movement, distribution, and exchange of cars and locomotives; to prescribe accounts, records, and memoranda; to make carriers liable for loss, damage, or injury to property caused by them; and to carry out various other functions.[35] The duties of the Commission are so varied and extensive that they are necessarily subdivided and handled by numerous bureaus and divisions.

It is obvious that in carrying out its functions the Commission will be compelled to deal with many controversies arising because of objections made by various corporations to certain requirements and orders. These disputes are handled in an investigatory and advisory way by the Bureau of Formal Cases, an agency of the Commission. The decisions are made by one of the divisions

---

[35] The functions of the Commission are bestowed by numerous acts of Congress, the most important of which are: The original Interstate Commerce Act of Mar. 2, 1889; the Elkins Act of Feb. 19, 1903; the Hepburn Act of June 29, 1906; the Mann-Elkins Act of June 18, 1910; the Transportation Act of Feb. 28, 1920; the Emergency Transportation Act of June 16, 1933.

of the Commission; or by the whole Commission, if the questions involved are especially interesting or important. The judicial courts will enforce (or set aside) the decisions of the Interstate Commerce Commission, under conditions which will be discussed elsewhere in this study.

2. *The Federal Trade Commission* is composed of five commissioners (not more than three of whom may belong to the same political party) who are appointed by the President with the advice and consent of the Senate. This Commission was established by a law of 1914,[36] which also declared unfair methods of competition unlawful, and empowered the Commission to prevent persons, partnerships, or corporations from using such methods in commerce.

When the Commission has reason to believe that any person or corporation is using unfair methods of competition in commerce, it may issue a complaint stating its charges in that respect and containing notice of a hearing. The person interested has a right to appear and show cause why an order should not be entered by the Commission, requiring such person to cease and desist from the practices mentioned. The testimony is reduced to writing and filed in the office of the Commission.

If upon such hearing the Commission shall be of the opinion that the method of competition in question is prohibited by this subdivision of this chapter, it shall make a report in writing in which it shall state its findings as to the facts and shall issue and cause to be served on such person, partnership, or corporation an order requiring such person, partnership, or corporation to cease and desist from using such method of competition.[37]

If the order is not obeyed while it is in effect, the Commission may ask the Circuit Court of Appeals to en-

[36] 38 Stat. L. 717.
[37] 15 U.S.C.A., Sec. 45.

force it, at the same time filing with its application a transcript of the entire record in the proceeding. The court thereupon has jurisdiction of the proceeding and of the questions determined therein,

> . . . and shall have power to make and enter upon the pleadings, testimony, and proceedings set forth in such transcript a decree affirming, modifying, or setting aside the order of the Commission. The findings of the Commission as to facts, if supported by testimony, shall be conclusive. If either party shall apply to the court for leave to adduce additional evidence, and shall show to the satisfaction of the Court that such additional evidence is material and that there were reasonable grounds for the failure to adduce such evidence in the proceeding before the Commission, the Court may order such additional evidence to be taken before the Commission and to be adduced upon the hearing in such manner and upon such terms and conditions as to the Court may seem proper. The Commission may modify its findings as to the facts, or make new findings, by reason of the additional evidence so taken, and it shall file such modified or new findings, which, if supported by testimony, shall be conclusive, and its recommendations, if any, for the modification or setting aside of the original order, with the return of such additional evidence. The judgment and decree of the court shall be final, except that the same shall be subject to review by the Supreme Court upon certiorari.[38]

Any party required to cease or desist from using unfair methods of competition may obtain a review of such order in the Circuit Court of Appeals by filing a petition praying that the order be set aside. A copy of the petition is served upon the Commission, which certifies and files with the court a transcript of its record. The court has jurisdiction to affirm, set aside, or modify the order of the Commission. The jurisdiction is exclusive.[39]

The Commission also has certain functions in respect to making investigations for the President under the

[38] The same.
[39] The same.

National Industrial Recovery Act,[40] and enforcing decisions made under this Act.[41]

3. *The Federal Communications Commission,*[42] which is composed of seven commissioners appointed by the President for a seven-year term,[43] has the function of regulating telephone, telegraph, cable, and radio communication. It has special licensing powers in respect to radio. The Commission is organized into three divisions, each of which includes at least three members. It has the power to make investigations either upon complaint or upon its own motion. It makes a report of each investigation, together with its decision, order, or requirement in the premises. There are three different methods of enforcing the orders of the Commission:

a) Upon application of the Attorney General of the United States, at the request of the Commission, alleging a failure to comply with, or a violation of, the provisions of the act, the district courts may issue a writ of mandamus commanding compliance.

b) For failure to obey an order of the Commission, other than for the payment of money, the Commission, an injured party, or the United States may apply to an appropriate district court for enforcement. If, after hearing, the court determines that the order was regularly made and duly served, and that there has been disobedience, the court shall enforce obedience by a writ of injunction or other proper process.

c) Upon request of the Commission any district attorney may carry on, under the direction of the Attorney General, all necessary proceedings for enforce-

[40] 48 Stat. L. 198.
[41] *NRA Bulletin No.* 7, p. 18.
[42] 73 Cong., Public No. 416.
[43] Except the first members, who are appointed for staggered terms ranging from one through seven years.

ment of the act or for punishment of violation thereof.

Persons deeming themselves aggrieved by the orders of the Commission may bring a suit (with certain exceptions) to enjoin, annul, set aside, or suspend the order in a district court. But no interlocutory injunction may be granted by any district court unless the application is presented to a circuit or district judge and is heard and determined by three judges. An appeal lies directly to the Supreme Court.

Penal provisions embodied in the act are made applicable as to both general violations of the act and violations of "any rule, regulation, restriction, or condition made or imposed by any international radio or wire communication treaty or convention to which the United States is a party."

In respect to the refusal of an application for a permit to construct a radio station, for a radio license, for the renewal of an existing radio station license, or for modification of an existing radio station license, the aggrieved party may appeal to the Court of Appeals of the District of Columbia.

4. *The Federal Power Commission* exercises a general administrative control over all power sites on navigable waters, public lands, and reservations of the United States. It supervises the location, designing, construction, maintenance and operation of power projects upon such sites. It sets up a system of accounting for the determining of net investment in licensed projects, and exercises a limited jurisdiction in respect to rates, services, and securities.[44] It holds hearings in connection with applications for permits or licenses, the making of re-

---

[44] 41 Stat. L. 1065; 41 Stat. L. 1353; National Emergency Council, *Current Organization Charts of U.S. Administrative Agencies*, p. 144, hereafter referred to as *Current Organization Charts*.

quired investigations, and the regulation of rates, services, or securities.[45] The district courts have power to enforce the orders and regulations of the Commission.[46]

5. *The Federal Reserve Board* examines the accounts, books, and affairs of Federal Reserve banks and exercises a general supervisory power over such banks. It may suspend reserve requirements; it supervises and regulates the issue and retirement of notes; it adds and reclassifies reserve and central reserve cities; and it requires the writing off of doubtful or worthless assets. It may cause the suspension of the operations of Federal Reserve banks, or permit national banks to act as trustees.[47] From the standpoint of the present study, some of these functions are definitely quasi-judicial in nature. The Circuit Courts of Appeal are empowered to enforce, set aside, or modify the orders of this Board,[48] under the Clayton Act. Other actions of the Board seem to escape judicial control.

6. *The Securities and Exchange Commission*, a bi-partisan body of five members appointed by the President for a term of five years, is charged with the regulation of securities, exchanges, and over-the-counter markets operating in interstate and foreign commerce.[49] The Commission has large powers to make rules and regulations to protect investors,[50] and to make other rules and regulations necessary for the execution of its functions. It may classify insurers, securities, exchanges, and other persons or matters within its jurisdiction.[51]

[45] U.S.C.A. Title 16, Chap. 12, Sec. 797(g).
[46] The same, Sec. 820.
[47] 38 Stat. L. 262 as amended by 46 Stat. L. 814.
[48] 28 U.S.C.A., Sec. 225(e).
[49] 73 Cong., Public No. 291.
[50] Sec. 11.
[51] Sec. 23(a).

The Commission has power to hold hearings. It has power to administer oaths and affirmations, subpoena witnesses, compel their attendance, and so on. In case of refusal, the Commission invokes the aid of the federal courts. The district courts and the Supreme Court of the District of Columbia have jurisdiction to issue writs of mandamus commanding any person to comply with the provisions of this law or with an order of the Commission made in pursuance thereof. Any person aggrieved by an order of the Commission to which he is a party may obtain a review of such order in a Circuit Court of Appeals of the United States. The court has jurisdiction to affirm, modify, enforce, or set aside an order of the Commission in whole or in part.

Findings of fact by the Commission, if supported by substantial evidence, are conclusive. If either party shall apply to the court for leave to adduce additional evidence, and the court is satisfied that it should be adduced, the court may so order. As a result, the Commission may modify its findings as to facts; and these new facts, like the first, are conclusive if supported by substantial evidence.[52]

The judgment and decree of the court is final, subject to review by the Supreme Court of the United States, upon certiorari or certification. The district courts of the United States, the Supreme Court of the District of Columbia, and the territorial courts have jurisdiction over violations of the law or the rules and regulations thereunder, and of all suits in equity and actions at law brought to enforce any liability or duty created by this law and the rules and regulations thereunder. The judgments and decrees so rendered are subject to review by

[52] Sec. 25.

the Circuit Court of Appeals,[53] and finally by the Supreme Court by way of certiorari.[54]

7. *The United States Shipping Board* administers the regulations governing the publication, posting, and filing of interstate rates, fares, and charges. It conducts hearings involving complaints which allege violations of the different regulatory provisions of the Shipping Act, the Merchant Marine Act, and the Intercoastal Shipping Act. It makes investigations regarding deferred rebates; "fighting ships;" retaliation against shippers; unfair contracts; preferential and prejudicial rates and practices; unfair devices; unjust discrimination against shippers and ports; and unreasonable rates, fares, charges, classifications, regulations, and practices. It makes examinations into agreements of carriers and other persons subject to the provisions of the Shipping Act.[55] It is controlled in its actions in much the same manner as is the Interstate Commerce Commission.

8. *The Petroleum Administrative Board* "assists and advises the Petroleum Administrator with respect to all matters incident to the administration and enforcement of the Code for Fair Competition for the Petroleum Industry; and acts as a quasi-judicial agency charged with holding hearings and assembling data necessary for the administration of the code."[56]

D. Primarily Executive Authorities

Various high executive authorities of the United States perform functions which are essentially acts of adminis-

---

[53] Secs. 27 and 28, and U.S.C.A., Sec. 225.

[54] Sec. 27, and U.S.C.A., Sec. 347.

[55] Shipping Act, 46 U.S.C.A., Chap. 23; Merchant Marine Act, 46 U.S.C.A. and 46 U.S.C.A., Supp., Chap. 24; Intercoastal Shipping Act, 46 U.S.C.A., Chap. 23A.

[56] *Current Organization Charts*, No. 93.

trative adjudication. This is true even of the President. For example, under the National Industrial Recovery Act,[57] the President was authorized for a limited time to license businesses which were "in or affecting interstate or foreign commerce," whenever, after notice and hearing, he found it necessary to do so in order to make effective a fair code of competition. No person could carry on any business which the President specified as subject to license, unless a license were first obtained. "The President may suspend or revoke any such license, after due notice and opportunity for hearing, for violations of the terms or conditions thereof. Any order of the President suspending or revoking any such license shall be final if in accordance with law."

The heads of the executive departments may also perform certain functions of administrative adjudication. For example, the Secretary of Labor until recently decided disputes concerning federal building construction projects under the Davis-Bacon Law; and the Postmaster General passes on controversies as to the use of the mails to defraud.

In some instances the executive officers have original jurisdiction over controversies; and, in other instances, only appellate jurisdiction. As we have already mentioned several examples of original jurisdiction in the preceding pages, we shall note at this point merely one or two examples of appellate jurisdiction. Thus, in controversies regarding the exclusion of immigrants, the decisions made by boards of special inquiry may be appealed to the Secretary of Labor for revision. The Secretary of the Interior is the highest administrative appellate authority in Land Office cases. Appeals lie to

---

[57] 48 Stat. L. 197 (Sec. 4(b), no longer in effect).

him from the decisions of the Registers and the Commissioner of the Land Office.

E. Primarily Administrative Authorities

A rather large proportion of the authorities in the federal government which exercise administrative judicial powers are primarily administrative in nature. That is, their fundamental work is not the settling of disputes, but the carrying on of particular fields of administrative activities. The settling of disputes is merely incidental to their general work. In every administrative department, the performance of day-by-day functions and duties must inevitably give rise to dissatisfaction on the part of a certain proportion of the individuals affected. Some of these individuals bring their complaints informally to the administrators themselves, with a request for the correction of an error or the reconsideration of a determination. The action taken by the administrators upon these complaints and requests is not administrative adjudication. In numerous instances, however, provision has been made for a formal hearing by the administrator of any complaint or controversy which has not been adjusted informally. Such hearing often conforms to all criteria of administrative adjudication.

F. Primarily Regular Courts Exercising the Functions of Administrative Tribunals

Both the Supreme Court of the District of Columbia and the Court of Appeals of the District have from time to time been given functions which, according to our criteria, make them act in the capacity of appellate administrative tribunals.[58] It is true that in several cases

---

[58] See pp. 91-100 for criteria.

the Supreme Court of the United States has treated the reviews of administrative decisions by the courts named above as merely administrative. From the viewpoint of this study, however, they are really administrative judicial decisions.

1. *The Supreme Court of the District of Columbia* acts as an appellate tribunal from two chief kinds of administrative action. It reviews the action taken by the Board of Education in issuing or revoking licenses to institutions to confer degrees.[59] It also reviews the action of the Public Utilities Commission of the District in respect to its regulation of the public utilities of the District;[60] and it may order the Commission "to vacate, set aside, or modify any such decision or order on the ground that the valuation, rate or rates, tolls, charges, schedules, joint rate or rates, or regulation, requirement, act, service or other thing complained of fixed in such order is unlawful, inadequate or unreasonable."[61] Regarding this last-named function, the Supreme Court of the United States has actually held that the Supreme Court of the District of Columbia, in revising decisions made by the Public Utilities Commission of the District, is revising a legislative act![62]

2. *The Court of Appeals of the District of Columbia* has had quite varied functions which involved administrative judicial matters, but at present these functions are not extensive. Under the Radio Act of 1927[63] Congress gave to this court the right to review the decisions of the Federal Radio Commission, with power to "hear, review,

---

[59] Code of the District of Columbia, Secs. 245, 247, pp. 28, 29.
[60] The same, Sec. 89, p. 392.
[61] The same.
[62] See *Keller* v. *Potomac Electric Co.*, 261 U.S. 428, 442.
[63] 44 Stat. L. 1169.

and determine the appeal" upon the record made before the Commission, and to "alter or revise the decision appealed from and enter such judgment as to it may seem just." The grant of such power, according to the Supreme Court of the United States,[64] made the court which received it "a 'superior and revising agency' in the administrative field." This position of the Court of Appeals was done away with by a later statute[65] which expressly limited appeals from the decisions of the Radio Commission to "questions of law," and which further provided "that the findings of fact of the Commission, if supported by substantial evidence, shall be conclusive unless it shall clearly appear that the findings of the Commission are arbitrary or capricious." This limitation to questions of law meant that in radio matters the court became a judicial rather than an administrative judicial reviewing authority. It occupies a similar position under the new law establishing the Federal Communications Commission.

The Court of Appeals of the District of Columbia was held to have administrative appellate power under the Act of 1893,[66] which permitted appeals from the decisions of the Commissioner of Patents.[67] This appellate jurisdiction was transferred to the Court of Customs and Patent Appeals by an act of March 2, 1929.[68]

The Court of Appeals of the District had administrative appellate jurisdiction in respect to trade-mark proceedings under an act of 1905.[69] In *Postum Cereal Co.* v.

[64] *Radio Commission* v. *General Electric Co.*, 281 U.S. 464; *Radio Commission* v. *Nelson Bros.*, 289 U.S. 274.
[65] 47 U.S.C.A., Supp., Sec. 96.
[66] 27 Stat. L. 436.
[67] *Radio Commission* v. *General Electric Co.*, 281 U.S. 464, 467; *Butterworth* v. *Hoe*, 112 U.S. 50, 60.
[68] 45 Stat. L. 1475.
[69] 33 Stat. L. 727.

California Fig Nut Co.,[70] the Supreme Court said regarding such jurisdiction: "The decision of the Court of Appeals under Section 9 of the Act of 1905, is not a judicial judgment. It is a mere administrative decision. It is merely an instruction to the Commissioner of Patents by a court which is made part of the machinery of the Patent Office for administrative purposes." This jurisdiction was transferred to the Court of Customs and Patent Appeals in 1929.[71]

At present, the Court of Appeals of the District of Columbia has original jurisdiction of an administrative nature in one type of case. If an individual permit to operate a motor vehicle has been denied, suspended, or revoked by the traffic director of the District of Columbia, the person affected may, under certain conditions, apply to any justice of the Court of Appeals of the District for a writ of error to review the order of the director of traffic. In case the individual has first applied for a review to the Commissioners of the District, and they have decided against him, he may ask the court for a writ of error to review the decision of the Commissioners.[72]

The Court of Appeals of the District has appellate jurisdiction from the Supreme Court of the District of Columbia in public utility cases.[73]

From this recital it is evident that the Court of Appeals of the District of Columbia may be given jurisdiction, as an administrative tribunal, at the option of Congress. This jurisdiction may cover not only cases arising in connection with the functioning of the District gov-

---

[70] 272 U.S. 693, 698.
[71] 45 Stat. L. 1475.
[72] *Code of the District of Columbia*, p. 56, Sec. 250.
[73] The same, p. 392, Sec. 89.

ernment, but also cases involving administrative operations of the federal government.

G. Primarily Fact-Finding Authorities

Although many agencies of administration must establish facts of various kinds as a part of their everyday work, only one primarily fact-finding agency need be discussed here because of its administrative judicial activities. That is the United States Tariff Commission.

The Tariff Commission consists of six members appointed by the President and confirmed by the Senate for terms of six years. It is primarily a fact-finding body, with the duty of investigating the fiscal and industrial effects of the customs laws of the United States, the tariff relationships between the United States and foreign countries, commercial treaties, preferential provisions, economic alliances, and so forth; and of studying conversion costs and costs of production of commodities, and differences in costs of production between domestic products and comparable foreign products.

The only function of a quasi-judicial nature performed by the Tariff Commission is in connection with unfair practices in import trade. The Commission makes investigations of practices which it has reason to suspect of being unfair, holds hearings, and makes findings. These findings, if supported by evidence, are conclusive; except that a rehearing may be granted. An appeal may be made by the importer or consignee to the United States Court of Customs and Patent Appeals on questions of law only. This court may order that further evidence shall be taken, and from this new evidence the Commission may modify its findings.[74]

[74] 19 U.S.C.A., Supp., Sec. 1337.

H. Licensing Authorities

From the viewpoint of this study, the licensing powers vested in several agencies of the government, especially the power to revoke or suspend, because of charges and after a hearing, licenses previously granted, must be looked upon as powers of administrative adjudication. For example: (1) The Licensing Division in the Bureau of Navigation and Steamboat Inspection reviews appeals from the decisions of supervising inspectors regarding the suspension and revocation of licenses and refusal to grant licenses.[75] (2) In respect to the issuance, suspension, or revocation of registration, aircraft, and airman certificates, or other certificates affecting aviation which are considered necessary by the Secretary of Commerce, a procedure of an administrative judicial nature is had. Within 20 days after notice that a certificate is suspended or revoked, the applicant or holder may file a request for a public hearing. The Secretary then arranges for such a hearing. Either the Secretary or any officer or employee of the Department of Commerce designated for this purpose may hold the hearing. The evidence taken is recorded and forwarded to the Secretary of Commerce as a basis for decision. The decision of the Secretary, if in accordance with law, is final. (3) The Federal Reserve Board has the right to issue a permit to a member bank to act as a correspondent bank, if, in its judgment, this is not incompatible with the public interest; and to revoke such a permit whenever it finds, after reasonable notice and opportunity to be heard, that the public interest requires such revocation.[76] There are several other agencies which exercise administrative adjudication in

---

[75] *Current Organization Charts*, No. 120.
[76] 48 Stat. L. 194, Sec. 32.

connection with the issuing, suspension, or revocation of licenses.

I. The Comptroller General

The Comptroller General of the United States, because of his peculiar functions, cannot be classified with any other administrative tribunal. Both he and the Assistant Comptroller General are appointed by the President for a term of 15 years.

The law charges the Comptroller General with the settlement and adjustment, independently of the executive departments, of all claims and demands whatsoever by the government of the United States, and of all accounts whatsoever in which the government of the United States is concerned as either debtor or creditor. Upon the application of any disbursing officer or the head of any executive department or independent establishment, he must render an advance decision on any question involving a payment to be made by or under such officer. This decision governs the settlement of the account.

It is necessary to distinguish carefully between the administrative functions of the Comptroller General and his adjudicatory functions. Although the settlement of accounts would seem to involve directly the interpretation of statutes, laws, regulations, and appropriation acts, and indirectly almost the entire body of federal law and at times state law, such settlement appears to be merely an administrative function. The Comptroller General is certainly performing an administrative judicial function, however, when he reviews, on his own motion, any accounts that have already been settled.

There is no direct method of appeal from the decisions of the Comptroller General. The person injured, however, may avail himself of a *de novo* suit in the Court of Claims, he may apply to the courts of the District of Columbia for a writ of mandamus, or he may apply in a court of equity for an injunction.

II. BORDER-LINE TYPES OF TRIBUNALS

The agencies which perform functions so closely related to those of administrative adjudication that a slight change in powers or relationships might transform them into the latter are primarily of three principal types: arbitrating authorities; advisory authorities on questions of administrative adjudication; and personnel authorities. So many of these agencies exist at present, that only a few of those included under each type can be mentioned here.

A. Primarily Arbitrating Authorities

There are several agencies which may be classed as mediating, conciliating, or arbitrating authorities. These are not, properly speaking, administrative judicial authorities, but it seems necessary to mention them here in order to give as complete a picture as possible of the various methods used in settling disputes by the administrative process.

It is the duty of the National Mediation Board to endeavor to bring about the prompt and amicable disposition of controversies between carriers and their employees concerning rates of pay, rules, and working conditions, and to administer the other provisions of the Railway Labor Act.[77] The former National Labor Board had authority to "adjust all industrial disputes, whether arising out of the interpretation and operation of the President's Re-employment Agreement, or other duly

[77] 44 Stat. L. 579; 45 U.S.C.A., Supp., Secs. 154, 155.

approved code of fair competition, and to compose all conflicts threatening the industrial peace of the country."[78] This Board has been superseded by the National Labor Relations Board created by executive order[79] in connection with the Labor Department.

The National Labor Relations Board has original jurisdiction over several matters. It is authorized (a) "to investigate issues, facts, practices, and activities of employers or employees arising under Section 7(a) of the National Industrial Recovery Act, or which are burdening or obstructing, or threatening to burden or obstruct, the free flow of interstate commerce;" (b) to order and conduct elections and on its own initiative to take steps to enforce its orders in the manner provided in Section 2 of Public Resolution 44, 73d Congress; (c) to hold hearings and make findings of fact regarding complaints and discriminations against or discharge of employees or other alleged violations of Section 7(a) of the National Recovery Act; (d) to prescribe, with the approval of the President, rules and regulations.

The Board has the following duties in respect to other labor boards: (a) to study activities of other boards in order to report, through the Secretary of Labor, to the President, whether such boards should be designated as special courts; (b) to recommend the establishment of regional labor relations boards and special labor boards; (c) to receive reports from such boards, and to review or hear appeals from them in cases where the lower board concerned recommends review, where there is division of opinion in the lower board, or where the National Labor

---

[78] Executive Order No. 6511, Dec. 16, 1933.

[79] No. 6763, June 29, 1934. The duties of this Board are of a mixed nature, so that its inclusion at this point is not entirely logical; but it is mentioned here because of its relationship to other authorities.

Relations Board deems review essential to the public interest.

The National Recovery Administration furnishes the most striking and complete example of an attempt to settle difficulties by way of mediation, conciliation, and administrative procedure generally, rather than by judicial or quasi-judicial action. The word "compliance" has been used to designate this process. The public officer in charge of enforcing the National Industrial Recovery Act is given the innocuous title of "Administrator." Neither the NRA nor any agency under its control has legal authority to coerce business enterprises into complying with the terms of codes. "All of its elaborate mechanism of compliance is therefore designed, first, to establish the fact of violation of a code, and, second, to 'persuade' the violator to mend his ways and to 'adjust' complaints. Only at the end of the procedure is the case passed on to the Department of Justice or the Federal Trade Commission for the exercise of the government's power to coerce."[80] Although the violation of a code is by statute a violation of the law, such violation is not immediately referred to enforcing authorities which seek to obtain the observance of the law by bringing suit; on the contrary, a series of attempts are made to adjust and settle the matter out of court. Much of the compliance power is vested in private industrial adjustment agencies, with which we are not here concerned. There are, however, a series of public agencies through which the compliance procedure operates. These are:

The state director of the National Emergency Council in each state, who co-operates with the National Compliance Director and the National Compliance Board of

[80] Charles L. Dearing and others, *The ABC of the NRA*, p. 97.

the Recovery Administration. These directors are given the assistance of field adjusters, when needed. It is contemplated that in each state there will also be one or more state adjustment boards, which are essentially boards of review. The findings of these state adjustment boards are set forth in the form of recommendations either to be acted upon by the state director, or referred, if necessary, to the National Compliance Director.

The National Compliance Director, who is head of the Compliance Division of the NRA, is charged with the duty of making an attempt to settle cases that are not settled by industry itself or by the public state agencies. When a case is referred to him, he may take such action as he deems advisable. In case he cannot adjust the complaint, or in case he considers it desirable for other reasons, he refers the case to the National Compliance Board.

The National Compliance Board, located at Washington, may take one of several steps. It may make further attempts at adjustment. It may call a public hearing upon the controversy. It may remove the Blue Eagle of the respondent and give wide publicity to this action. It may recommend to the Administrator that the case be referred to one of the two chief enforcement agencies, the Department of Justice or the Federal Trade Commission. Up to the time that the case is undertaken by one or the other of these last two authorities, there has been nothing but an administrative compliance procedure.[81]

[81] For the details of procedure, see "Manual for the Adjustment of Complaints," *NRA Bulletin No. 7;* also NRA first release, *Information for Code Authorities,* Jan. 22, 1934; and Dearing and others, *The ABC of the NRA,* pp. 104ff. While this book was in press, important changes were made in the organization of the National Recovery Administration; but so far as can be ascertained at present, the general duties and functions of this agency are not altered.

B. Primarily Advisory Authorities on Questions of Administrative Adjudication

In many of the government departments and agencies there are boards, sections, or bureaus which do not actually make administrative judicial decisions, but which investigate cases and give reasoned advice on the basis of which an administrative or executive authority may make the final determination. Thus, within the Interstate Commerce Commission there is a Bureau of Formal Cases, which consists of boards of review and examiners who act for the Commission in the adjudication of rate cases arising either upon complaint or upon the initiation of an action by the Commission. Hearings are held either at Washington or near the residence of the private party by examiners who go on circuit throughout the United States. The examiners draft proposed reports to which exception may be taken by the contending parties. Oral arguments may be made before one of the divisions of the Commission or before the entire Commission.[82]

A Board of Review in the Department of Labor reviews the opinions and the recommendations of the examiners of the legal branch of this Department in exclusion and expulsion cases, to decide whether the conclusions previously reached are correct in fact and law. "The action of this body is advisory merely and need not be followed by the Secretary [of Labor] if he decides to ignore it. In practice, however, its recommendations are usually followed and therefore become in fact decisions."[83]

These authorities are established in various ways: sometimes by law, sometimes by executive order, at times by the order of the Department itself. In some instances

[82] See *Current Organization Charts*, p. 136.
[83] W. C. Van Vleck, *The Administrative Control of Aliens*, pp. 78-82.

they are full-time authorities; in others they are merely *ad hoc* authorities, appointed as need for their action arises.

C. PRIMARILY PERSONNEL AUTHORITIES

In connection with personnel administration there are a variety of functions which are carried out by several different agencies. The chief of these functions have to do with acting upon applications for examination; making inquiries in respect to character; placing individuals in classes and grades; allocating persons to particular positions; grading examinations; giving efficiency ratings as a basis for retention in the service or promotion; making investigations as to political activity; acting on such matters as reduction in rank, grade, or salary, suspension from duty, and dismissal from the service; determining upon the compensation that a person should receive if injured in the service; and passing upon retirement claims. All of these functions are in the first instance administrative in nature, involving administrative investigation and administrative determination.

Administrative adjudication, whether officially recognized as such or not, takes place when reviews are permitted in respect to any decisions made in the course of performing any of the above functions.

There are several functions carried out by different officers or agents of the Civil Service Commission, over which, in theory at least, the Commission itself exercises an appellate power. These include, among others, investigations in respect to character, allocation of positions, classifications, examination ratings, and under a new executive order, review of decisions in respect to retirement pensions. There is organized within the Commission itself a Board of Appeals and Review, which reviews all such matters. In theory, its decisions are merely advisory. In practice, they are final, unless a question of policy is involved. It should be especially noted that neither the Commission (except in the one case given below) nor the Board of Appeals and Review has jurisdiction to review administrative determinations made by other administrative authorities having to do with personnel, such as the government departments and agencies and the Employees' Compensation Commission.

In respect to efficiency ratings, the first mark is given by the immediate superior of the employee. This mark is passed on to a reviewing officer for the particular division in which the employee is located. Finally, a reviewing board in each department or independent agency passes on all the marks of that service. The purpose of these reviews would seem to be partly administrative —that is, to bring harmony into the rating system in the service; and partly judicial—that is, to adjust any unfairness or discrimination in respect to individuals in the service. The reviewing process is not primarily administrative adjudication, since it takes place even when there is no definite objection on the part of employees to the ratings given. Since within the past year or so great dissatisfaction with this system has been expressed, in several departments review boards have been set up whose function is decidedly that of administrative adjudication, for they hear and determine upon complaints. No appeals on efficiency ratings go to the Civil Service Commission, unless they involve merely questions of procedure.

At present the decisions made by administrative and executive officers in respect to reduction in salary, rank, or grade, suspension from duty, or dismissal from the service, are purely administrative, and are not appealable to any administrative judicial authority. The Civil Service Commission and its Board of Appeals and Review have no appellate jurisdiction over such acts, and the possibility of court action is almost negligible.

The decisions of the Employees' Compensation Commission, which passes finally and conclusively upon compensation to those injured in the federal service and the service of the District of Columbia, are considered as being entirely administrative in nature, since compensation is considered merely a boon and not a right. No appeal lies from them either to any administrative tribunal or to the courts.

Certain changes might easily make of the Civil Service Commission and its Board of Appeals and Review real administrative tribunals. If, as the Civil Service Commission itself has advocated for the past few years, there should be created under the supervision of the Commission a statutory board or "court of appeals" to hear and determine finally appeals of employees in the classified service who have been reduced in salary, rank, or grade, suspended from duty or dismissed from the service, this agency would undoubtedly have the status of a real administrative court. If the functions of the Employees' Compensation Commission were transferred to the Civil Service Commission, another change which has been advocated, appeals regarding these functions might also go to the proposed administrative court, despite the fact that theoretically speaking, such cases involve no rights, but merely favors granted by the government.

III. SUMMARY

From the foregoing classification of administrative adjudicatory authorities, it is obvious that practically every administrative agency and function is in some way connected with the work of administrative adjudication. Either the organizational unit which is carrying on a given function makes decisions of a quasi-judicial nature as a regular part of its operations, or there is within it, beside it, or above it, some authority that in one way or another carries out this task.

The types of administrative adjudicatory authorities are quite numerous, and there are striking differences within each type. There is much variety as to the relationship of the administrative function to the adjudicatory function. There are great differences in the organization of such authorities, in their size, the term of office of their members, the way in which their members are selected, the way in which the various authorities operate, their constitutional and legal position, and their relationship to other authorities and agencies. Much of this is undoubtedly due to the fact that these authorities were organized almost always as an incident to the carrying on of administrative activities.

As we shall see later, there are vast differences in the methods and procedures employed in the hearing of cases before the various administrative judicial authorities, in the rules of evidence that they use, and in the manner by which they make their decisions. Equally great differences appear in the methods by which the orders and decisions of such authorities are enforced, and the means by which their decisions are further controlled. In a word, there is complete confusion in respect to the organization of the function of administrative adjudication.

Despite the fact that there are many types of administrative adjudicating authorities, for some purposes it is desirable to classify all the different authorities which are carrying on administrative adjudication into but two categories: authorities which are primarily administering and merely adjudicating in connection with this function, and authorities which are primarily deciding administrative cases and controlling administration.

From this viewpoint, more than one-half of the authorities acting in a quasi-judicial capacity are chiefly engaged in administration, and are adjudicating only incidentally, in connection with their other functions. In several instances the adjudicating process, as far as it is being accomplished, is carried out by an agency within the administrative organization, which acts in the last analysis as a sort of controlling authority.

The chief administrative authorities that are only incidentally exercising the function of administrative adjudication are: The Federal Communications Commission, the Federal Power Commission, the Securities and Exchange Commission, the Interstate Commerce Commission, the Employees' Compensation Commission, the Deputy Commissioners under the Longshoremen's and Harbor Workers' Act, the National Labor Relations Board, the National Recovery Administration, the General Accounting Office with the Comptroller General, the Land Department, the Patent Office, the Federal Trade Commission, the Veterans' Administration, the Petroleum Administrative Board, the Agricultural Adjustment Administration, the Aeronautics Branch of the Department of Commerce, the United States Shipping Board, the Food and Drug Administration, the Bureau of Plant Quarantine, the Licensing Division of the Bureau of Navigation and Steamboat Inspection, the United States Tariff Commission, the Civil Service Commission, the Co-ordinator of Transportation, the Secretary of the Interior, the Secretary of Labor, the

Postmaster General, the Secretary of Agriculture. In several instances, subdivisions within the larger units are also exercising quasi-judicial powers.

There are nearly a score of authorities whose primary function is that of administrative adjudication. In various ways these authorities pass upon and control administrative action; sometimes by giving advisory opinions, sometimes by deciding cases and controversies between the government and an individual, sometimes by reviewing the administrative decisions of administrative authorities, and sometimes by reviewing the decisions of other authorities that are exercising the function of administrative adjudication.

The authorities that are exercising a controlling function (no attempt is given here to state the particular nature of that control) are as follows: The United States Customs Court, the Court of Customs and Patent Appeals, the Board of Tax Appeals, the Court of Claims, the Board of Appeals in the Patent Office, the Board of Appeals in the Veterans' Administration, the Board of Labor Review in the Emergency Public Works Administration, the Supreme Court of the District of Columbia and the Court of Appeals of the District of Columbia acting as administrative tribunals, the Comptroller General, the Bureau of Formal Cases in the Interstate Commerce Commission, the Board of Review in the Department of Labor, the Board of Review in the Civil Service Commission, the review boards in the various departments which pass upon efficiency ratings, the actions of certain heads of departments in controlling, not in an administrative way but in a quasi-judicial way, the actions of their inferiors, the Board of Discipline in the United States Patent Office, the Board of Wage and Salary Review in the Government Printing Office, the Board of Review in the Department of War in the Office of the Judge Advocate General.

From this analysis it can be seen that consciously or unconsciously, an attempt has been made in the federal government to establish some sort of quasi-judicial or administrative judicial control over administrative action and over quasi-judicial action resulting from the review of administrative action. It is true that there is a bewildering variety in the types of organization employed; that many of the administrative authorities which adjudicate lack an adequate legislative basis for this function; that some of the work done by such authorities at present is largely advisory in nature; and that there is little logic or system in the establishment of the various authorities. Nevertheless these agencies of administrative adjudication perform an indispensable task. Careful and well-considered reorganization could lessen the number of types of administrative adjudicatory agencies, introduce order and system into their procedures, supply adequate appellate tribunals, and greatly increase the general efficiency with which the work of administrative adjudication could be accomplished.

CHAPTER VIII

PROCEDURE AND ENFORCEMENT

Much of the success of any system of administrative adjudication depends upon the procedures by means of which the system is operated, and the methods employed for enforcing the decisions made under it. Appropriate and adequate procedures not only assist the individual to secure justice in his dealings with the administration, but also save the government much needless confusion, litigation, time, and expense. Proper methods of enforcement uphold the independence of administrative judicial authorities, prevent undue interference by the ordinary courts, and help to keep the administrative judicial process in harmony with the administrative process. Because of the important results which depend upon procedures and enforcement methods, it is necessary at this point to devote a few pages to each of these subjects.

I. METHODS OF PROCEDURE

There is variety so great as to be indistinguishable from confusion, in regard to the methods of procedure employed by the administrative judicial authorities connected with the federal government.[1] The law itself may prescribe or at least outline the procedure to be followed by a given authority, as it does in respect to the Interstate Commerce Commission; or it may say little or nothing on the subject of procedure, as in the case of the law governing the Federal Trade Commission. Some authorities are given the power to make their own rules of procedure; others have not received such a grant

[1] See Harold M. Stephens, *Administrative Tribunals and the Rules of Evidence*, pp. 7 and 8.

of power; still others are empowered to make their own rules, subject to certain conditions or limitations. Thus, the United States Board of Tax Appeals is authorized by law to conduct its proceedings "in accordance with such rules of practice and procedure (other than rules of evidence) as the Board may prescribe and in accordance with the rules of evidence applicable in courts of equity in the District of Columbia."[2]

The rules of procedure prescribed by law, or adopted by the administrative judicial bodies which may make their own rules, are so different in content, in style, and in attention to detail, that any summary or classification of them is impossible. Both the rules themselves and the proceedings under them range all the way from remarkable informality to formality approaching that of a court. No rules of procedure govern the actions of the executive and administrative authorities when they make decisions of an administrative judicial nature; except such vague statutory directions as that the President shall examine into the facts, and "if he shall be satisfied" of certain conditions, he shall then take certain action.

The most important subdivision of procedural rules is certainly that of rules of evidence. Yet it happens quite frequently that even when rules are prescribed or adopted for the guidance of administrative tribunals, no rules of evidence are included. This is true in respect to the Interstate Commerce Commission, the Federal Trade Commission, the United States Customs Court, the Land Department, the United States Shipping Board, and various other authorities.

When courts review the decisions of administrative judicial tribunals, they sometimes refuse to uphold these

[2] Revenue Act of 1924, Sec. 907 (a), as amended by Revenue Act of 1928, Sec. 601.

decisions because they consider that evidence was taken in an improper manner, or that the rules of evidence employed in arriving at a decision were not such as to safeguard all the interests concerned. The judicial courts thus have a certain influence upon the rules of evidence employed by agencies of administrative adjudication. Yet this influence is considerably less powerful than might be expected, for the courts have displayed a marked tendency to assume, on the whole, a fairly liberal attitude on the matter of evidence.

An interesting example of this tendency is the attitude taken by the courts in regard to rules of evidence in cases coming from the Interstate Commerce Commission. This is summarized by Stephens as follows:

But these cases [where the question of rules of evidence was actually in point] and the dicta in the other four have set a pattern, which, summarized, may be said to be that the Interstate Commerce Commission is not to be too narrowly constrained by the "technical" and "narrow rules" which prevail at common law trials, or by the "strict rules" prevailing in suits between private parties, or by the rules which in judicial proceedings would make matter incompetent, or by "mechanical rules," or by "mathematically correct rules," and these cases, particularizing, sanction the use of hearsay and of unidentified signatures, the disregard of admissions of parties, the use of a formula or method of adjusting rate divisions which is not in evidence, and of evidence in another cause. But these cases also, it should be noted, require the production of relevant testimony and documents, forbid the use of the Commission's own information not formally proved at the hearing, or the use of anything as evidence which is not introduced as such . . . and assert that "the more liberal the practice in admitting testimony, the more imperative the obligation to preserve the essential rules of evidence by which rights are asserted or defended."[3]

[3] Stephens, *Administrative Tribunals and the Rules of Evidence*, pp. 30, 31. See also *Radio Commission* v. *Nelson Bros. Co.*, 289 U.S. 266, at 276.

Only one case has come before the courts involving the failure of the Federal Trade Commission to apply rules of evidence. In this case[4] the question was raised as to whether the Commission was restricted to the taking of legally competent and relevant testimony.[5] The court held that it was not so restricted, saying: "We incline to think that it is not by the statute, and, having regard to the exigencies of administrative law, that it should not be so restricted. We are of the opinion that evidence or testimony, even though legally incompetent, if of the kind that usually affects fair-minded men in the conduct of their daily and more important affairs, should be received and considered; but it should be fairly done."

The assumption of this position by the courts is explicable only on the ground that the regulatory bodies are performing functions of several different types, and should therefore have greater freedom than if their work were wholly judicial. Since they make rules of a sub-legislative character, they must necessarily have some of the attributes of a legislative body; that is, they must be able to use a wide variety of facts and of considerations of policy as a basis for their actions. It is evident, however, that in exercising the quasi-judicial function, they are dealing with a different subject matter. Here proof should be required; and proof is not and cannot be the resultant of common knowledge, hearsay evidence, and irrelevant testimony. This the courts seem to have realized to quite a degree. It is only when both functions are performed together that difficulties arise. For example, if sub-legislation is incidental to the mak-

[4] *John Bene and Sons, Inc.* v. *Federal Trade Commission*, 299 Fed. 468.
[5] For fuller discussion, see Stephens, *Administrative Tribunals and the Rules of Evidence*, pp. 31 and 32.

ing of a quasi-judicial decision, as is the case in respect to the fixing of rates by the Interstate Commerce Commission, or the making of a cease and desist order in respect to unfair methods of competition by the Federal Trade Commission, two contrary methods in respect to evidence are at work, causing confusion. Most of the inconsistencies and contradictions in the position taken by the courts as to rules of evidence before regulatory bodies may be traced to this improper hybridization of functions.

Rules of evidence before other types of administrative judicial authorities differ very greatly. Like other rules of procedure, they are practically non-existent in respect to the quasi-judicial decisions of certain high executive and administrative officers. On the other hand, the rules of evidence may be identical with those used in the regular courts. We have already seen that the United States Board of Tax Appeals is governed by the rules of evidence applicable in courts of equity of the District of Columbia. Between these two extremes, there is an indescribable variety of written rules and of rules that are merely understood to govern practice. These often, but not always, reflect the special functions of the various tribunals.

II. METHODS OF ENFORCEMENT

Much of the efficiency of any administrative adjudicative body, as well as the independence and authority of its position, must depend upon the manner in which its orders or decisions are enforced. In the federal administration there is no uniformity as to methods of enforcing the decisions of administrative tribunals. The methods employed vary according to the type of authority, the adjudicative process, and the type of function that is being carried on. In many instances the methods of enforcement used seem to depend entirely upon the whim or caprice of Congress. Among the methods of enforcement that should be examined are the following ten: making orders or decisions self-executing; execution of orders or decisions by further administrative action; execution as the result of further legislative action, such as the making of an appropriation; placing the burden upon the administrative judicial body itself, to secure enforcement through court action in case of violation of its orders; providing that the courts shall enforce obedience by "the proper remedies;" providing that public prosecuting authorities shall enforce obedience through court action; placing heavy penalties upon those who disregard orders and decisions, and permitting equitable relief from the order or decision; making the decision final, with right of appeal; using the boycott; enforcing obedience by mandamus.

Because of the lack of system in enforcement, the methods used are at times confused, inconsistent, and roundabout. Any classification of methods must therefore be more or less unsatisfactory, particularly since there will be an inevitable overlapping among some classes. It must also be understood that some of the methods of enforcement used apply equally to ordinary administrative decisions and orders, and to administrative judicial decisions. Despite these difficulties, we shall endeavor to survey in a brief and cursory fashion the principal methods by which the decisions of federal administrative judicial agencies are enforced.

A. In respect to practically all licensing activities, the decision of the administrative or administrative judicial authority which grants, suspends, revokes, refuses, or withholds a license is self-executing. In some instances the person who is injured by such an act has rights of appeal; but until a change is brought about through the action of the appellate authority, the decision of the licensing authorities is effective as it stands. For example, when the Licensing Division of the Bureau of Navigation and Steamboat Inspection, the Federal Communications Commission, and the Federal Power Commission are exercising the licensing function, their decisions are self-executing. It is difficult to see any other method of executing such decisions.

B. In a number of instances the decisions of the administrative tribunal are executed through the action of another administrative authority. Thus, after the President has decided that a certain article is to be excluded from entry into the United States, the Secretary of the Treasury, through the proper officers, enforces the President's decision.[6] After the Board of Tax Appeals has made a decision in a tax case, the Commissioner of Internal Revenue executes it just as though it were a part of the law. The decisions of the United States Customs Court become the mandate for the Collector of Customs.[7] The decisions of the Court of Customs and Patent Appeals in customs cases are in the last analysis enforced by the Collector of Customs,[8] while its decisions in respect to patent and trade-mark appeals are enforced by the Commissioner of Patents. The decisions of the chief examiners in the Patent Office and of the Board of Appeals in patent and trade-mark cases are also enforced

---

[6] 46 Stat. L. 703, Sec. 337(e).

[7] See Rules of the U.S. Customs Court, 1930, No. 29, which states: "The court's judgment order shall be the collector's mandate and shall constitute his authority for the reliquidation of an entry, if such be the order of the court."

[8] It is true that this court issues a final mandate to the U.S. Customs Court for such further proceedings as shall be proper (see Rules of Feb. 28, 1931, Rule 22) but in the last analysis it is the Collector of Customs who enforces the decision.

by the Commissioner of Patents. This must necessarily be so, since he is the officer who issues patents. In any case involving the expulsion of immigrants, after recommendation by the Board of Review that an alien be deported (unless the Assistant Secretary of Labor disapproves of this recommendation) a warrant of deportation is issued by the Secretary of Labor.

The method of administrative enforcement is particularly applicable when some sort of administrative tribunal acts as an appellate authority to review decisions made by administrative agencies, and when the government is granting a favor. The decision of the tribunal then becomes a part of the law which the administrative agency is executing.

C. Occasionally the decisions of administrative tribunals depend in theory for their execution upon further legislative action, particularly the making of an appropriation. This is so in respect to all claims against the United States decided by administrative tribunals. Thus, the decisions of the Employees' Compensation Commission, the Comptroller General, and the Court of Claims all depend in the final analysis upon the fact that an appropriation is made by Congress in settlement of the claims which are allowed in such decisions. In actual practice, claims are settled administratively through the payment of the warrants of the Comptroller General by the Treasury. In practice, to all intents and purposes the general rule is administrative enforcement.

D. The method of placing the burden upon the administrative judicial authority itself, to secure enforcement of its orders through court action, has been adopted in respect to several authorities. For example, under the original Interstate Commerce Act, the orders of the Commission were not made binding upon the carriers affected, who might disobey them with impunity, unless the Commission obtained enforcement of the same through the courts. By the Hepburn Act, the orders of the Commission were made binding; but even now the Commission cannot enforce its own decisions and orders. If any carrier refuses obedience, the Commission must seek enforcement through a circut court; the latter must enforce any order which it finds to have been "regularly made and duly served." It is seldom necessary for the Commission to resort to this method of enforcement. The penalties for disobedience of an order, which become operative from its effective date, are made so severe that dissatisfied carriers no longer await a move for enforcement by the Commission, but go directly to the courts to ask relief by initiating proceedings to enjoin, suspend, or invalidate a given order. This action by the carriers "has become the established method of subjecting the Commission's determinations to judicial review."[9]

The law governing the Federal Trade Commission places upon the Commission the burden of securing enforcement of its orders through the courts. Upon refusal to obey the orders of the Commission by those concerned, the Commission may apply to the Circuit Court of Appeals of the United States, within the circuit where the method of competition declared to be unfair was used, or where the party concerned resides or carries out its business, for the enforcement of its orders.[10] A decision of a circuit court of appeals, in a case of this nature, may be reviewed in the Supreme Court by means of the writ of certiorari. Much of the weakness of the Commission is due to this method of enforcement, for the result is to

[9] I. L. Sharfman, *The Interstate Commerce Commission*, Vol. 2, p. 388.
[10] 38 Stat. L. 719, Sec. 5; 43 Stat. L. 939, Sec. 2.

"make the procedure for securing obedience to the statute very cumbersome, tedious and expensive,"[11] and to enable those opposing an order of the Commission to postpone indefinitely the enforcement of the law.

Under the National Recovery Act, the authorities who make administrative judicial decisions on matters governed by this statute must depend upon the Federal Trade Commission and the Department of Justice for the enforcement of their orders. The experience of the Federal Trade Commission suggests reasonable doubt as to the wisdom of this method of enforcement.

E. Whenever any order of the United States Shipping Board, other than an order regarding a money payment, is violated, either the Board, the party injured, or the Attorney General may apply for enforcement to the district court having jurisdiction of the parties. The court enforces obedience by writ of injunction or other proper process, mandatory or otherwise.[12]

Under the Packers' and Stock Yards Act of 1921, besides making violations of cease and desist orders subject to penalty, the Secretary of Agriculture may also apply to the district court for enforcement of such orders. The court is required to enforce obedience if, after hearing, it determines that the order was "lawfully" made and duly served.

F. Another method of enforcing administrative judicial decisions is to provide that action to compel obedience may be brought before a court by public prosecuting authorities. Thus, the Water Power Act provides that the Attorney General, either on the request of the Water

---

[11] *Annual Report of the Federal Trade Commission*, 1928, pp. 78 and 79.

[12] 46 U.S.C.A., Sec. 828. In case of violation of orders of the Board for money payment, see the same, Sec. 829.

Power Commission or on that of the Secretary of War, may institute proceedings in equity in the district court for the purpose of revoking for violation of its terms any permit or license issued, or "for the purpose of remedying or correcting by injunction, mandamus or other process any act of commission or omission in violation of the provisions of this chapter or of any lawful regulation or order promulgated thereunder."[13] When the former National Labor Board decided that an employer had interfered with the Board's conduct of an election or had declined to recognize labor unions or to bargain collectively, the Board made a formal finding to that effect, and made recommendations concerning enforcement to the Attorney General or to the Compliance Division of the National Recovery Administration.[14] The Compliance Division also sought the assistance of the Department of Justice for the enforcement of its decisions.

G. The placing of penalties upon those who disregard the orders or decisions of administrative tribunals has been tried in several instances. We have already seen that heavy penalties are provided for failure to observe the orders of the Interstate Commerce Commission; and that violations of the orders of the Secretary of Agriculture under the Packers' and Stock Yards Act are also subject to penalty. There are several other instances of this method of enforcement, as, for example, under the Federal Communications Commission Act. In all instances equitable relief is provided. That is, the parties affected by an order may test its validity by means of injunction proceedings or some other action in equity. The burden is thus placed upon them of convincing the court that there is good reason to enjoin or modify an order or de-

[13] 16 U.S.C.A., Sec. 820.
[14] Executive Order of Feb. 23, 1934.

cision, rather than upon the administrative judicial authorities of acting to enforce it.

H. The method of making decisions of an administrative tribunal final, with right of appeal, has been adopted in several instances during the past few years. Under this method, the appropriate administrative authorities are empowered to enforce any such decision unless its validity is disputed by the party affected, through an appeal as provided by the law. Thus, decisions of the Communications Commission in respect to certain matters over which it has jurisdiction are final, subject to the right of appeal to the Court of Appeals of the District of Columbia.[15] In case the court reverses the decision of the Commission, it remands the case to the Commission to carry out its judgment.[16]

I. Under the National Recovery Act the boycott, through the withdrawal of the Blue Eagle, has been used as a method of enforcement.

J. In some instances statutes have provided for the use of the mandamus as a method of compelling obedience to the decisions of administrative tribunals. Thus, the Federal Trade Commission Act[17] provides that: "Upon application of the Attorney General of the United States, at the request of the Commission, the district courts of the United States shall have jurisdiction to issue writs of mandamus commanding any person or corporation to comply with the provisions of the act or any order of the Commission made in pursuance thereof."

III. SUMMARY

There are no general rules of procedure applicable to the authorities that are carrying on administrative ad-

[15] 73 Cong., Public No. 416, Sec. 402.
[16] The same.
[17] 38 Stat. L. 717, Sec. 9.

judication. Procedure is so varied that no lawyer knows how to proceed with a case without examining the particular rules of the authority with which he is dealing. Even when he does so, he may find the rules so vague and indefinite that he hardly knows with any degree of certainty what is required. Although several elaborate general treatises have been written on the subject of federal procedure and practice, as well as many special treatises dealing with the procedure of particular administrative adjudicating bodies and administrative tribunals, lawyers as well as litigants are often at a loss regarding the proper steps to take.

Rules of evidence range all the way from those almost as strict as the rules applied in ordinary judicial courts to practically no rules, except, perhaps, those of ordinary common sense. In some administrative tribunals, the hearings are very formal. In others, they are scarcely more formal than conversations. Informality is generally most pronounced in the case of mixed authorities where the quasi-judicial function is as yet hardly recognized. Yet even before some of the authorities that are acting as controlling agencies over administrative action, there is very little formality and the rules of evidence are almost negligible.

At least ten different types of methods are used for the enforcement of decisions made by authorities exercising quasi-judicial functions. Some of these are almost inherent in the nature of the particular function that is being carried on. For example, the decisions regarding licenses are practically self-executing. The execution of orders or decisions by further administrative action is particularly applicable when the decision made by an administrative authority is controlled by a superior judicial or administrative judicial authority. Here the decision of the controlling authority becomes the rule of law governing the future decisions and actions of the administrative authority. The two methods of self-execution and enforcement by further administrative action would seem to be applicable, if properly organized, to practically all authorities except the regulatory authorities in their present form and the authorities whose decisions require further legislative action to make them enforceable.

There are great advantages in the method of enforcing the decisions of administrative tribunals by further administrative action. It is simple, free from cost, and effective. It is not necessary to drag the courts into the matter; hence the courts are not able to interfere in the administrative or administrative judicial process, as they are when enforcement depends upon their action.

The method of enforcement by further administrative action is not applicable to decisions made by the regulatory type of administrative judicial authorities as now organized. When regulatory commissions exercise their quasi-judicial functions, they are not passing on the acts of other administrative agencies, but are, so to speak, working in relation to their own administrative activities. Consequently, their decisions cannot be enforced by any lower administrative authority which they are controlling.

The acts of a regulatory authority, although self-executing in nature where there is obedience to them, are not so when obedience is refused or when an order or decision is violated. Its orders are in the nature of judicial orders or decisions, and yet it is not vested with the powers of a court. It does not possess its own enforcement methods, enforcement agencies, and the right to punish for contempt. When the orders of a regulatory authority are violated, therefore, it must depend upon some other authority for their enforcement. Various types of enforcement methods have been used in various instances.

Several serious difficulties are connected with the customary requirement that regulatory bodies must call upon the ordinary courts to enforce their orders and decisions. This requirement not only makes procedure for enforcement long drawn out and expensive, but it also enables the courts in many instances to arrogate to themselves the delegated legislative powers which Congress intended to be exercised by independent boards and commissions. "Administrative agencies are ordinarily created to exercise powers previously in the hands of legislatures and, on principle, Congress cannot impose legislative functions on the courts. If the Federal Trade Commission Act, as was intended and as is generally assumed, delegates legislative power, then the courts have reached the very curious result of taking that authority as a proper field of judicial competence to the exclusion of the administrative commission."[18]

Providing that the courts shall "enforce obedience by the proper remedies" is a related method of enforcement which is equally unsatisfactory. In many instances the courts, when theoretically exercising discretion as to whether or not a certain remedial writ should issue, assume actually the discretionary power or even sub-legislative power which was vested in the commission or other regulatory body.

Either a heavy penalty for the disobedience of an order, which places the burden upon the violator to appeal to the courts for relief by injunction or other

---

[18] Carl McFarland, *Judicial Control of the Federal Trade Comission, 1920-30*, p. 9.

appropriate remedy, or an inducement to obey the administrative judicial decision or order in the form of a provision for the prosecution of those who refuse obedience or violate the order, is a much more effective method than the last two discussed. The imposition of a penalty and the right to prosecute release the government from the ignominious and helpless position of lacking all effective sanction for its work of control unless it calls for aid. The individual may still ask the courts for relief, or defend himself if prosecuted; but he cannot ignore or defy the regulatory authority with impunity. The method sometimes adopted, of making the decision of a regulatory body final, subject to appeal by the individual or corporation affected, also relieves the government of the burden of calling upon the ordinary judicial courts to enforce its decisions.

A very serious objection to the enforcement methods employed by the judicial courts is the fact that the courts confuse the question of enforcement with the question of control. When the law requires them to enforce the decisions of administrative regulatory bodies, it does not give them the right to control the actions of such bodies, by going into the question at issue. Yet the courts have repeatedly assumed the power of control, often carrying it to the extreme point of examining into the facts and making their own decisions to replace those of the expert commission. Much thought should be given to the matter of separating enforcement and control. Means of relief should certainly be provided and made accessible to those affected by regulatory decisions and orders; but relief should not mean a confusion of enforcement methods with control over regulatory bodies or other administrative judicial tribunals.

CHAPTER IX

CONTROLS AND REMEDIES

There is no unified system of controlling the actions and decisions of the various federal administrative tribunals. This statement applies both to the extent of review and to the types of remedies that are available.

Most of the remedies and controls which apply to the acts of administrative judicial authorities are exercised by the regular judicial courts. This, however, is not always the case.

I. GENERAL CONTROLS

Review over the decisions of certain administrative tribunals, in the first instance, and in a few cases in the second instance, is in the hands of superior administrative tribunals. For example, the decisions of the regional review boards and the Insurance Claims Council in the Veterans' Administration are brought on appeal to the Board of Appeals of this Administration. The decisions of the Customs Court, the Commissioner of Patents, the examiners in chief in the Patent Office, and the Board of Appeals in the Patent Office, are subject to appeal in either first or second instance to the Board of Customs and Patent Appeals.

The extent to which the decisions of administrative tribunals will be reviewed by the judicial courts is provided, in some instances, by statute; in others it has grown up as a result of judicial decisions. In a very general way it may be said that the extent of review over the decisions of heads of departments and other high executive and administrative officers, when acting in an administrative judicial capacity, has been fixed by judicial decisions; whereas the extent of the review of most of the special administrative courts, both those inside government departments and those which act independently, and of the great regulatory tribunals, has been partly provided for by law, and has been defined broadly or narrowly by judicial decisions.

In several instances a law or regulation specifically provides that there shall be no review of the decisions of administrative judicial agencies. This is the case in respect to the decisions of the Board of Labor Review in the Public Works Administration, as to which a resolution by the Board of Public Works provides: "Decisions of the Board of Labor Review shall be binding upon all parties."[1] The contract form of the Public Works Administration also provides that the decisions of this same Board "shall be final and conclusive upon the parties . . ." in respect to labor disputes. No appeal is provided for. The law provides no appeal to the courts from the Board of Appeals in the Veterans' Administration, but on the contrary, states that: "All decisions rendered by the Administrator of Veterans' Affairs[2] under the provisions of this title . . . shall be final and conclusive on all questions of law and fact, and no other official or court of the United States shall have jurisdiction to review by mandamus or otherwise any such decision."[3] There is no appeal from the decisions of the Employees' Compensation Commission, since the courts have held that the compensation in question is a favor rather than a right. Awards made in violation of the Compensation

[1] *Federal Emergency Administration of Public Works Bulletin 51,* Sec. 54.

[2] This power of decision has by executive order been largely delegated to the Board of Appeals. See Executive Order No. 6230 of July 28, 1933.

[3] 48 Stat. L. 9, Sec. 5.

Act, however, may be disallowed by the Comptroller General.[4] No appeals lie to the courts from the decisions of the Civil Service Commission, since the courts hold that it is enforcing rules and regulations which do not have the force of law.[5] In respect to the exclusion and the expulsion of aliens, no statutory provision for review is made. On the contrary, there are express statements that the decisions of the administrative officers are final.[6]

It happens in several instances, that even though laws provide no method for direct review of decisions and orders made by administrative judicial bodies, indirect review takes place either in connection with enforcement, or by some sort of collateral attack. Thus, judicial control over acts of the Interstate Commerce Commission[7] is exercised, if at all, either as the result of the Commission's action in attempting to enforce its orders, or through an injunction suit brought by the party aggrieved by an order, in the attempt to prevent its application.

Again, no statutory right of review exists in respect to the decisions of the Comptroller General. The individual injured is restricted to the use of some collateral attack, such as bringing suit in the Court of Claims, applying to the courts of the District of Columbia for a writ of mandamus, or applying to an equity court for an injunction.[8]

In many instances, the courts will refuse to review the subject matter of administrative judicial orders or

---

[4] G. A. Weber, *Employees' Compensation Commission*, p. 25.

[5] *Morgan* v. *Nunn*, 84 Fed. 551; *Flemming* v. *Stahl*, 83 Fed. 940.

[6] Act of 1917, Sec. 19. For a discussion of judicial review despite these provisions, see W. C. Van Vleck, *The Administrative Control of Aliens*, Chap. V.

[7] 49 U.S.C.A., Note 21, p. 49.

[8] Albert Langeluttig, "Legal Status of the Comptroller General of the United States," *23 Ill. Law Review* 563.

decisions, on the ground that the authority is exercising functions that are legislative, executive, or political in nature. Thus, the courts have said that they "cannot exercise any direct appellate jurisdiction of the land officials, because such a function is not judicial; it is administrative, executive, and political in nature. The right to interfere in such cases would break down the distinction, so important and well defined in our system, between the several separate and distinct branches of government."[9] For similar reasons, the court will not undertake to control by mandamus or injunction the actions of high executive authorities,[10] even when these actions are, from the viewpoint of this study, administrative judicial decisions.

The courts have not hesitated to interfere, however, in respect to the quasi-judicial acts of the land authorities, or the executive authorities, when these acts are in excess of power. In all cases the courts will compel administrative or executive authorities to remain within their respective jurisdictions.[11]

Abuse of power, furthermore, always seems to be ground for judicial review, even though no statutory basis is given for such review. Freund has said: "Well established principles of common law and equity permit a judicial review of administrative determinations, wherever there is a question of jurisdiction, and where there is an abuse of power."[12]

[9] *Craig* v. *Leitensdorfer*, 123 U.S. 189.

[10] See pp. 186 ff.

[11] See *St. Louis Smelting and Refining Co.* v. *Kemp*, 104 U.S. 636; *Newhall* v. *Sanger*, 92 U.S. 761; *Davies* v. *Manolis*, 179 Fed. 818. See also J. B. Cheadle, "Judicial Review of Administrative Determination," 2 *Southwestern Political Science Quarterly* 1, to the effect that "no administrative tribunal can finally determine its own jurisdiction."

[12] "The Right of Judicial Review in Rate Controversies," 27 *West Va. Law Quarterly* 207.

In a number of recent statutes governing the orders or decisions of administrative judicial bodies, an attempt has been made to limit review by the courts to questions of law. Thus, the findings of the Federal Trade Commission, "if supported by testimony, shall be conclusive."[13] The findings of the Tariff Commission in respect to unfair methods of foreign competition, "if supported by evidence, shall be conclusive."[14] The Longshoremen's and Harbor Workers' Act[15] provides that a compensation order made by a deputy commissioner may be suspended or set aside only if it is not in accordance with law. In respect to the Communications Commission, the law provides: "That the review of the court [Court of Appeals of the District of Columbia] shall be limited to questions of law, and that findings of fact by the Commission, if supported by substantial evidence, shall be conclusive unless it shall clearly appear that the findings of the Commission are arbitrary or capricious."[16]

In practice, the courts have found several ways by which they can take jurisdiction over fact-finding, even when statutory provisions make the fact-finding of an administrative judicial body final. Sometimes the courts make their own examination and determination of facts, if they believe that this is required as a step toward the enforcement of constitutional rights.[17] Again, the courts may take jurisdiction over questions of fact which must be decided as a preliminary to determining whether or not a certain administrative judicial authority has juris-

---

[13] 15 U.S.C.A., Sec. 45.

[14] 19 U.S.C.A., Supp., 1337(c).

[15] 33 U.S.C.A., Sec. 921.

[16] 73 Cong., Public No. 416, Sec. 402(e).

[17] See *Crowell* v. *Benson*, 52 Sup. Ct. 285, 1932, in respect to the finality of fact-finding by the deputy commissioners under the Longshoremen's and Harbor Workers' Act.

diction in a particular case. A fact which falls into this category is generally called a "jurisdictional fact."[18]

Occasionally the attitude of the court to all intents and purposes transforms what have been called "derivative facts," that is, determinations of fact which are derived from evidence and the interpretation thereof, into questions of law. This has been done in respect to certain decisions of the Federal Trade Commission as to unfair methods of competition, which the courts have reviewed on the ground that what constitutes an unfair method of competition is not a question of fact but a question of law.[19] Even when a statute provides for finality of fact-finding on the part of an administrative tribunal, the regular courts may intervene by holding that judicial interpretation of the statute is needed. When a statute contains such an expression as "crime involving moral turpitude," "likely to become a public charge," and so on, there is a strong probability that the courts will say that the meaning of this expression is a question of law requiring judicial interpretation.

It is possible for the courts to say that a finding of fact by an administrative body, without substantial evidence or testimony to support it, does violence to the law. "And an inquiry into the facts before the Commission, in order to ascertain whether its findings are thus vitiated, belongs to the judicial province."[20]

Therefore, despite legislative provisions which may seek to bestow upon administrative judicial authorities

[18] The same.

[19] See *Federal Trade Commission* v. *Gratz,* 253 U.S. 421 at 427, where the court held: "The words 'unfair method of competition' are not defined by statute. . . . It is for the courts, not the Commission, ultimately to determine as a matter of law what they include." For a criticism of the failure of Congress to give the Commission power to lay down rules in respect to unfair methods of competition, see pp. 54-55.

[20] *Radio Commission* v. *Nelson Bros. Co.,* 289 U.S. 277.

finality in respect to fact-finding, there can be no certainty that such an authority enjoys this power completely, until one has examined all the decisions bearing upon the subject that have been handed down by the higher courts. Even then, if various important questions have not been raised in the cases decided, certainty is impossible.

The courts display a growing tendency, nevertheless, to refuse to review findings of fact made by administrative tribunals;[21] though they hold firmly to the fundamental principle, expressed in both statutory law and court decisions, that the ordinary courts shall review the decisions of administrative tribunals involving questions of law. "The courts are loath to relinquish any of their ultimate jurisdiction over legal questions, and will not accept as conclusive the decisions of administrative tribunals on points of law; at least not where in the opinion of the court a statute is open to only one construction and such construction has not been given to it by the administrative agency."[22]

II. PARTICULAR REMEDIES

One of the most important problems of control over the action of administrative tribunals, from the standpoint of individual rights, is that of establishing remedies which are simple yet comprehensive, which are easily available and effective, but which do not hamper the administration unnecessarily in its functioning.

The remedies that may be sought by a person who considers himself injured by federal action are usually classified as common law remedies and statutory remedies. It must be recognized, however, that even though a statu-

[21] See A. Morton Tollefson, "Administrative Finality," *29 Mich. Law Review* 840, for numerous citations.
[22] The same, p. 844.

tory remedy is given, it is in many instances implemented by the common law remedies, such as the injunction or the mandamus.

Among the most important of the common law remedies that may be available against the acts of administrative tribunals are the mandamus, the injunction, the certiorari, and the writ of habeas corpus. Actions for damages are much less important, since they are inapplicable to any judicial or quasi-judicial act.

A. The mandamus. By virtue of the criterion laid down by the courts, that discretionary acts and acts judicial in nature are not subject to the writ of mandamus, it seems that in no case would this writ lie directly against the quasi-judicial decisions of administrative tribunals. The Supreme Court has held[23] that even errors of law committed in the discharge of a function essentially judicial in nature cannot be corrected through the writ of mandamus. In the case of *Board of Tax Appeals* v. *United States*[24] it was held that the writ of mandamus will not lie to control the exercise of the judicial or quasi-judicial jurisdiction of an executive board or officer. In the case of *Wilbur* v. *United States*,[25] it was said: "It follows that the Secretary, being called upon to examine and pass upon evidence on which to form his judgment in a matter wholly within his jurisdiction, was exercising a quasi-judicial discretion which cannot be controlled by mandamus."

Although the writ of mandamus cannot be used to control the quasi-judicial discretion of administrative tribunals, it can be used to compel them to take jurisdiction in respect to a statutory duty requiring official

[23] *Interstate Commerce Commission* v. *United States*, 53 Sup. Ct. 607.
[24] 59 App. D.C. 151.
[25] 60 App. D.C. 328.

decision or action; and the refusal of such jurisdiction will warrant the issue of the mandamus.[26]

From what has been said, it is evident that the writ of mandamus is practically useless as a remedy against erroneous decisions which may be made by most of the types of administrative tribunals—the special independent administrative tribunals, the special administrative tribunals within the government departments and agencies, the regulatory authorities in so far as they are exercising either quasi-legislative or quasi-judicial powers, and the President and the heads of departments in so far as they are making quasi-judicial decisions. It may be used, however, in respect to most of these administrative judicial authorities as a crude method of determining their jurisdiction; of causing them to take action that is clearly required of them by law; and especially of compelling them to act when their refusal to do so seems to be based upon arbitrariness, capriciousness, or illegality.

Today, the writ of mandamus is used chiefly to compel the performance of duties imposed by law upon the departments, offices, and agencies which, in the course of their functions, bestow or withhold rights or privileges, funds, grants, and so forth. The great majority of mandamus suits are brought against the Land Department, the Postmaster General, and the Comptroller General. Even in such suits the remedy is almost valueless, since the courts will not employ it against quasi-judicial decisions as such, or in general against any action involving the use of judgment or discretion. It operates (despite a few notable exceptions) almost entirely in causing action to be taken as regards "ministerial" or mandatory functions.

[26] *New York, New Haven, and Hartford R.R. Co.* v. *Interstate Commerce Commission,* 60 App. D.C. 403.

This restricted use of the mandamus has been caused largely by the courts themselves, which have adopted various criteria that serve as limitations. Among the more important of such criteria are: That the writ may not be used to establish legal rights, but only to enforce those already existing; that the writ will issue only upon sound judicial discretion; that the interests involved must be substantial and concrete, and not abstract; that no other remedy shall be available; that all administrative appeals must have been taken; that the writ will not lie against a political or executive act, or where judgment and discretion are involved, or where the granting of the writ would be idle. Finally, the writ can be issued by no federal court except the Supreme Court of the District of Columbia without statutory authorization.

B. The injunction. Another common law remedy which is sometimes used to control the acts of federal administrative tribunals is the equitable writ of injunction. This writ has a broader field of application than the mandamus. Moreover, it can be granted by every federal district court, as well as by judges of the United States Supreme Court.[27] In some instances it is made a feature of statutory remedies. For example, the provisions for review of the determinations of deputy commissioners under the Longshoremen's and Harbor Workers' Compensation Act, state: "If not in accordance with law, a compensation order may be suspended, or set aside, in whole or in part through injunction proceedings. . . ."[28]

There are several criteria employed by the courts in determining whether or not an injunction will issue. As a matter of principle (to which there are but few exceptions) the injunction, whether temporary or permanent,

[27] Judicial Code, Art. 378.
[28] 33 U.S.C.A., Supp., Sec. 931.

cannot be sought as of right, but will be granted or refused at the discretion of the court. This writ is used
primarily to prevent an irreparable wrong from being
done. The person who requests the issuance of an injunction must show that he is threatened with specific
injury through the violation of some legal or equitable
right. He must also, as a rule, show the absence of any
other adequate legal remedy.

From the viewpoint of control over administrative
legislation, perhaps the most important criterion that the
courts have laid down regarding the issue of the injunction against public officers is the distinction between its
use in respect to discretionary and ministerial actions.
Only the latter are normally controllable by this writ.
Thus, it was held in the case of *Tidal Osage Co.* v.
West,[29] that the decision of the Secretary of the Interior
cannot be reviewed by injunction, when, in exercising
the broad jurisdiction vested in him respecting the disposition and control of Indian lands, he must determine
his power to act through the interpretation of statutes
and of rules and regulations lawfully made in compliance
therewith. Nor will the writ lie to review the power conferred upon the Secretary of the Interior to hear and
determine the rights of contestants for patents to public
lands, for this function is quasi-judicial in nature.[30] Again,
the writ of injunction cannot be used to review or control a judgment of the Interstate Commerce Commission which involves the exercise of its discretion, which
is within its jurisdiction, and which depends upon questions of fact.[31]

[29] 57 App. D.C. 41.
[30] *Perry* v. *Work*, 56 App. D.C. 92.
[31] *Pittsburgh and West Virginia Railway Co.* v. *Interstate Commerce
Commission*, 54 App. D.C. 34.

Another important criterion is whether the decision of the administrative tribunal deals with questions of law or of fact. In respect to the Interstate Commerce Commission, the courts have often refused to issue injunctions, on the ground that the question whether or not certain acts of carriers amount to unfair discrimination is one of fact, upon which the Commission has power of final determination.[32]

The general rule of the courts as to issuing injunctions against the acts of heads of departments is summarized in the case of *Bates and Guild Co.* v. *Payne*,[33] where it is held that when the "decision of questions of fact is committed by Congress to the judgment and discretion of the head of a department, his decision thereon is conclusive; and even upon mixed questions of law and fact, or of law alone, his action will carry with it a strong presumption of its correctness, and the courts will not ordinarily review it, although they may have the power, and will occasionally exercise the right of so doing."

Other criteria which the courts apply in deciding whether or not they will issue injunctions against administrative or quasi-judicial actions of government agents are: Whether the statute or order on which an action was based has been interpreted or construed in the same way for a long period of time; whether the interpretation of law by an administrative officer is or is not specifically required; and whether the officer or agency has been arbitrary or capricious in exercising a discretionary power.

It is obvious that the criteria set up by the courts, as to when they will or will not issue a writ of injunction,

---

[32] *United States* v. *Louisville and Nashville Railway Co.*, 235 U.S. 314; *Manufacturers' Railway Co.* v. *United States*, 246 U.S. 457.

[33] 194 U.S. 109, 110.

very greatly limit the use of this writ as a remedy for erroneous decisions by administrative judicial authorities. The elimination of discretionary acts, quasi-judicial acts, questions of fact, acts where an administrative officer must construe the law, action under procedures or interpretations of statutes that have continued for a long time, and questions involving abstract rights rather than concrete rights, must evidently leave relatively few actions of administrative bodies or administrative tribunals to be controlled by this remedy. There would be still fewer so controlled if it were not for the statutory requirements mentioned above.

C. Habeas corpus. Since the function of the writ of habeas corpus is to inquire into the detention of a person, it can be readily seen that this remedy has very little place in controlling the decisions of administrative tribunals. Its chief use in respect to such tribunals is in immigration cases, Chinese exclusion cases, and deportation cases, decided upon by the Secretary of Labor.[34]

D. Writ of certiorari. Certain decisions of administrative judicial authorities in the federal government may be reviewed in either first, second, or third instance through the writ of certiorari. This use of the writ is, however, merely incidental and occasional, for reasons that will appear later.

The present use of the certiorari by the Supreme Court of the United States is based chiefly upon the so-called Judges' bill of 1925,[35] which provided:

In any case, civil or criminal, in a circuit court of appeals, or in the Court of Appeals of the District of Columbia, it shall be competent for the Supreme Court of the United States, upon the

---

[34] On judicial review in such cases, see Van Vleck, *Administrative Control of Aliens.*

[35] Now incorporated into the U.S. Judicial Code as Sec. 347.

petition of any party thereto, whether government or other liti-
gant, to require by certiorari, either before or after a judgment
or decree by such lower court, that the cause be certified to the
Supreme Court for determination by it with the same power and
authority, and with like effect, as if the cause had been brought
there by unrestricted writ of error or appeal.

The provision just quoted, and certain other statutory
enactments,[36] attempted to give to the Supreme Court,
in the writ of certiorari, a means of controlling and unifying the practice and the jurisprudence of the lower
courts; as well as to simplify the process of bringing
cases up from the latter, and to reduce the burden of the
Supreme Court by leaving the granting of the writ to its
own discretion.

In the exercise of this discretion, it has applied certain
criteria. The writ of certiorari will generally be issued
when a case involves a federal question of substance not
previously decided by the Supreme Court; when the
decision by a lower court appears to conflict with previous
decisions of the Supreme Court; in case such a decision
is made by a circuit court of appeals, if it conflicts with
that of another circuit court of appeals on the same matter; or under similar circumstances.[37]

Since the writ is limited to action "from court to
court," it does not apply to several kinds of administrative judicial decisions which are not reviewable by a
court. Moreover, it will not be issued to review decisions
that are advisory only,[38] actions of courts that merely
instruct administrative officers or are mere appellate administrative decisions,[39] decisions of courts that merely

---

[36] In particular the abolition of the writ of error and the substitu-
tion of the appeal therefor. 45 Stat. L. 54, as amended by 45 Stat. L.
466.

[37] See Rules of the Supreme Court, especially Rules 38-41.

[38] Ex parte *Bakelite Corporation,* 279 U.S. 438.

[39] *Postum Cereal Co.* v. *California Fig Nut Co.,* 272 U.S. 693.

"revise legislative discretion,"[40] or decisions of courts which are acting as superior revising agencies in the field of administration.[41]

Despite all these negative criteria, various statutes governing certain administrative tribunals provide that certiorari to the Supreme Court shall be the method by which their decisions are controlled.[42] Law and practice combined have brought about the possibility of a considerable degree of control by the Supreme Court over administrative judicial decisions through this writ. Thus, in primary instance the decisions of the Court of Customs and Patent Appeals and the Court of Claims are reviewable by the Supreme Court by the writ of certiorari. In secondary instance the decisions of the Commissioner of Patents, the Board of Appeals in the Patent Office, and the Board of Tax Appeals; certain decisions of the Interstate Commerce Commission, the United States Shipping Board, the Federal Trade Commission, the Securities and Exchange Commission, the Communications Commission, and the Federal Reserve Board in respect to orders under the anti-trust acts; and the orders of the Secretary of Agriculture under the Grain Futures Act and the Packers' and Stock Yards Act, are reviewable by the Supreme Court by the writ of certiorari. In third instance the decisions of the examiners in chief in the Patent Office are reviewable by the Supreme Court by way of certiorari.[43]

[40] *Keller* v. *Potomac Electric Power Co.*, 261 U.S. 428.

[41] *Federal Radio Commission* v. *General Electric Co.*, 281 U.S. 464, 467; *Radio Commission* v. *Nelson Bros. Co.*, 289 U.S. 266, 274.

[42] For example, acts of the Communications Commission are reviewable by certiorari (73 Cong., Public No. 416); also decisions of the Board of Tax Appeals under the Revenue Act of 1926.

[43] It has been held in certain cases that the Supreme Court of the District of Columbia may also issue writs of certiorari against the acts of various special tribunals exercising judicial or quasi-judicial functions;

This possibility of control is realized only to a very slight extent. The Supreme Court uses the writ of certiorari less as a means of redressing judicial or quasi-judicial mistakes and guaranteeing that justice will be done to individuals, than as a means of supervising and controlling the federal judicial system. Its rules for the exercise of its own discretion in the granting of the writ are constructed for this express purpose, rather than for that of protecting individual rights (which has largely become a function of the lower courts) or of controlling the actions of special authorities or tribunals exercising judicial or quasi-judicial powers. Indirectly, and, so to speak, sporadically, it may accomplish both of the last-named functions in those few instances where it takes jurisdiction over a case. The actual control over administrative judicial bodies, however, except in rare instances, ends with the decisions of the Circuit Courts of Appeals, the Supreme Court of the District of Columbia, the Court of Appeals of the District of Columbia, the Court of Customs and Patent Appeals, and the Court of Claims. There is no one court to unify and control all the decisions of administrative tribunals.

Another factor which makes the use of the certiorari relatively unimportant as a method of final control over administrative action is the wholesale denial of petitions for this writ. During the six years from 1926 to 1931, inclusive, there were 3,919 petitions brought before the Supreme Court, of which only 747 were granted.[44]

---

but petitions of this nature have not been granted. See *Padgett* v. *District of Columbia*, 17 App. D.C. at p. 262; *Guy* v. *District of Columbia*, 25 App. D.C. 119; *District of Columbia* v. *Burgdorf*, 6 App. D.C. 465.

[44] Derived from statistics prepared by Frankfurter and Landis, published in the following articles: "The Business of the Supreme Court at October Term, 1930," *45 Harvard Law Review* 284; and "The Business of the Supreme Court of October Term, 1931," *46 Harvard Law Review* 238.

Though no statistics are available as to the exact number of petitions for the writ of certiorari that arise from the original decisions of administrative tribunals and authorities exercising quasi-judicial powers, a rough estimate based upon the number of cases arising under anti-trust laws, the "commerce clause," the Federal Employers' Liability Act and related acts, the laws on immigration and naturalization, Indian affairs, public lands, national banks, taxation, and so on, indicates that about one-third of all certiorari cases come up as the result of the original action of administrative tribunals and related authorities. This means that the Supreme Court receives each year about 250 petitions for writs of certiorari involving final determination of some administrative judicial question. Since barely 50 of these petitions are granted, evidently the certiorari is not an important remedy for mistakes and faults in administrative adjudication.

E. Writ of prohibition. The writ of prohibition is used for the purpose of preventing an unlawful assumption of jurisdiction by a court of peculiar, limited, or inferior jurisdiction,[45] and can be used only to restrain the exercise of judicial functions. In theory, it might be applied to control those courts which we have classified as special administrative courts, and which the Supreme Court classifies as "legislative courts"; but it would not lie in respect to the courts of the District of Columbia acting as authorities for the review of administrative or administrative judicial acts, since according to the Supreme Court of the United States they are then acting as superior administrative reviewing agencies. The power of the Supreme Court to issue writs of prohibition has never been clearly defined either by statute or decision.

---

[45] Ex parte *Gordon*, 104 U.S. 515; *Smith* v. *Whitney*, 116 U.S. 167.

In the Bakelite Case,[46] the Supreme Court was called upon to issue a writ of prohibition against the Court of Customs Appeals (now the Court of Customs and Patent Appeals). The Supreme Court held that it was not necessary in the particular case to decide whether or not it had this power, but admitted that the question whether the writ of prohibition would lie was not free from doubt. It is evident that the writ of prohibition is virtually of no effect as a means of controlling the action of administrative adjudicative authorities.

F. Appeals to judicial courts. The word appeal is often used in a broad sense to denote the review of the decisions or orders of one authority by another. In order to give a true picture of the appeal as a remedy co-ordinate with the other remedies which we have been discussing, however, it is necessary to limit ourselves to its technical meaning: a remedy by which a superior court re-examines and retires a case brought before it from another authority or court.

Before discussing the significance of the appeal as a means of controlling quasi-judicial decisions and orders, we must say a few words about the general nature of the remedy. In the first place, in the federal government, the right to an appeal is purely statutory.[47] Consequently, unless there is special statutory authorization, no appeal lies from the decisions or orders of administrative adjudicating bodies. In the second place, where the appeal does lie it is a remedy to which a party to the case has a right, and is therefore not discretionary with the court. In the third place, the appeal may be used either as a first or second instance remedy, or as a final remedy.

---

[46] See ex parte *Bakelite Corporation*, 279 U.S. 448, for statement of Supreme Court to this effect.

[47] *Heike* v. *United States*, 217 U.S. 423.

An examination of all the remedies available against all the chief federal authorities which make quasi-judicial decisions or orders shows that a direct appeal from these authorities to an ordinary judicial court is seldom given by statute. In some instances the decisions of the administrative judicial authorities are final; in several instances there is provision for review by higher administrative authorities; in some instances the reviewing authority, although a regular judicial court, is acting in an administrative or legislative capacity; in two instances, at least, certiorari is the remedy used; and in several instances the review is either a step in enforcement proceedings, or else, though called an appeal, it is too closely connected with enforcement methods to be an appeal in the technical sense here employed.

The best examples of administrative judicial authorities whose decisions are controlled by a true appeal are the Board of Tax Appeals and the Federal Communications Commission.

The decisions of the Board of Tax Appeals may be appealed to either a Circuit Court of Appeals or the Court of Appeals of the District of Columbia. The appellate court will consider only questions of law which appear upon the record of a case.[48] There is a possibility of final review, by certiorari to the United States Supreme Court.[49]

Decisions of the Communications Commission modifying, suspending, or revoking radio station licenses, or refusing to grant or renew licenses, may be appealed to the Court of Appeals of the District of Columbia. The review of the court is limited to questions of law. The

[48] Hugh C. Bickford, *Court Procedure in Federal Tax Cases* (1929 ed.), p. 21.
[49] 26 U.S.C.A., Supp., Sec. 1224.

findings of fact, if supported by substantial evidence, are conclusive, "unless it shall clearly appear that the findings of the Commission are arbitrary or capricious." The judgment of the court is final, except for a possible review by certiorari by the Supreme Court of the United States.[50]

The Circuit Courts of Appeals have appellate jurisdiction over the decisions of several administrative judicial authorities. For example, the Federal Trade Commission Act[51] provides that any party required by an order of the Commission, after a formal hearing, to cease and desist from using unfair methods of competition, may obtain a review of such order in the Circuit Court of Appeals by filing in the court a petition praying that the order be set aside. Upon examining the transcript of the hearing, the court may affirm, set aside, or modify the order of the Commission. The findings of the Commission in respect to facts, however, are conclusive. The Circuit Courts of Appeals also have power to review the orders of the Federal Trade Commission in respect to the enforcement of certain sections of the Clayton Act. The procedure is quite similar to that just described.[52]

Section 2 of the Clayton Act[53] gives power to the Interstate Commerce Commission to enforce compliance with certain sections of the act, in respect to common carriers, and a similar jurisdiction to the Federal Reserve Board as to banks, banking associations, and trust companies. Any party required by an order of the Commission or Board to cease and desist from a violation charged, may obtain a review in the Circuit Court of Appeals. The

[50] 73 Cong., Public No. 416, Sec. 402(e).
[51] 15 U.S.C.A., Sec. 45.
[52] The same, Sec. 21.
[53] The same.

court has power to affirm, set aside, or modify the order of the Commission or Board. The findings of fact of such bodies, however, are final and conclusive.

According to the Packers' and Stock Yards Act of 1921, a Circuit Court of Appeals may review the orders of the Secretary of Agriculture issued under this act.[54] Procedure is along the same general lines as in the other instances just given. The decree of the court may affirm, set aside, or modify the orders of the Secretary. Such a decree is final, except that it is subject to review by the Supreme Court of the United States upon certiorari.

Control over the orders of the Securities and Exchange Commission, established by the law of 1934,[55] is in the hands of the Circuit Courts of Appeals or the Court of Appeals of the District of Columbia. A written petition is presented to the court, praying that a specified order be modified or set aside in whole or in part. The Commission certifies to the court a copy of the transcript of the record. The court has exclusive jurisdiction to affirm, modify, enforce, or set aside the order in whole or in part. The findings of the Commission as to fact, if supported by substantial evidence, are conclusive. The judgment of the court is final, subject to review by the Supreme Court upon certiorari or certification.

It is necessary to mention the fact that the jurisdiction of the judicial courts over appeals from orders of the Federal Trade Commission, the Interstate Commerce Commission, the Federal Reserve Board, and various other authorities, is closely related to the question of enforcement methods. In general, the administrative judicial authority may also appeal to the court for the en-

[54] 7 U.S.C.A. 194.
[55] 73 Cong., Public No. 291, pp. 23, 24.

forcement of its orders; and it is sometimes a question of strategy whether it will do so, or will allow the corporation or private party affected to make the first move. This situation is at times rather confusing. Occasionally it works out in such a way that the court, in acting on an appeal, becomes in fact an arbiter of policy.

Review of quasi-judicial decisions by way of appeal to a regular judicial court in final instance occurs relatively seldom. In many situations, some of which we have noted above, the Supreme Court of the United States may review by way of certiorari the decision on an appeal rendered by a lower court. In a few instances, however, it is possible to appeal directly to the Supreme Court.

Thus, an appeal may be taken from an order of a district court, granting or denying an interlocutory injunction in respect to the orders of the Interstate Commerce Commission,[56] to the United States Supreme Court. An appeal from the final judgment or decree of a district court in respect to a request for enforcement of the orders of the Interstate Commerce Commission (with certain exceptions),[57] may be taken to the United States Supreme Court. When a case is brought before a district court by the party affected, seeking to enjoin, set aside, annul, or suspend, in whole or in part, an order of the Interstate Commerce Commission,[58] an appeal lies to the Supreme Court. A direct appeal to the Supreme Court is allowed from the decisions of district courts under the Packers' and Stock Yards Act of 1921,[59] reviewing the orders of the Secretary of Agriculture.

[56] 28 U.S.C.A., Sec. 47.
[57] 28 U.S.C.A., Supp., Sec. 47(a) and Sec. 41, par. 27.
[58] 28 U.S.C.A., Sec. 41, par. 28; the same, Supp., Sec. 47(a).
[59] 7 U.S.C.A., Sec. 217.

III. CONCLUSIONS

The foregoing pages show that there is no systematic control over the administrative judicial authorities, and that there are no certain remedies for any injustice toward individuals which may be caused by the decisions of these authorities. The methods and the extent of review over the acts of administrative tribunals vary according to many different factors, including legislative provisions, the character of the reviewing authority, and even the particular subject involved. As we have remarked above, no plan or system governs judicial review of quasi-judicial decisions and orders.

A complete picture of court control over the decisions and orders of such bodies would almost necessitate a separate treatment of every individual agency. Plausible reasons could no doubt be given for the particular method followed in respect to each administrative judicial authority. It may well be asked, however, whether it is not possible to create a far simpler and more unified system.

CHAPTER X

ADVANTAGES OF ADMINISTRATIVE ADJUDICATION

In Chapter VII we saw that it is possible from one viewpoint to classify most of the authorities that are carrying on the function of administrative adjudication into two main groups: (1) those which are primarily administering and only incidentally adjudicating; and (2) those which are primarily concerned with the function of settling disputes and controlling administrative action.

In examining the advantages of administrative adjudication, it is necessary to keep clearly in mind the distinction between these two types of authorities; for although certain advantages are common to both types, other advantages belong pre-eminently to one type or the other. The present chapter will consider first the advantages which are claimed for each separate type, and next the common advantages. As a matter of fairness, so-called advantages which the authors consider only specious, or outweighed by disadvantages, will be listed here. Later pages will examine them critically and attempt to evaluate them.

I. ADVANTAGES OF ADMINISTRATIVE ADJUDICATION AS A PART OF THE PROCESS OF ADMINISTRATION

The advantages which are usually claimed for administrative adjudication as a part of the administrative process are eight in number. They are briefly discussed below.

A. Administrative agencies can settle cases coming be-

fore them, both on their merits and also with the avowed
purpose of furthering a particular social or economic
policy that has been initiated by the legislature or the
executive. "Of all the characteristics of administrative
law, none is more advantageous, when rightly used for
the public good, than the power of the tribunal to decide the cases coming before it with the avowed object of
furthering a policy of social improvement in some particular field; and of adapting their attitude towards the
controversy so as to fit the needs of that policy."[1] Thus,
the decisions of the authorities connected with the National Recovery Administration almost of necessity must
be made in harmony with the aims of the program of
industrial recovery. Such authorities are not administering an abstract law, but are administering a social and
economic policy.

B. Administrative adjudication is important in times
of emergency when a large degree of freedom and discretion on the part of the administration seems to be
of more importance than a precise legal regularity in the
functioning of the administrative services. In times of
great stress it often happens that the functions of government are more concentrated than in normal times,
so that unified and effective action may be taken. To attempt a scientific differentiation of function in such cases,
however desirable it may be in itself, might lead to such
delays and hindrances to effective action as to endanger
the state and the general welfare.

C. Where the subject to be regulated is so new and
untried that neither the legislature nor the executive
authorities deem themselves capable of laying down in
advance rules and regulations governing it, it may seem

---

[1] See W. A. Robson, *Justice and Administrative Law*, p. 275.

advisable to develop economic policy, standards, norms, and criteria case by case rather than to attempt to regulate in advance. This is the trial and error method. By proceeding in this way, it is believed that principles, viewpoints, methods, and standards will gradually develop, which may either form the basis of further legislative or regulatory action or may become a sort of "common law" on the subject.

D. When new legal and juridical standards must be developed and integrated into public administration, either because new policies demand them or because the legal standards and criteria formerly applied to administrative policies or acts must be changed to meet present-day needs, it may be advantageous to have the adjudication necessary for the performance of such acts accomplished by the administration itself, which is in sympathy with the new type of social or economic policy. For example, new legal norms and standards became almost a necessity when the government attempted to regulate competitive methods under the Federal Trade Commission Act. The establishment by the legislature of the principle of workmen's compensation likewise demanded the introduction of new legal standards and the abolition of old standards. The present far-reaching interference with business and industry under the National Industrial Recovery Act and the Agricultural Adjustment Act undoubtedly demands that property rights shall be viewed by all judicial agencies in a different way than ever before in the history of this country.

E. Even when the legislature itself establishes new standards and norms which change and modify the common law concepts, it may seem necessary that these be interpreted by administrative judicial authorities which have been established for the purpose of administering cases arising under them, rather than by the courts, in order that the decisions may be in harmony with the new law. This is due to the tendency of the ordinary courts to look always to the past; to their deep immersion in common law concepts; to their wish to place new situations within ancient categories. This tendency has often, it is claimed, caused the courts to demonstrate that they are either definitely hostile to new economic, social, or legal principles, or are so committed to old principles as to be unable to make their decisions conform to new social trends, new policies, or new types of social action.

It is interesting to observe that when the legislatures of certain states have created a statutory liability of the state and its subdivisions for certain types of injuries occasioned to individuals, the courts have in many instances so twisted and bent the new creation as to make it conform in every way possible with the ancient concepts of the common law rather than the manifest intent of the legislature. Our federal courts have rather consistently declined to consider any economic practices restraining or interfering with trade as being "unfair methods of competition" except those so adjudged by the common law.

Years ago the Federal Trade Commission, when attempting to introduce into the concept of "unfair methods of competition" certain practices now recognized as unfair by various codes made under the National Recovery Act, found itself blocked at every turn by the courts, which refused to go beyond the common law doctrine. The old common law standard of "reasonableness" was read by the courts into the Sherman Anti-Trust Act with such effect as to change entirely the character of the act. These are but a few stray examples of the inability shown by the ordinary courts to adopt the views of the legislature on new lines of policy, and of their determined insistence upon old legal concepts which has often defeated the express will of the legislature. From both domestic and foreign experience, it is fair to conclude that administrative adjudicating authorities generally take a much more modern and liberal attitude, in greater harmony with present social trends and legislative intention, than is taken by the ordinary courts.

F. Administrative tribunals are valuable where public law standards should be developed to supplement and fill in the deficiencies of inadequate standards of private law. For instance, when the state is exercising the taxing power or the police power, or when it is regulating and controlling business and industry, the ordinary norms that govern the relationship of one individual to another are not applicable. The relationship of the state to the individual in such cases is not that of one private person to another and should not be governed by the same standards and principles.

In respect to such functions as exercising control over the conditions affecting public health, working for the prevention of infectious diseases and the elimination of plant diseases, controlling hours of labor, and so on, the powers which the state exercises are not the powers which one individual can exercise toward another. Moreover, when controversies arise in respect to the administration of these functions, the decisions which are made must have the double purpose of enforcing individual rights and promoting social welfare. In all decisions involving such subjects, judgment must be based to a certain extent upon new standards of social morality and social needs, as well as on mere questions of legality or illegality.

The Federal Trade Commission and the National Recovery Administration, to mention concrete instances, have been given the task of developing economic ethics and morality in connection with their functions of control. The Interstate Commerce Commission is required to perform the social task of securing a cheap and efficient service on the part of railways. The Securities and Exchange Commission is attempting to prevent fraud and chicanery in the sale of securities. The Federal Communications Commission has, among its other duties, that of creating and maintaining conditions in radio transmission which will work to the best advantage of the public. All decisions of such bodies involve not only individual rights but also collective needs. It is claimed by many enthusiastic believers in this type of administrative agency that its complex work is necessary and inevitable, and, if properly safeguarded, will work out equitably, since the tendencies mentioned above do not imply ruthless sacrifice of individual rights to social needs, but rather a fair evaluation of individual rights by standards which at the same time serve social needs.

It is claimed that when the ordinary courts are called upon to decide cases in which the administration and a private person are opposing parties, they habitually make their decisions according to the old familiar standards governing the relationships of one individual to another, rather than the new standards fitted to the needs of the social situation. They apply the individualistic concepts of the common law, instead of developing new public law concepts applicable to a highly integrated society with a growing consciousness of common needs and common purposes. Likewise, although the state itself has rapidly changed from a police state to a complex group of specialized services, the ordinary courts have refused to recognize the altered relationship of the individual to the state which this change has brought about. Although the administrative tribunals have not been permitted to disregard certain criteria which the ordinary courts have considered basic, they have nevertheless been very useful in the development of new criteria in the domain of public law.

G. Many persons feel that the function of adjudicating, particularly in the regulatory activities of government, is so closely integrated with the making of policy and the exercise of a wide discretion, and also with the administrative function, that it is impossible to separate them. The function of adjudicating may be so interwoven with the function of fact-finding that it often seems as if the determination of the facts virtually constitutes a decision. It is also difficult to separate the exercise of administrative discretion from the judicial function. For these reasons it is believed that an administrative tribunal exercising all three functions of government is desirable.

H. It is frequently argued that in the first instance, at least, what is needed is merely the settlement of a controversy by a method which combines the factors of an administrative decision with those of a quasi-judicial decision. The purpose here is not that of controlling an administrative act, but merely of making a decision upon the facts, as to the rights in controversy. The administrative authorities, because of the very nature of the subject matter before them, must perform functions which closely resemble those performed by the courts. They must interpret law, hold hearings in order to determine the facts of any controversial matter, and make a decision.

II. ADVANTAGES OF AUTHORITIES THAT MERELY ADJUDICATE AND CONTROL

We saw in Chapter VII that at present there are several authorities, particularly the independent administrative courts and the special administrative courts within various departments and agencies, which do not administer, but merely settle disputes resulting from administrative action, and control the administration to keep it within the bounds of legality.[2] The advantages of having this type of tribunal settle administrative cases fall into two groups: First, advantages as regards the decision of such cases by the regular courts; second, advantages as regards the decision of such cases by agencies which combine administrative and judicial functions.

A. ADVANTAGES OVER ORDINARY JUDICIAL COURTS

1. Administrative courts can handle public law cases much better than the ordinary courts. We have already had occasion to observe that the aims, the subject matter, and the criteria of public law are of quite a different nature from those of civil law. In private law the aim of courts is to adjust the differences between private individuals. In public law the aim of adjudication is not only to adjust the relationship of the state to the individual, but also to keep the administrative machine functioning within the bounds of legality, either by compelling it to act, by restraining it from acting, by causing it to act according to standards laid down for it by laws and regulations, or by requiring it to act with due regard to equity and justice. One of the prime functions of adjudication, then, is the protection of the objective legal order. In other words, a very large number of administrative cases involve an element of control over the

[2] See pp. 122 ff.

administration as well as the mere settling of a dispute.

In public law controversies, the judicial authorities are dealing with a subject matter which in the majority of instances is quite separate and distinct from the subject matter of private law. In the granting of public lands, the exclusion or deportation of aliens, taxation, the regulation of public utilities, the regulation and control of business, and so forth, the situations to be adjudicated are not those of private law and cannot be settled properly according to private law standards. Not only is the subject matter different from that of private law, but it is often so complex and technical that only a judge who is thoroughly familiar with its intricacies can possibly make a reasonable and properly balanced decision.

In many instances, the criteria of public law are essentially different from the criteria of private law. This is due in part to the fact that the state is using force, in part to the fact that it is controlling the actions of its own agencies as well as adjudicating, and in part to the differences in subject matter which have just been mentioned.

The relationship of the parties in public law suits is quite different from the relationship of the individuals to one another in civil law suits. In civil law suits, the state acts merely as a judge, mediator, or umpire between equal parties. In public law suits, as a rule, the state is both the judge or mediator, and also a party to the suit. In civil law suits, the courts are dealing with the relationships of individuals with one another. In public law suits, the courts or adjudicatory agencies are generally dealing with the relationship between the individual and the state. The state always appears as a superior and not as an equal. It has behind it unlimited force. The individual, on the other hand, appears as an inferior, without any method of compelling the state to deal fairly with him, unless it consents to be compelled.

But why, it may be asked, do these differences between public law and private law demand a different type of court?

It has been mentioned already that the subject matter of public law is so complex and highly specialized as to require a degree of expert knowledge not to be found or expected in the ordinary courts. But this is not all. Authorities that are settling public law disputes should not only have a wide technical training in the field of public law, but should also see clearly the difference in its aims and purposes from those of private law.

Instead of merely thinking of law in the terms of individual rights, they should also be able to see in public law a system of state-individual relationships. They should be thinking of adjudication in terms of control of the state over its own actions. They should be thinking of protecting the objective legal order quite as much as of protecting individual rights. They must of necessity think in terms of public administration as well as in terms of judicial tradition. They must work upon the basis of an ever broadening theory of public law, its meaning, its significance, its purposes, its applications.

A correct theory of public law cannot well be developed by the ordinary courts, which are not only steeped in the feelings and traditions of private law, but which do not handle a sufficient number of cases in the whole vast field of public law to develop broad and significant theories regarding it. Administrative tribunals, especially those which handle appeals from many lower authorities and hence know a great deal about many phases of administration, may be expected to work out a sound theory of public law.

2. Another advantage of special administrative tribunals over the ordinary courts, particularly in second instance, is the fact that they can handle cases that are not definitely "cases and controversies" under Article III of the United States Constitution and so cannot be handled by the regular constitutional courts. These courts have refused to take jurisdiction over appeals from decisions made by administrative adjudicatory agencies, on the ground that such a decision is not final; that it is of an administrative, supervisory, or legislative nature; or that it deals with matters which might be handled by the legislature, the executive, or the administrative authorities. It is also possible for administrative tribunals to handle that class of controversies (such as civil service cases) over which the regular courts at present refuse to take jurisdiction, on the ground that the regulations of the President do not have the force of law and so[3] cannot be handled by the courts.

In respect to cases arising out of a contest as to the validity of administrative action where so-called favors or grants are involved, as in land cases, immigration cases, postal cases, employers' liability cases, pension cases, and so on, the administrative courts are not hindered from taking jurisdiction on the ground that since only grants and favors are involved, rather than rights, there is no case or controversy within the meaning of Article III of the Constitution. Such cases could certainly be handled by administrative courts, which would thus be able to enforce the law by judicial means in several important fields where satisfactory adjudication is now impossible.

[3] *Morgan* v. *Nunn*, 84 Fed. 551.

B. Advantages over Agencies Which Both Administer and Adjudicate

1. When authorities are established which merely settle disputes and control administrative action, a separation can be made between the function of administration and that of adjudication. The advantages of this separation of functions are discussed in the next chapter.

2. Entrusting the work of adjudicating and controlling to special authorities which have no other primary duties makes possible a separation of the function of administrative fact-finding from the function of administrative adjudication. This is important; for if administrative fact-finding is interwoven with administrative adjudication, the confusion of functions may result in great injustice. The finding of facts may be considered as sufficient basis for a decision, whereas in many instances it is but a preliminary task. The decision should be made in view of not only the facts, but also the law, and the needs of social and individual justice.

3. By establishing administrative adjudicating authorities that are separated from the active administration, it is possible to prevent the same agencies from exercising the inconsistent and conflicting powers of prosecutor and judge, as happens from time to time under our present organization. It is very difficult for an authority "to impress upon its findings that stamp of impartiality and of disinterested justice"[4] which is needed in both good government and good administration, when it acts as prosecutor, judge, and perhaps interested party, all in the same case.

4. It is possible, when administrative adjudication is separated from administration, to eliminate much of the

---

[4] Gerard C. Henderson, *Federal Trade Commission*, p. 328.

difficulty which results from the fact that the government is one of the parties in the case, and often the aggressive party. By this separation, although in the last analysis the government is still a party, at least one and the same government agency is not a judge in its own cause. The administrative authority becomes the party against whom suit is brought. The adjudicating authority assumes the function of checking and controlling the action of the administrative authority. As far as possible, therefore, the circumstances resemble those of an ordinary suit, in which there are two opposing parties with an impartial judge deciding between them.

5. The separation of the function of administrative adjudication from that of active administration makes possible the exercise of a definite control over the legality of acts performed by the administration, by an authority that is established largely for this purpose. In respect to a very great number of administrative actions, the individual does not wish to have his rights adjudicated; he merely wishes to have the administration controlled in respect to the exercise of its power. He wishes it to remain within its jurisdiction; he wishes it to act according to the rules, procedures, and methods laid down for it. He is anxious that it shall not abuse its powers by acting to injure him for personal, political, religious, social, or any other reasons. He wishes it to do what it is required to do, and to refrain from doing that which it has no right to do.

The situation here is quite different from that where the individual is suing the government on a contract; or where, the law permitting, he is suing for damages wrongfully done to him or his property by the administration. When the function of administrative adjudication is combined with the function of active administration, control over the legality of administrative acts is not present in the first instance, but must be exercised in a second or third instance. This leads us naturally to another advantage.

6. Where administrative adjudication is separated from active administration, it is possible to break away from the control of the ordinary courts over administration and to substitute a system of control by administrative courts. In case administrative adjudication results from the administrative process, two objectionable features appear. First, the administrative process is not surrounded by the safeguards necessary for proper adjudication. Second, the act of the administration is not controlled by an impartial outside authority.

Many persons maintain that, in order to overcome these objections, after the decision of the administrative tribunal there should be an appeal to the courts. If, however, the administrative tribunal in the first instance is an authority which not only adjudicates but also controls the administrative authority, the initial process of control over administrative action has already taken place. There is no need to call upon the ordinary courts for assistance. It is an easy step to provide for appellate administrative tribunals, and thus complete the system of administrative adjudication.

7. Administrative tribunals of the type which we are discussing are necessary as a means of developing and harmonizing administrative law. No true system of administrative law can develop so long as it continues to grow up as the confused result of innumerable decisions of various administrative authorities established at different times to carry out different kinds of functions; using many kinds of procedure, rules of evidence, and methods of making decisions; having decisions enforced

in diverse ways; and being subjected to various types of control by administrative courts and judicial courts.

When, however, a system of administrative courts which adjudicate only administrative cases is established, under a superior administrative court, a well-rounded and unified system of administrative law will naturally develop. Since it will be differentiated from the ordinary law, it can be studied by scholars, and known and understood by the legal profession and by those working in the government departments. The Board of Tax Appeals and the Court of Customs and Patent Appeals, for example, acting as administrative adjudicating authorities, have done much to develop and systematize the tax, customs, and patent law.

III. ADVANTAGES COMMON TO BOTH TYPES OF ADMINISTRATIVE TRIBUNALS

A. Thorough knowledge of specialized subject matter by the court is a very great advantage of administrative adjudicating agencies of every kind. Where a high degree of expertness and administrative knowledge is necessary for a correct and fair decision, or where facts and figures must be gathered and correlated in order that the decision may correspond with present-day reality, some special kind of administrative tribunal is likely to be the best means of meeting the situation. Thus, patent cases, tax cases, and customs cases, to give only a few examples, involve the application of very technical law to extraordinarily technical facts. Those judging such cases must be steeped in the complexities of the subject matter.

B. An administrative tribunal is highly desirable where the decision should be made from the administrative as well as the legal point of view. The administrative point of view may and should be the result of the study of a vast amount of factual material; of living, as it were, with present-day problems; of considering and discussing problems in terms of social and economic realities; of habitual contact with many persons working on similar problems. The legal point of view, on the contrary, may be chiefly concerned with constitutions, with laws and former court decisions, to the exclusion of many practical considerations and relevant facts.

Who can doubt that the point of view of the members of the Interstate Commerce Commission, formed after working for years with problems of railway valuation, after settling thousands of cases in respect to rates, after making complete and exhaustive studies of the railway system of the country, places them in a better position to determine what factors should be taken into consideration in the valuation of a railway property, than are the members of any ordinary court? Certainly no practical administrator will feel any doubts as to the superior value of special knowledge combined with long experience, in the administrative adjudication of controversies involving both law and technical information.

C. Administrative tribunals are superior to the ordinary courts as regards the exercise of the sub-legislative function. It has been pointed out that a certain amount of sub-legislation or rule-making by all courts, tribunals, or adjudicatory authorities is inevitable, even though the legislature and the executive authorities have exercised their respective legislative and sub-legislative powers carefully and fully, and even though the administration has used its broad powers of discretion wisely and prudently. Since administrative adjudicatory authorities handle only administrative cases, they can secure a far better and more detailed knowledge of the subject matter involved in the different branches of administration than can the ordinary judicial courts, which must deal with the wide fields of criminal and civil law as well as with public law. Hence, their sub-legislative work is superior, from the administrative viewpoint, to that of the ordinary courts.

Since administrative tribunals are, or should be, composed partly of persons who have had wide administrative experience, the viewpoint of administrative needs and necessities will enter into such of their decisions as must supplement or fill in the gaps found to exist in legislative or sub-legislative enactments. The Board of Tax Appeals, for instance, can know and understand the complex tax laws and the rules and regulations of the Bureau of Internal Revenue better than can an ordinary court. Consequently, when it is necesary to interpret or supplement the tax laws and regulations in order to decide a case, this special tribunal is in a more advantageous position than an ordinary court.

D. Administrative adjudication is especially useful where many cases of a more or less technical or standard nature, or many cases involving much the same subject matter, must be decided rapidly; or where, because of the great number of cases, and the small amounts involved, speed and cheapness become important factors. Thus, it may be necessary to make some 15,000 to 20,000 decisions each year in immigration cases, and many thousands of decisions in tax cases, workmen's compensation cases, veterans' cases, and land cases. It is scarcely necessary to emphasize the immense advantage of having special tribunals make decisions in such fields. The ordinary courts, on the one hand, could not possibly handle so large a number of cases, even if they had the special knowledge which they lack; whereas the active administrator, on the other hand, is hardly an unprejudiced judge, and may be sadly lacking in legal knowledge. The special tribunal may be the golden mean.

E. An advantage possessed by administrative tribunals, which, if properly safeguarded, is also an advantage to the public, is the relative simplicity and flexibility of their methods, procedures, rules of evidence, and manner of making decisions. In many cases such tribunals are given power to establish their own procedure, to create their own rules of evidence, and to control to a very large extent the factors which will govern the making of their decisions. Even when they are not given complete power in such matters, they are generally left a much freer hand than the ordinary courts possess.

Moreover, the judicial courts themselves have been very liberal in leaving such authorities a free hand in these matters, instead of insisting on the application of ordinary judicial procedure and criteria. It is generally the practice of administrative boards and tribunals to conduct their hearings in a much freer manner than the judicial courts would employ. Thus, the hearings are generally expedited, rules of evidence are reduced to a minimum, cases are frequently presented without counsel or by public accountants, and the decisions are based not merely on the evidence presented in the hearing of the case, but also on facts gathered by the commission or administrative tribunal itself.[5]

F. Administrative tribunals can often enforce a policy, unhampered by antiquated rules of law and judicial precedents. They are not necessarily bound, as are the courts, by the doctrine of *stare decisis;* hence they may readily change their doctrines in case the old ones seem inapplicable.

[5] See Harold M. Stephens, *Administrative Tribunals and the Rules of Evidence,* Chap. VI.

IV. SUMMARY

The administrative tribunals connected with the federal government may be divided, from the functional viewpoint, into two main classes: those which adjudicate in connection with their administrative functions; and those which have no administrative or sub-legislative functions but which merely adjudicate—that is, settle cases and control administration. Although these classes have certain common advantages, such as the development of expertness, the possibility of presenting the administrative point of view rather than the merely legal, the ability to handle a great number of cases of a technical or standard nature, and the advantage of flexibility as to methods, procedures, rules of evidence, and methods of making decisions, there are several advantages that are peculiar to each type.

The advantages peculiar to the administrative tribunals which carry on administrative functions and also adjudicate are (according to those who favor such a type of tribunal): the ability to settle cases for the avowed purpose of furthering a particular social or economic policy; to handle cases in a more or less summary way in times of emergency; to develop economic policies, standards, and norms in new and untried social and economic situations; to develop new legal and judicial standards and norms and integrate them into public administration; and to interpret the new principles, standards and norms laid down by the legislature in concrete cases, thus keeping adjudication in harmony with public policy. It is often claimed, also, that the function of administrative regulation is so closely related to the function of administrative adjudication that it is impossible to separate them, and that they must consequently remain in the hands of the same authority. A similar argument, often advanced by those who favor the retention of agencies with mixed powers, is that ordinary administrative decision and quasi-judicial decision are so interwoven, particularly in the first instance, that it is inadvisable to attempt to separate them.

These arguments will not be answered at the moment; but the questions will be raised for later discussion: Could not the advantages claimed for the mixed authorities be obtained through authorities of the other type? Does not the mixture of functions involve serious disadvantages, which make it expedient to place administrative adjudication in the hands of the second type of administrative tribunal?

The advantages of authorities which merely adjudicate and control must be considered as regards both the handling of administrative cases by the ordinary courts, and the making of quasi-judicial decisions by authorities which also perform administrative functions.

Administrative tribunals which merely adjudicate, that is, decide cases and thereby control administrative action, are superior to the ordinary courts as authorities to decide administrative cases, for several different reasons. Administrative tribunals necessarily develop expert and detailed knowledge of particular fields of administration, and make their decisions from the administrative point of view as well as the legal. They can also handle a vast number of cases of a technical and standard nature; develop flexibility and simplicity as to methods, procedures, and rules of evidence; and break away from the doctrine of *stare decisis*.

Since many of their members are chosen from among administrators, these tribunals are able to perform the necessary task of sub-legislation as a part of adjudication better than could the ordinary courts in the highly specialized fields of public administration. Since they handle only public law controversies, such tribunals develop the viewpoint and the theory of public law, and are able to apply it to the cases that come before them, rather than confining themselves to the conceptions and the philosophy of private law. They begin to see cases in relationship to social and economic situations, rather than merely in relationship to fixed and more or less arbitary private rights.

They should develop a feeling for the protection of the objective legal order, quite as much as for the protection of individual rights; since their duty is to control administrative action as well as to protect the individual. Another advantage of administrative tribunals consists in the fact that they can handle types of cases which the ordinary courts refuse to handle, as they are not considered "cases and controversies" within the meaning of Article III of the Constitution.

The type of administrative adjudicatory authority which merely adjudicates administrative controversies and thus controls administrative action has several advantages over the type which exercises the two functions of administration and adjudication. In the work of the authority which merely adjudicates, various important and necessary distinctions can be used; especially between the function of administrative fact-finding and that of adjudication, and between the work of prosecutor and that of judge.

The difficulty of allowing the government, which appears as an interested party, to be the judge in its own case, can be practically eliminated by the establishment of the administrative judicial type of authority. Another marked advantage of this type of authority is that it makes possible an effective control over administration in the first instance. The separation of the function of administration from that of administrative adjudication also makes it easier to establish an administrative court system which can perform the valuable function of developing and harmonizing administrative law.

CHAPTER XI

FAULTS AND DISADVANTAGES OF EXISTING ADMINISTRATIVE ADJUDICATION

It is necessary to consider the reverse of the picture presented in the preceding chapter. Administrative adjudication has not only its advantages, but also its dangers, which must be recognized and so far as possible eradicated. Most of its dangers and difficulties, fortunately, lie not in the function itself, but in faulty organization of the agencies which perform it, or in unsatisfactory relationships between these agencies and other organs of government, and in improper methods. It is therefore quite reasonable to hope that patient effort may succeed in removing, or at least in minimizing, the dangers and disadvantages, and in developing the advantages.

An analysis of the administrative tribunals and other agencies of the federal government which perform quasi-judicial functions shows that, as these tribunals are now constituted, some of the difficulties, disadvantages, and faults connected with their organization and functioning are rather general in nature and apply to nearly all such authorities; whereas several are solely or largely connected with particular types of authorities. A few are associated with some particular organization.

I. GENERAL DISADVANTAGES

A. One of the most outstanding general difficulties connected with administrative adjudication in the federal government is the fact that there is no comprehensive administrative, legal, or political theory underlying this function. Such little theory as exists has been drawn largely from private law or from constitutional law. The administrative judicial authorities have grown up rather haphazardly as emergencies have seemed to demand. No general theory underlies their organization, their relationship to other authorities, the nature of their powers, the position of their members, their procedures, the nature and effects of their decisions, the extent to which they should be controlled, or even the methods to be used for controlling them.

Should administrative judicial authorities be organized as collegial bodies, or should individual administrators be endowed with quasi-judicial functions? Should the same persons be active administrative agencies as well as quasi-judicial authorities? Should any doctrine of separation of powers exist as to their activities? Should administrative judicial authorities be organized within government departments and agencies, or should they be organized independently? In the former case, should members of the active administration also serve as members of a collegial adjudicatory body within a given agency, or should the members of this body be free from other duties, and act simply in the capacity of administrative judicial authorities?

Should such authorities be under the administrative control of the heads of the agencies within which they function, or removed from this control? In case they are under the administrative control of a government department or agency, should certain means be established to make their decisions at least free from external control? Should the position of administrative judicial authorities be as independent as that of judges, or should their position be of a political nature? Should such authorities be chosen from the active administration, from among judges, from among laymen, or from a combination of such persons? Should the members of such authorities be selected by civil service examination, or appointed without reference to the civil service?

Should the procedure and rules of evidence used by quasi-judicial authorities be primarily of an administrative nature, or primarily of a judicial nature? What should be the nature of their decisions? Should they be binding upon the parties concerned? Should they be *res judicata*? Should such authorities pass finally and conclusively upon questions of fact, or should such questions be reviewable by the courts? Should such authorities have wide discretionary power, within which they operate uncontrolled by the courts?

By what methods should the decisions of such authorities be enforced? What types of control should be exercised over these decisions? What kinds of remedies may be used against the acts of such authorities? What should be the type of reviewing authority? Should it be an administrative authority, an administrative court, or a regular court or courts? What should the reviewing authority do in respect to the decisions made? Should it annul them, set them aside, make a *de novo* decision, suspend them, remand them?

To all of these questions no general theoretical answer has been found. The answer seems to depend at present partly upon the nature of each authority, partly upon the time when it was established, partly upon previous judicial decisions, and partly upon the particular circumstances, and the pressures that were exerted, when the bill creating the authority was passed. It is not to be supposed that an absolute uniformity under all conditions is possible or desirable. There is no reason, for example, why certain types of questions cannot be decided by individual administrators, and others by special administrative courts. On the other hand, there is no reason why the decisions of both types of authorities just mentioned should not be reviewed by one higher administrative court, which will serve to make administrative jurisprudence consistent. The failure to work out any general theory, as a framework within which a reasonably varied and flexible organization can operate, has led to an almost unbelievable complexity and confusion in respect to our administrative judicial system, if system it can be called.

B. The statutory and other documentary basis for administrative adjudication is extremely faulty. A careful examination of the laws governing the administrative judicial authorities in our federal government shows that most of them do not cover all the factors involved in the proper organization and functioning of such agencies. This is true especially in respect to procedures, rules of evidence, finality of decision, the type of decision that is given, the methods by which decisions are to be executed, and the extent to which decisions are to be controlled. Such criticism is applicable as regards nearly all the types of authorities that we have listed; though less so in respect to the independent administrative courts and the regulatory commissions than in respect to most other quasi-judicial agencies.

The failure to establish a proper legislative basis for such authorities leads to confusion in their functioning, uncertainty as to their procedure, and the bringing of many suits before the judicial courts, which painfully and gradually settle points that should have been established by statutory provisions. It means, also, that until the courts have done this—and for so long as new questions arise—litigants and their lawyers, as well as the government, must lack a reasonable understanding of their rights and the methods by which these may be secured.

In several recent instances administrative tribunals have been established, not by statute, but by executive order or departmental regulation. In a few instances, at least, the documentation is so scanty as to leave not only the public but the authority itself completely in the dark in respect to the various important factors governing its functioning. For example, a press release of August 5, 1933, establishing the National Labor Board, and the executive orders providing for its functioning,[1] failed to make clear the real nature of this authority, the extent of its powers, or the methods by which its duties are to be performed. Was it merely an advisory, conciliating, mediating authority, or did it also have quasi-judicial functions? The governing documents were incredibly vague in many respects, and absolutely silent as to the nature and legal effects of the Board's decisions. Another example of insufficient documentary basis for proper functioning is found in the Board of Labor Review in the Emergency Public Works Administration.

C. No supreme or final administrative court exists in the United States. One of the prime methods of unifying administrative jurisprudence, and of controlling authorities that hear appeals from administrative judicial decisions, is that of having a secondary appeal to a final tribunal. Much of the proper control over administrative adjudication depends upon what kind of authority hears final appeals, the conditions under which these appeals may be brought, the question whether they are of right or at the discretion of the appellate authority; the pleas which are allowed, and the juridical effects of each

[1] Executive Order No. 6511, Dec. 16, 1933; Executive Order No. 6580, Feb. 1, 1934; Executive Order No. 6612-A, Feb. 23, 1934.

plea; the problem whether questions of both fact and law will be heard; and such procedural problems as whether the supreme administrative tribunal remands certain cases to some other tribunal, or whether it makes all decisions; and whether, for any reason whatsoever, another appeal lies to some other type of court.

If the final authority is primarily an authority for the settlement of constitutional law controversies, its decisions will be controlled by this fact rather than by the principles of administration. If appeals are not a matter of right but a matter of discretion, the final appellate authority will almost inevitably lay down criteria as to when an appeal will lie, based on considerations of procedure which may not be significant from an administrative standpoint.

Such criteria may virtually eliminate from consideration cases that are important as regards administration, but are not important from the viewpoint of the court. For example, the criteria used by the Supreme Court of the United States as to when it will or will not take jurisdiction of a case by certiorari, are applicable as a method of testing out constitutionality, or of controlling the lower courts in order to make their decisions uniform; but are not designed in any way as criteria for controlling administrative action.

Whether the highest appellate tribunal is to hear questions of both fact and law, is important for several reasons. If the position be taken that the highest tribunal for deciding appeals from administrative judicial decisions is established largely to do justice in individual cases, such tribunal may well be given the power to hear questions of both fact and law. On the other hand, if it be held that its function is largely to unify administrative jurisprudence and to maintain a uniform interpretation of law, it will hear appeals on questions of law alone.

D. The wide scattering of jurisdiction is another serious disadvantage of administrative adjudication, as it is practiced in England and the United States. The power to make quasi-judicial decisions may be given to boards, commissions, and other authorities, variously organized, variously controlled, endowed with various powers and functions, rules, and procedures. In some instances, decisions by executive or administrative officers or boards or commissions are made only after "compliance with rigid formalities of notice and hearing; in other instances an informal procedure is observed; and in the vast majority of cases there is no notice or hearing whatsoever."[2] The result is a scattered and incoherent jurisprudence as to the conditions under which suits may be brought, the manner of bringing them, who may be parties to suits, what pleas may be advanced, the conditions under which various pleas will be received, the rules of procedure, the rules of evidence, the powers of the authority making the decision, the methods by which the decision is to be enforced, the administrative and judicial remedies available against the decision, and the appeals which will lie from administrative judicial decisions to higher courts. As a consequence of this confusion, there is an almost complete lack of knowledge, even on the part of lawyers, as to how to attack various kinds of administrative actions. In such a system, also, there is no rhyme or reason in administrative law.

E. The failure to give administrative judicial authorities power to execute their own orders, and the requirement that they must resort to the judicial courts for en-

---

[2] American Bar Association, advance program to be presented at the 50th annual meeting, p. 184.

forcement, may prevent really effective action by these authorities. Thus, in respect to the Federal Trade Commission, the law provides: "If . . . such corporation fails or neglects to obey such order of the Commission while the same is in effect, the Commission may apply to the Circuit Court of Appeals of the United States, within any circuit where the method of competition in question was used or where such . . . corporation resides or carries on business, for the enforcement of the order. . . ."[3]

Under the original Act to Regulate Commerce of 1887, "the Commission's orders, as such, did not become binding upon the parties affected thereby; the carriers were free to ignore them without penalty. Upon neglect or refusal of the carriers 'to obey any lawful order or requirement,' the burden was placed upon the Commission to secure its enforcement in the courts. Not only did such enforcement necessarily involve a review of the Commission's determination, but since the Commission's report, on such judicial hearing, was merely to be 'prima facie evidence of the matters therein stated,' there was no obstacle to the admission of new evidence and thus to a hearing *de novo*."[4] It would appear that if the President, under the National Industrial Recovery Act, establishes quasi-judicial authorities to decide upon controversies that will arise under the act, an appeal must be made to the district courts for the enforcement of the decisions.[5]

The almost inevitable result of such a practice is not only to weaken the administrative tribunal, but to place the control of economic and social policy in the hands of

[3] 38 Stat. L. 720.
[4] I. L. Sharfman, *The Interstate Commerce Commission*, Vol. II, p. 386.
[5] Title I, Sec. 3(c).

the judicial courts; since the real decision is the judicial decision and not that of the administrative tribunal.[6]

F. Although in many instances acts of Congress declare that findings of facts made by quasi-judicial authorities, when supported by testimony, are to be held to be conclusive, and although it is undoubtedly true that the findings of administrative officers or tribunals, on matters properly within the sphere of their jurisdiction, are binding upon the courts if supported by substantial evidence,[7] there is a decided tendency for the courts, when property interests are involved, to substitute their own findings of facts. There is a tendency to permit administrative fact-finding to be final and conclusive in respect to acts where the granting of a so-called privilege or favor is involved, as for instance in public land cases, immigration cases, the use of the mails, and so on; but to review carefully, and at times to replace by the findings of the judicial court, fact-findings of an administrative agent or commission in cases involving vested rights or property interests.[8]

It is manifest that if the courts can substitute their findings of fact for those of administrative bodies or tribunals, the usefulness of the latter is much impaired. If they are established to carry on a specific function

---

[6] "Federal Trade Commission—False and Misleading Advertising," *31 Mich. Law Review* 806-07.

[7] See Note, *27 Harvard Law Review* 943.

[8] In several cases involving state commissions the courts have held that due process of law requires independent judgment by the courts both as to law and to facts. *Ohio Valley Water Co.* v. *Ben Avon Borough,* 253 U.S. 287; *Bluefield Waterworks and Improvement Co.* v. *Public Service Commission,* 262 U.S. 679. In the O'Fallon decision (279 U.S. 461) the Supreme Court virtually substituted its judgment for that of the Interstate Commerce Commission as to the weight that should be given to different factors to be taken into consideration in determining value. See F. Rodell, "Regulation of Securities by the Federal Trade Commission," *43 Yale Law Journal* 279.

which they are particularly qualified to perform, and yet are not allowed to perform that function, the whole purpose of their existence—to save the courts from work which the latter have neither the time nor the training to perform, and to entrust such work to trained specialists—loses its meaning.

G. One of the very grave difficulties of administrative adjudication, as at present organized in the United States, is the fact that it is too intimately bound in with a system of constitutional law and a system of common law which tend to impede its proper growth and operation.

The doctrine of separation of powers has not developed in the United States, as it has in France, in such a way that the ordinary courts may not interfere with administrative acts and therefore administrative courts had to be established; but rather in such a way that the ordinary courts, unless especial provision is made otherwise, control the administration. This control is exercised under the hypotheses and criteria of the common law rather than under the principles and criteria of public law. On the other hand, our courts have not so interpreted the doctrine of separation of powers as to make it impossible to confer legislative power upon quasi-judicial bodies. Nor have they objected that there is lack of due process of law, when the same authority virtually legislates at the same time that it is rendering a decision. The due process of law clauses of the federal Constitution have not been used to bring about a well-planned, well thought out, and well-controlled system of administrative adjudication, but have been used primarily as a method of controlling substantive law.

H. It has always been considered one of the prime virtues of a court that its rules of evidence protect individuals in the presentation of cases; that through rather rigid rules of evidence the truth of the matter can be found. With the development of administrative justice there has been a tendency to regard the old juridical rules as no longer applicable—to hold "That their obstructive and irrational technicalities have made the system nauseous and futile in its native habitat; and that to transplant it to new fields would be an error amounting to a folly."[9]

In so far as the legislatures have laid down rules for administrative judicial authorities, they have generally adopted the viewpoint just mentioned. The same thing is true of commissions, acting as rule makers.

The courts themselves, reviewing the refusal of commissions to apply the rules of evidence, have, with exceptions, sustained the commissions. . . . Commissioners, it is believed, can weigh the evidence, whatever its nature and however informally presented, better than courts. Their expertness enables them to know the worth of hearsay, the probable authenticity of unidentified signatures, the comparative value of evidence taken in other causes—without being confused or misled by, or obliged to sift out, the collateral issues involved; to know the value of the conclusions of lay witnesses without presentation of the data upon which they are based; to understand how far to give credence to matters not within the witnesses's knowledge; to judge of the correctness of secondary evidence as to the contents of books; to know whether or not to consider testimony not shown to be connected with the case; to judge the value of letters and telegrams and copies of contracts; to sense the accuracy of commercial ratings, investors' manuals, recitals in deeds, interviews, newspaper clippings; to know the worth of common knowledge; to understand the statistical reports of carriers, and the scientific reports of engineers without examination of the makers; to give proper weight to the affidavits of prostitutes and the *ex parte* statements of their "customers;" to evaluate impeachment without explanation; to tell how far to

[9] J. H. Wigmore, *Evidence*, 2d ed., 1923, Sec. 4(b), p. 28.

treat contradictions as affirmative evidence; to value the testimony of wife against husband; to know to what extent proof of the commission of one act is proof of the commission of a similar one; to take evidence for what it is worth without discrimination at the outset as to competency; and to act dependably and fairly upon their own information undisclosed to parties or to reviewing courts—all better than judges and juries.[10]

Is there not the possibility of danger that we have gone too far in doing away with rules of evidence? If so, can we go back to any appreciable extent? Do new methods make many rules of evidence obsolete? In respect to an increasing number of administrative determinations, there is no statutory provision for review.[11] For example, provisions for any adequate review are almost entirely lacking in the laws establishing the NRA and the AAA. Sometimes no judicial remedy of any sort is available, although in numerous instances an administrative review is allowed. In many cases review is possible through suits for extraordinary remedies, such as the injunction, the mandamus, or habeas corpus proceedings; but these remedies are so narrow in their application, so difficult to apply, so discretionary in nature, present so many difficulties of application, and are tied in with so great a number of special criteria, as to give little effective relief against quasi-judicial decisions.

Even where statutory provisions exist for judicial review, there is no uniform method for securing such review. There is great variety in respect to the reviewing courts and also in respect to the scope of the review. The latter depends to a large extent upon the decisions

[10] Harold M. Stephens, *Administrative Tribunals and the Rules of Evidence*, p. 92.
[11] See Securities Act of 1933, 48 Stat. L. 80, Sec. 9(a), providing that findings of fact of the Federal Trade Commission, if supported by evidence, are conclusive.

of the Supreme Court, which seems to have no logical or coherent basis for determining either the scope or the conditions under which review is permitted or required. The decisions of the Supreme Court are so inconsistent on these points as to make it impossible for one to determine with any certainty whether or not review will be permitted in a given case.

Such a situation presents serious difficulties. Since administrative adjudication has already become a method of settling great numbers of disputes, its operations should be properly controlled. Some sort of appeal or review should be a matter of right, rather than lying at the discretion of the court; the method of bringing the case before the reviewing authority should be simple, easy, and inexpensive; in so far as possible all cases to be reviewed should go before one tribunal with general jurisdiction. At the present time there is a bewildering variety of appellate authorities. In several instances there is a choice of appellate authorities, as in tax appeals, patent appeals, and so on. All this makes for confusion.

The criteria as to when the reviewing authority will or will not take jurisdiction should be simple and well known; [12] and the pleas that the injured individual brings should have a direct relationship to what he wishes to have accomplished by review. For example, if he believes that the authority has abused its power, this should be the direct plea. The review should be upon this point, and the decision should pass definitely upon the question whether the act complained of does constitute an abuse

[12] Nothing will so far remove the difficulties in respect to criteria as to provide that a review is a matter of right, rather than discretion. So long as one must depend upon extraordinary and equitable remedies as a method of bringing his case before the court for adjudication, all of the vague criteria historically connected with these remedies may be so applied as to cause uncertainty.

of power. The appellate authority should be able in its decision to provide the kind of relief from the administrative act which the nature of the case requires; and the petitioner should know the nature of the relief that will be afforded if his plea is granted.

I. The procedures by which administrative judicial authorities act, unless they are established and safeguarded with the greatest care, may not be based upon sound principles of either administration or justice. Since administrative tribunals have been established largely in reaction against the inadequacies, delays, costs, and technicalities of judicial processes, it is entirely possible that they have gone too far in the direction of speed and simplicity, even to the point of doing away with basic safeguards. There is all the more danger that this may happen when, as is very generally the case, these authorities establish their own rules of procedure. But mere rules of procedure may not be sufficient to guarantee a proper process of law. Both France and Germany have come to realize that equal or greater importance attaches to the nature and quality of the authority that administers them.

II. SPECIAL DISADVANTAGES OF REGULATORY AUTHORITIES ACTING AS ADMINISTRATIVE TRIBUNALS

A. One of the greatest sources of danger in administrative adjudication, particularly in the United States and England, is the fact that the judicial decisions of administrative authorities may often contain material which is really the equivalent of supplementary legislation, or in some instances of basic legislation. This places the administrative authority charged with making a decision in the position of legislating at the same time that it is adjudicating. When the legal basis for administrative action is inadequate, and when it is insufficiently supplemented by regulations, such a confusion of functions is quite likely to occur.

Although, as we have remarked above, administrative tribunals can do much toward developing public law and assisting in the growth and development of progressive social policies, this good work should be done in the course of interpreting existing laws and rules and regulations. New substantive law should not be made in the course of rendering a decision, which is properly an adjudication of the rights of parties under law that already exists. In case the same authority is given both sub-legislative and quasi-judicial powers, these powers should always be exercised separately, so that parties bringing suit may know beforehand all the substance of the law, including rules and regulations.

It must be admitted that when the work properly belonging to the legislature and the regulatory authorities has not been done in a full and sufficient manner, courts of every type feel themselves compelled to "find" and "interpret" some principle or concept which can be applied to a question at issue; and that substantive law—however vigorously the courts deny the fact—is often created in the effort to make such application. This situation can be avoided in large part if the agencies whose task it is to make statutes, rules, and regulations will do their duty.

B. The combination of the quasi-legislative and the quasi-judicial functions in the same administrative authority prevents an adequate control over either of these functions.

It is a very common practice, in both England and the United States, to bestow upon the same administrative authority the power of promulgating rules and regulations on a certain matter, and the power of making decisions in respect to the enforcement of the law applicable to the said matter, including its own rules and regulations. This means that one authority is given both the function of administrative legislation and that of administrative adjudication. One of the most deplorable results of such a combination of functions is the impossibility of establishing a proper control over either. This is due to the fact that the nature, aims, purposes, and methods of the two functions are radically different.

When administrative bodies are exercising sub-legislative power, manifestly their regulations should harmonize not only with the letter of the law, but also with the general policies of the government. In order that such policies may be carried out efficiently and without unnecessary friction, the authority which is assisting in the process of sub-legislation should share the viewpoint of the government. This means that the higher administrative officers must be removable at the will of the government in power, so that the persons who are actually responsible for sub-legislation may be depended upon to act in harmony with governmental policies. In other words, control over sub-legislation should be a political control, since sub-legislation is so frequently concerned with matters of policy, and with questions of adapting means to the ends sought by the government.

When administrative bodies are making judicial or quasi-judicial decisions, on the other hand, they should be in as independent a position as possible. In order that this may be so, they should be free from the immediate control of both the legislature and the executive. In case members of such bodies are removed when a new legislative or executive policy comes into effect, there can be no such thing as independence in their decisions. Their decisions will almost of necessity be based upon considerations of policy, rather than upon the duty of comparing an administrative act in an objective way with the law, rules, and regulations applicable when the act was performed. In view of these considerations, it is evident that appropriate control over the authorities called upon to make administrative judicial decisions cannot be political in nature, but must be judicial. The questions that arise in respect to such decisions are such as would arise in respect to the decisions of any judicial body.

When the same authority which makes rules and regulations also makes administrative judicial decisions, a serious dilemma is inevitable. In case political control, whether legislative or executive, is attempted, the authority loses its value as a judicial agency. In case no political control is attempted, its line of policy may be entirely out of harmony with the general lines of legislative and executive policy. Obviously, therefore, the sub-legislative function should be lodged with either the chief executive operating through the Cabinet, or with members of the Cabinet; in other words, with the chief political authorities. To give the sub-legislative function to either independent administrative authorities such as boards and commissions, or permanent authorities engaged in active administration, not only results in confusion but makes any system of control impossible.

Policy must be controlled by political methods. Administration must be controlled by administrative methods. Judicial determinations must be controlled by judicial methods. Where all three functions, the determination of policy, the conduct of active administration, and the making of decisions judicial in nature, are in the hands of the same authority, any control attempted by one method must interfere with the proper conduct of either administration, the determination of policy, or the making of decisions. If it be held that certain governmental functions, such as rate regulations,[13] are of a mixed or composite nature, then care should be taken to place these functions under a controlling authority capable of exercising a composite control. To date, however, no really satisfactory authority of this sort has been developed.

The problem of attempting to control the substance of administrative rate regulations by the courts on the ground of constitutionality shows the confusion that may result from inappropriate types of control. If one takes the position that since these regulations are sub-legislative or legislative in nature, they may be declared unconstitutional, one is immediately confronted by the fact that they are also judicial in nature. But substantive judicial action may never be subjected to the test of constitutionality. "A court may lay down a judgment affecting life, liberty, or property which, however arbitrary the aggrieved party may consider it, affords no grounds for the federal question of deprivation of property without due process of law."[14]

C. There is a danger that the authority which is exercising the function of administrative adjudication may be at the same time a fact-finding authority, a prosecuting authority, and a judging authority. It may thus be placed in the position of issuing rules and regulations, making examinations as to whether these rules and regulations are being obeyed, haling before it the individual or corporation that disobeys the rules and regulations,

[13] A. A. Berle, Jr., "The Expansion of American Administrative Law," *30 Harvard Law Review* 430 ff.

[14] Laurence Curtis, 2d, "Judicial Review of Commission Rate Regulation," *34 Harvard Law Review,* 867 ff.

and hearing and deciding the case. This is contrary to any proper process of law, which demands not only that rules and regulations shall be laid down in advance of the making of a decision in a particular case, but also that the authority which is to decide the case shall not be the same authority that gathers evidence and facts upon which prosecution is based.

D. Administrative adjudication is sometimes too uncertain and too inconsistent to be fair to all interests affected. Even though the pragmatic trial and error approach in respect to economic and social policies may have advantages from the viewpoint of the government and its regulatory program, it may be absolutely unjust to the individuals and organizations controlled. We have already noted the fact that, unless these can know definitely their rights under the law before they act, they are left in doubt as to the legality and the propriety of their actions until the time when they are prosecuted and the court has rendered a decision. This situation arises quite often, when regulatory agencies render quasi-judicial decisions.

Under our present system, the trial and error method of working out social policy in part through quasi-judicial decisions made by administrative boards and commissions, can lead only to one of two results: either a high degree of uncontrolled arbitrary discretion; or a judicial control over discretion, which makes the courts, rather than the administrative authorities, the dictators of social policy. The latter, in turn, leads to complete confusion. The courts lose their character as judicial bodies, and become bodies essentially legislative in nature. Instead of testing out administrative action to see whether it conforms to laws, rules, and regulations made in advance by responsible authorities—whether an administrative agency has abused its powers, has failed to observe the proper forms, or has violated some rule of law—the courts are compelled to determine whether the action is socially expedient. A confusion of powers in the hands of the administrative authority thus leads inevitably to a confusion of powers in the hands of the courts, completing the vicious circle of uncertainty as to the legality of contemplated action.

E. The very fact that the authority which makes administrative judicial decisions may also be developing new social concepts, new social values, new ideas of social and economic morality, that it is acting for the benefit of society as a whole, and is endeavoring to do justice to the social aspects of the problems with which it must deal, may make it blind to individual rights and individual welfare, if these run counter to the general policy that is to be carried out. A certain fanaticism or ruthlessness may develop regarding the significance of social protection as against individual rights. Thus, it might be easy for an agency whose duty it was to work for the eradication of plant or animal diseases to come to the conclusion that society must be protected at all costs, and that the rights of any individual are negligible in comparison with social needs.

Where such an authority is exercising wide regulatory power, and also the power of enforcing its own regulations, there is grave danger that the individual will be injured, particularly if he does not have at his disposal means to contest the validity of both the general regulation and the special decision which fixes his own rights. The tendency in human nature to find arguments for justifying action already taken or about to be taken, which is particularly powerful when any one detailed action is a part of a general action, must not be permitted to operate ruthlessly for the ease of the administration in enforcing its policies, regardless of the plight of the individual. Administrative adjudication should be sufficiently separated from active administration to safeguard individual rights against this tendency.

F. A different type of thinking from that necessary in making a proper judicial decision is involved in administrative work. The essence of administrative work is action. Things must be accomplished. Work must be cleared. Decisions must be made rapidly. To give adequate time to the case of one person may prevent the giving of any time whatsoever to others. As a rule, the functions of active administration mean that no thorough examination of documents or evidence is possible. Who has not had the experience of seeing a busy administrator give five minutes of time to a proposal that for any proper investigation would take half a day; of seeing documents of great importance thumbed over with such rapidity as to make any intelligent examination of them impossible; of having a vital interview cut short by the arrival of an important personage; of being unable to present witnesses who would help to sustain the viewpoint or the claim advanced; of having a "snap judgment" take the place of a real decision? Who has not felt that the very position of the administrator standing on his own ground, with complete power to determine manner of presentation, time to be given to presentation, subject matter that may be presented, and so on, places the ordinary individual at a disadvantage in seeking an adequate examination of his cause?

These disadvantages are partly or entirely eliminated if provision is made for a careful administrative judicial hearing. Procedure can easily be provided whereby the individual may have plenty of time to prepare and present his case, may be represented by legal advisers, may bring evidence and have witnesses summoned. Under such procedure, the administrator ceases to stand in a position of arbitrariness, since he, like the individual, must be bound by the rules and regulations governing the hearing, and must appear as a party rather than as a dictator. Perhaps the greatest advantage of improved administrative judicial procedure is the fact that it necessitates the provision of a judge or bench trained to judicial thinking—one who is not a party to the dispute; whose function is not that of pushing through a vast amount of administrative business, but is simply that of judging.[15]

G. The authority that hears and determines the case may not operate as a unified body or authority that has charge of the case from inception to finish, as a court does. It may consist of a department which is subdivided into offices, bureaus, agencies, and so on, several of which may have a hand in the same case. Thus, in the expulsion process in immigration cases, there is a hearing before a local immigration officer, a review of the record by the Board of Review in the department at Washington, and finally a decision by the Assistant to the Secretary of Labor.[16]

In actual practice the decision of important cases may be left, for all intents and purposes, to an unknown subordinate in a department, a person without adequate training, experience, or background. The duty may be discharged in a rather perfunctory manner by an officer who has no such rigorous training, professional experience, or high character as should be demanded of judges.

[15] On the importance of the judicial attitude, see W. A. Robson, *Justice and Administrative Law*, Chap. V.

[16] W. C. Van Vleck, *The Administrative Control of Aliens*, p. 83.

In many instances, the administrative authority, unlike a court, is compelled to rely almost entirely upon the findings of persons belonging to its own staff. It may, therefore, be practically impossible for the individual affected by a decision to know who decided his case, or to have the decision reviewed by a better qualified person. This situation is particularly dangerous when the administrative authority making the decision is a vast government organization where manifestly no one or even several persons can be held responsible for all the decisions that are being made.

H. There is always the danger, when an administrative authority is exercising quasi-judicial powers, that neither the parties interested nor the public may know the real reasons for the exercise of its powers in particular ways. The authority may not let it be known what principles it is following or why they are being followed. The result is that the public not only lives in uncertainty as to how it is expected to act, but also develops the suspicion that the authority is acting in a purely arbitrary way; or even that it may be consciously favoring its friends and injuring its enemies.

Several administrative authorities do not "motivate" their decisions, or publish them in any systematic way. The failure to give and publish reasons for decisions leads to several undesirable results. It makes impossible the evolution of general principles to serve as a guide in the making of future decisions. Without the publication of reasons, those interested in the subject matter of such decisions will not be able to build up for themselves a systematic foundation for further thinking. More important still, from the standpoint of the individual, there is no proper basis given for appeal. In order that there may be such a basis, the decision should lay down the principles on which it was based, and should give rather detailed reasons for its conclusions. Among the more important administrative judicial authorities in the United States, several are not open to criticism on this point; but others, such as the Federal Trade Commission, have been greatly lacking in this respect.[17]

I. Administrative judicial authorities may not investigate facts in a satisfactory way. This may be due to the numerous cases which they must handle with a small staff; to lack of time; or to the fact that the procedure followed does not give an opportunity for the proper presentation of materials, that rules of evidence are rudimentary or altogether missing, or that the personnel of the authority is not such as to guarantee impartiality in fact-finding. That this fault is not inherent in administrative adjudication, and can be overcome quite easily by ordinary and reasonable precautions, may be seen from an examination of the work done by such authorities as the Interstate Commerce Commission or the Board of Tax Appeals.

J. There is danger that the administrative authority will exercise such a wide power of interpretation or construction of law as virtually to legislate; and yet that it will not be checked in the exercise of this power, since there is no supreme administrative court, and the judicial courts may hold that the executive or administrative authority has a large degree of judgment and discretion in the interpretation of statutes. This lack of control by the courts is particularly noticeable when the provisions of statutes involve what the courts are pleased to call "questions of privilege" rather than questions of rights. In respect to the entrance of immigrants into the United States, in respect to land office determinations, in respect

[17] T. C. Blaisdell, *The Federal Trade Commission*, p. 38.

to postal determinations, and so on, the courts take the attitude that since no rights are involved, but only privileges, it is not necessary for them to interfere with officers exercising these functions, even when such officers are interpreting statutes, unless there is a gross and manifest misinterpretation. Thus, the Supreme Court said, in the case of *Riverside Oil Company* v. *Hitchcock*:[18]

Neither an injunction nor mandamus will lie against an officer of the Land Department to control him in discharging an official duty which requires the exercise of his judgment and discretion. . . . The head of an executive department in the administration of the various concerns of his office is continually required to exercise judgment and discretion. He must exercise his judgment in expounding the laws under which he is from time to time required to act. . . . Whether he decided right or wrong is not the question. Having jurisdiction to decide at all, he necessarily had jurisdiction, and it was his duty, to decide as he thought the law was, and the courts have no power whatever under those circumstances to review his determination by mandamus or injunction.

In respect to the relationships of officers to the government, involving questions of appointment, promotion, dismissal, and the respective rights and duties of superior and inferior officers, the courts take the attitude that they will not interfere to enforce regulations by procedure in equity,[19] since vested interests are not involved, and since the rules and regulations of the civil service do not have the force of law. It has been held that the civil service rules promulgated by the executive, in so far as they deal with the executive's right of removal, are only expressions of the will of the President, and are regulations imposed by him upon his own action, or on

[18] 190 U.S. 316.
[19] *White* v. *Berry*, 171 U.S. 366; *Carr* v. *Gordon*, 82 Fed. 373.

the heads of departments appointed by him.[20] Civil service regulations, it has been held, do not have the force of law, and the courts cannot enforce them or review cases involving the removal of employees.[21]

K. Closely associated with the difficulty just mentioned, is the fact that the judicial courts have established complex and questionable criteria as to when they will or will not take control over administrative action. Some of these criteria are obviously based on no well thought out principles, but are largely historical in origin, having been developed for the purpose of being applied to a relatively simple administrative system. The criteria may vary according to the nature of the authority that is functioning, according to different types of administrative acts which it is sought to control, according to the sovereign or non-sovereign field of government activity, and so on and so on, often without logic or consistency. Some of the criteria may be applicable even under modern conditions, whereas others are useless or worse than useless.

It should be clear that the validity and the effectiveness of control over both administrative and quasi-judicial action depend to a large extent upon the criteria established, as to when judicial control is or is not to be used. If these criteria are uncertain, based on unrealities, difficult to apply, and numerous, it is entirely possible for the courts to refuse control where they should exercise it, or to apply control where for the good and proper functioning of the administration it should not be applied. If, on the other hand, the criteria are few and simple, are based upon the realities of the present-

---

[20] *Morgan* v. *Nunn*, 84 Fed. 551.
[21] *United States* v. *Lapp*, 244 Fed. 377; *Carr* v. *Gordon*, 82 Fed. 373; *Eberlein* v. *United States*, 53 Ct. Cl. 466.

day situation, are easy to apply, and are fairly certain in their application, a control can be established that gives the administration the greatest possible freedom in carrying out its functions, yet at the same time forces it to act within the bounds of legality and justice.

L. The remedies and controls which are applied to the decisions of administrative judicial authorities in our federal government are both unsystematic and inadequate. In some instances—especially when heads of departments make quasi-judicial decisions as to matters within their jurisdiction—no real controls or remedies are available. In other instances, higher administrative authorities may review findings and decisions; in still others, the function of review is performed by the judicial courts. There is no order or system whatever in the work of the higher administrative authorities. No attempt is made to have the acts of these authorities unified or controlled by a superior administrative tribunal. When the judicial courts intervene, they are handicapped by their own interpretation of the doctrine of separation of powers, by the criteria which they have established as limitations upon the use of remedial writs, and by statutory provisions (even though they can often evade such provisions). Hence they neither control the jurisprudence or even the procedure of the administrative tribunals in a systematic way, nor assure the protection of individual rights. A satisfactory and practical system of controls and remedies is greatly needed as a fundamental improvement in the administrative jurisprudence of the United States.

III. FAULTS IN RESPECT TO TRIBUNALS WHICH ARE ONLY ADJUDICATING AND CONTROLLING AUTHORITIES

We have seen in the chapter on types of administrative adjudicating authorities that there are two types of authorities which have no administrative function, but only settle disputes and control administration; namely, the independent administrative courts, and the special administrative courts within government departments or agencies. These tribunals, as organized at present, are involved in several difficulties.

A. The first is that their constitutional position is confused and anomalous. The Court of Claims, the United States Customs Court, and the Court of Customs and Patent Appeals should not be called "legislative courts,"[22] but should be expressly recognized as administrative courts. The Board of Tax Appeals, instead of being considered as "an executive or administrative board, upon the decision of which the parties are given an opportunity to base a petition for review to the courts after the administrative inquiry of the Board has been decided,"[23] should be designated as a regular administrative court. To refuse to view these independent administrative courts in their true light, simply lends more confusion to an already confused situation.

B. In patent appeals and tax appeals cases, the practice of giving other courts concurrent jurisdiction with the special authorities established to settle them has nothing to commend it. There seems to be no good reason why the administrative courts should not have exclusive jurisdiction in such matters.

C. The final review of the decisions of all the independent administrative courts is by writ of certiorari to the Supreme Court. As we point out in another connection, this type of review is not a suitable and appropri-

[22] As far as the authors are aware, no decision has expressly called the United States Customs Court a "legislative" court. From the criteria laid down in several cases, however, it would have to fall within this category.
[23] *Old Colony Trust Co.* v. *Commissioner*, 279 U.S. 716.

ate method of controlling the action of administrative tribunals.

D. In respect to the special administrative courts within the government departments, the criticism may well be made that these courts do not have as independent a position as they should, and that their decisions may therefore be influenced by administrative pressure. There would seem no good reason, in case such authorities as the Board of Appeals in the Veterans' Administration are to continue, why they should not be placed in an independent position.

IV. FAULTS IN RESPECT TO ADVISORY ADJUDICATORY AUTHORITIES

The existence of numerous boards of appeal and review in various government departments and agencies seems to be due to the feeling that some sort of judicial procedure and judgment in regard to certain types of action is necessary, even though the legislature has not established proper administrative tribunals to settle such cases. Although not organized for assuming the functions of administrative courts, either in respect to the qualifications of their members, their terms of office, their manner of appointment, or any other factor making for their independence, these agencies prepare opinions which to all intents and purposes are the real decisions in the respective cases. While it is true that some high administrative authorities assume responsibility, this does not as a rule prevent the decisions from being really those of the advisory authority.

The seeming advantage of having such an authority is that it saves litigation, and yet gives an appearance of a more nearly judicial process than if the case were decided by the administrative authority without some sort of quasi-judicial advice. The writers believe that if a proper system of administrative courts were established, the advisory authorities could be either eliminated, or confined to their proper task of collecting and examining materials and expressing their views on the questions at hand.

V. FAULTS IN RESPECT TO THE COURTS OF THE DISTRICT OF COLUMBIA ACTING AS ADMINIS-TRATIVE COURTS

In several instances, particularly in the past, Congress has placed upon the courts of the District of Columbia the function of settling cases of an administrative judicial nature. This practice seems to have been due to the fact that no other appropriate administrative tribunal was available for handling cases involving questions of an administrative or legislative nature. The establishment of a unified system of federal administrative courts would make it unnecessary to give such powers to the courts of the District of Columbia, which, when all is said and done, are placed in a somewhat anomalous position by them. The transference of patent and trade-mark cases from the Court of Appeals of the District of Columbia to the Court of Customs and Patent Appeals, a real administrative court, was a step in the direction of freeing the District courts from administrative cases.

VI. DIFFICULTIES IN RESPECT TO SEVERAL MEDIATING, CONCILIATING, AND ARBITRATING AUTHORITIES

The chief difficulties in respect to mediating, conciliating, and arbitrating authorities have been in connection with the National Recovery Administration. These difficulties have been due to two principal factors: first, the failure to develop a clear line of policy as to the part that the government was to take in the regulation and control of business; and second, the failure to realize that in the process of the making and enforcement of codes there should be a separation of the three functions of government. Consequently, although not only administration, but also administrative legislation and administrative adjudication, were necessary parts of the work of the NRA, the whole set-up was largely administrative in nature. Within the past few months, experience has shown the need of organizational changes. There has been a tendency to lay some stress upon the judicial functions, in particular. Thus, the recently created Labor Relations Board is interpreting its functions as largely quasi-judicial or judicial in nature. Undoubtedly, a real administrative court for labor disputes is needed, as well as other special administrative courts.

VII. DIFFICULTIES IN RESPECT TO PERSONNEL AUTHORITIES

The chief difficulty of administrative adjudication in respect to personnel authorities seems to consist in the fact that this function is not properly recognized, and consequently no adequate provision has been made for handling it. In case a real administrative court system is established, care should be taken to provide that all acts affecting the rights and status of civil service employees should be reviewable by administrative tribunals.

VIII. SUMMARY

The faults and difficulties in respect to administrative adjudication as now organized are both general or common, and particular to special types of authorities.

The chief general faults and difficulties are: that no theory or philosophy underlies our whole system of administrative adjudication; that the documentation upon which administrative judicial authorities are established and act is unsystematic and sketchy in nature; that there is an unnecessarily large number of such authorities, so differently organized, with such different methods, procedures, and superior controls, as to cause bewilderment and confusion; that there is no final court or authority to develop, systematize, and harmonize federal administrative law; that the constitutional law system and the administrative law system are not well integrated; that in many instances proceedings before such bodies are inadequate and rules of evidence are often too meager; that the present-day system of remedies is cumbersome, complex, expensive, and inadequate; that the system of control over administrative adjudication is extremely inadequate and faulty.

The disadvantages that are found chiefly in administrative tribunals which exercise one or more other functions of government in connection with the functions of adjudication are: that their decisions may often contain material sub-legislative in nature; that their judgments are often too uncertain and inconsistent to be fair to all interests concerned; that, because of being too strongly impregnated with the view of general public interest, they may lose sight of individual rights; that they are thinking too exclusively in terms of administration rather than in terms of adjudication; that the various factors necessary for the determination of a case may be handled by several different hidden authorities; that there will not be the same careful examination of facts as there is before a court; that the administrative authority may be at one and the same time a fact-finding, a prosecuting, and an adjudicating authority, and a party in the case; that the combination of two or three functions of government in the same authority prevents adequate control over any function; that the judicial courts have developed inconsistent, complex, and questionable criteria as to when they will take control over the acts of such authorities; that the establishment of independent boards and commissions to carry out the three functions of government results in scattering administrative responsibility, preventing the proper integration of administrative activity, and making impossible a proper system of administrative control.

There are relatively few difficulties peculiar to the administrative tribunals which do not legislate or administer, but only adjudicate. The chief of these are: that the constitutional position of some of them as "legislative courts" is rather anomalous; that in several instances other authorities have concurrent jurisdiction over the same subject matter; that there is no superior administrative court to control them and unify their jurisprudence, but that they are generally controlled through the writ of certiorari, which is used primarily for the purpose of unifying the jurisprudence of the ordinary courts rather than for that of controlling administrative courts and their decisions.

The existence of advisory adjudicatory authorities is, as a rule, due to failure to establish a proper system of administrative adjudication. Although these authorities are not organized for assuming the functions of administrative courts, their decisions are often final in effect.

Among the great variety of decisions made by personnel authorities, some are really of a judicial nature, but no adequate organization has been established to handle these cases. Personnel cases today are handled almost entirely on a purely administrative basis, and the judicial aspects of such cases are largely neglected.

In respect to agencies connected with or placed under the NRA which, during the first year, have acted almost exclusively as administrative, mediating, and conciliatory authorities, there was at first a dire confusion of functions, with little recognition of the fact that there is a separate and distinct function of administrative adjudication. This fact now seems to be recognized, and it is probable that the NRA will soon provide for better organized administrative adjudicatory agencies.

Fortunately most of the faults, dangers, and difficulties of administrative adjudication do not lie in the function itself, but rather in factors which can be changed. It is evidently possible to organize the function in such a way as to insure to a large degree its manifest advantages and to do away with its more serious disadvantages. The following chapter will sketch an outline of a system which appears more simple and workable than that which exists today.

CHAPTER XII

CONCLUSIONS AND RECOMMENDATIONS

Administrative legislation and administrative adjudication have become, as the preceding pages have shown, two of the most important methods used by the modern state in making the many delicate adjustments required by the complex functions of the present day. The government of the United States has increased its use of these methods during recent years, until at present there is hardly an individual citizen who is not affected by them in many different ways. In concluding our brief study, we shall summarize the principal facts which it has established and the conclusions which it has reached, and shall make certain recommendations for systematizing and strengthening both administrative legislation and administrative adjudication.

I. ADMINISTRATIVE LEGISLATION

There are nearly 600 agencies in the federal government today which are exercising the function of making rules and regulations affecting the lives and property of individuals, and operating to all intents as a part of the law of the land. These authorities include not only Congress, the President, and the heads of the government departments, but also bureaus and divisions within departments, special independent administrative bodies, courts and administrative courts, proprietary corporations, and nearly 500 economic code authorities.

The rules and regulations issued by these administrative agencies are sometimes made prior to the taking of administrative action; but it may happen, and very often does happen, that they are made in the course of such action, and are thus its product, rather than its guide. The result of this situation, added to the number and diversity of the administrative regulatory authorities, is such a mass of rules and regulations issued in such various forms that it is virtually impossible for the individuals affected thereby to know what their rights and duties are. To answer this question in any particular instance it is necessary to know the Constitution of the United States and the statutory law; the rules, regulations, and executive orders issued by the President; the rules, regulations and orders issued by various administrative authorities; and, finally, a multitude of court decisions. A large proportion of the essential information regarding certain questions can be found only through long and painstaking research in Washington or a few other important centers of legal information.

No serious attempt has been made by Congress to require the issuance or publication of rules and regulations governing each field of administrative activity before such activity is undertaken. There is no system of imposing upon some appropriate authority the duty of seeing that legislative action is properly implemented; nor, as a rule, does Congress give to the authority which is to carry out a given function the power of making rules and regulations completing and filling in the laws passed by Congress regarding this function. No authority exists to see that rules and regulations are prepared in definite and prescribed form, that they fulfil the purposes and respect the provisions of the law under which they were passed, and that they are not in conflict with other rules and regulations issued by the same or other authorities. No policy exists as to the conditions and methods under which rules and regulations shall be issued. There is no attempt to separate the rules and regulations into different classes according to their legal significance, or to publish them so that they are readily available.

To do away with the present confused situation, it is suggested:

A. That Congress itself shall establish a broad and general basis upon which such legislation may rest.

B. That rules and regulations be classified in accordance with their effect. The four different classes will be: Those whose purpose is merely to carry out the provisions of the law, without affecting the rights, duties, or property of individuals; those which do affect the rights and property of individuals; those which merely organize or reorganize government departments, services or agencies; and those which apply only to the internal operations of a department, an agency, or a service.

C. That all rules and regulations which further implement the law, which organize or reorganize a government department, agency, or service, and which affect the rights and property of individuals, shall be issued by the President, even though they originate in a government department, agency, or service. The President should have the help of a special bureau or board for this function.

D. That all rules and regulations, other than unimportant departmental regulations, shall be prepared for publication and published by a bureau of the President or similar agency, which shall take care that each document appears to have a legal basis; that it appears to be in harmony with the law and with other rules and regulations; that it is in correct form; and that it is properly classified as to its legal significance. Where executive orders, rules, or regulations are in the nature of measures implementing the law, both the law and these orders, rules, or regulations should be published together in such a way as to give a complete statement of the legal situation.

E. That there shall be established an Official Gazette which will publish, as soon as possible after they are issued, all rules and regulations, as well as laws and other matters of general interest. Any rules and regulations which particularly affect certain interests, such as agriculture, shipping, mining, banking, and so on, shall be collected and published in trade journals as well as in the Official Gazette; and all rules and regulations on special subjects shall be published from time to time in collected form. There should be proper classification of rules and regulations and they should be adequately indexed.

F. That both the Official Gazette and the published collections of special rules and regulations shall be kept at numerous official depositories where they can be available to all interested persons.

II. ADMINISTRATIVE ADJUDICATION

In the federal government of the United States, as the preceding pages have shown, a large number of agents and authorities exercise the function of administrative adjudication. These agents and authorities are of several different general types, and of many individual forms. There is no definite relationship among them, binding them into any sort of unity. No general political, legal, or administrative theory underlies either their organization or their functioning. No system of administrative tribunals exists, within which every separate one finds a logical place; no system of administrative judicial procedure exists, by which all the tribunals might be controlled. Without system, without theory, the individual authorities of administrative adjudication have been created to meet particular situations or conditions.

An almost indescribable confusion is found when any attempt is made to study these agencies in respect to form and organization, relationships with other authorities, functions, methods of procedure, rules of evidence, finality of decision, agencies and methods by which their decisions and orders may be enforced, remedies and types of relief that may be used in respect to their actions, and agencies and methods by which they are controlled. So great is this complexity, that not merely an ordinary citizen seeking to protect his rights, but even a competent lawyer practicing in federal administrative and constitutional law, can scarcely find his way through the jungle. Many agents of the government itself— sometimes the actual authorities who must make quasi-judicial decisions—are uncertain and bewildered concerning these matters.

Either of two methods might be adopted in the hope of alleviating the present situation. A series of individual amendments, improvements, and reforms could be introduced. A scientific system of administrative adjudication might be established after a thorough study of the experience of the United States and various other countries.

A. Gradual reform. To those who believe that government institutions, particularly such as deal with problems largely legal in nature, must be the result of slow and painful evolution, this method may seem preferable. "Trial and error," operating by means of the gradual introduction of individual changes, seems to such persons a desirable means of developing more satisfactory organizations, relationships, and working methods.

There is no possible refutation of such a position, as regards proposals that are wholly new and untried, and conditions which allow indefinite time for the gradual change and development of existing institutions. Several factors indicate, however, that the evolutionary process has already gone so far in the matter now under discussion that it is unnecessary to depend upon it any longer.

In the first place, there is no lack of American or foreign experience to guide and direct the organization of a system of administrative tribunals. In Germany, and especially in France, such systems exist, and have existed for a long time. Their nature, their operations, and the effects of their work can be studied by anyone who is desirous of information in this field. But even more important is the fact that both England and the United States have had sufficient experience with administrative tribunals to make the problem of organizing these into a system far more a question of orderly arrangement and improvement affecting tried and tested institutions, than a venture into new and unknown territory.

To await further evolutionary process means a long continuance of the present confusion. This is a disadvantage both to the individuals who feel themselves injured by some act of administration, and to the government itself. Uncertainty that justice will be done—and on the part of certain individuals and corporations, the hope that in the general confusion, they may acquire some advantage as against the government or against society at large—must tend toward weakening popular respect for government. Incidentally, the present lack of system is very costly to the taxpayers.

Finally, there is no guarantee that unguided evolution will ever result in a satisfactory system. Such a system demands carefully thought out answers to the problems raised in the course of this study, and to many more; it demands deliberate and intelligent integration of the various administrative tribunals, and delicate adjustment of the relationships among men. Piecemeal reform can never bring about such an integration. Since the federal government has already developed a far-reaching and intricate network of administrative adjudication, it is fair to conclude that the point in evolution has now been reached when trial and error on a large scale can be replaced by systematic reorganization based largely on American experience.

B. Establishment of a scientific system. The second method named above, that is, the establishment of a scientific system of administrative tribunals and administrative adjudication, is evidently both possible and advisable. It is not the purpose of this study to outline such a system in detail. A few suggestions will be given, however, drawn largely from the practical experience of the most successful of our federal tribunals and from the experience of other countries with the same matter.

At this point the question must inevitably arise, as to how far it is possible to bring all federal administrative tribunals into a unified system. Because of the various types of the functions performed by these tribunals, is it possible to organize them as parts of a single whole? The answer to this very fundamental question depends on certain conditions. Probably the most important of these is the extent to which it is possible to separate the legislative, the administrative, and the quasi-judicial functions in practice. As we have seen, the frequent combination of these three functions in the hands of the same agency has made necessary the organization of different types of authorities from those which merely administer or merely adjudicate; and has, furthermore, complicated the problems of remedies, of enforcement, and of types of control.

The problem does not seem difficult in respect to customs administration, tax administration, the settling of claims against the government, Veterans' administration, civil service administration, land disputes, immigration cases, postal cases, tariff cases, and all other such cases where there are definite statutory or regulatory provisions to be enforced by administrative authorities, and where there is, or should be, the possibility of a review of the decisions rendered by these authorities.

Is there any inherent reason why regulatory functions in general, such as the regulation of banks, stock exchanges, public utilities, business and economic enterprises, may not be controlled and regulated in the same way?

It is true that many persons consider the legislature incapable of laying down any detailed norms which the administration can enforce as it enforces the detailed provisions of tax laws or customs laws. The legislature itself, while hardly sharing this opinion, has displayed a disinclination to establish definite fundamental norms for the guidance of the regulatory agencies. Because of the separation of powers as interpreted in the United States, and because of the impossibility of holding the executive branch of the government responsible to the legislature, the latter has generally preferred not to bestow a wide rule-making power in these fields upon the President or members of the Cabinet. It has chosen, instead, to bestow directly upon regulatory bodies a type of authority which is really a combination of administrative and quasi-legislative powers. The attitude of the legislature was doubtless influenced by the common belief that no reasonable general norms can be established for regulatory activities, but that each case must be decided on the basis of the particular factors involved. It was necessary, accordingly, to add the function of making quasi-judicial decisions to the functions of sub-legislation and administration. All three functions were given to the same authority; and control over regulatory authorities in the exercise of their powers was vested in the ordinary courts. Another reason advanced for vesting the three functions in the same authority was that each regulatory body would be enabled, because of its extensive powers, to perform any social experimentation necessary for establishing a proper system of control.

A distinct break in this system was made with the establishment of the NRA codes. Here there is an implied theory that the factors which make for unfair competition can be analyzed to a very great extent, and that general norms can be established and organized into codes. There is also a distinct break in the doctrine of separation of powers; for in the last analysis the President of the United States is the code authority. This is undeniable, since no matter how important may be the action of the code authorities in formulating codes, it is the action of the President alone that gives them the force of law.

The new departure means, in the opinion of the authors, that there is no reason why the legislature, in view of past experience, and with the assistance of experts, cannot lay down far more detailed norms than it has done in the past as regards the regulatory functions. There seems to be no reason, moreover, why the President, assisted by the experience of the commissions and his own expert staffs and department staffs, cannot add to these norms sufficiently to make a clear, comprehensive, and workable basic law for the regulation of business and industry, which can be administered with a rather high degree of certainty, as are the tax laws. This would virtually eliminate the great degree of legislative activity now exercised by various administrative authorities, boards, and commissions, and would either make of them merely authorities for the administration of the law, or would leave the way open for their transformation into administrative courts.

With such separation of the legislative and the administrative function, there would no longer be any reason why the regulatory authorities should exercise any extensive administrative judicial functions. They would be enforcing definite laws, and could be controlled in so doing, as other administrative authorities are controlled. Such a system would tend to eliminate many difficulties which now exist in respect to the organization, the functioning, and the control of regulatory authorities. In the opinion of the authors, it would also facilitate the establishment of a completely unified system of administrative courts.

If this proposition appears inadvisable, the regulatory bodies might at least be organized with some degree of uniformity, as a special type of administrative tribunal possessed of functions that differentiate it in various ways (as procedure, enforcement, and rules of evidence, for example) from the other types which are organized under one governing code. Even so, the regulatory bodies could and should be made a part of the general system of administrative adjudication, since remedies and controls in respect to their decisions should be vested in the same higher administrative tribunals which hear cases coming up from other administrative judicial authorities.

1. Changes in organization. If the plan of administra-

tive legislation and administrative adjudication which we have suggested were adopted, significant changes would be needed in many of the independent regulatory boards and commissions. Their functions of rule-making would be taken over largely by the President and the bureau which would be organized to assist him in the preparation and publication of rules and regulations. Controversies between the regulatory authorities and industries in respect to the acts of the latter would be handled by administrative tribunals. This would leave the regulatory authorities in the position of administrative bodies. As such they might well be subordinate to the large government departments.

Certain exceptions to this arrangement might possibly be made, as in the case of the Interstate Commerce Commission, which, because of its long experience, the fact that there is a separation of the administrative and the adjudicatory powers within its own organization, and its demonstrated success in developing a rather satisfactory set of relationships, might function quite well as now organized. On the other hand, it might be relieved of all duties save those of a lower administrative court. There is the possibility of adding other quasi-judicial functions to it, such as cases arising from decisions made by other administrative authorities regulating other means of interstate transportation and communication. Under such circumstances its present administrative functions could be transferred to an agency within the Department of Commerce. Under either arrangement its decisions should be subject to appeal to the highest administrative tribunal.

These suggestions are merely examples of the way in which relatively slight changes could bring even the independent regulatory commissions into an integral relationship with a systematically worked out organization of administrative tribunals.

2. Clarification of functions. Another basic condition in the establishment of an administrative court system is the working out of a distinction between the purposes, functions, and methods of administration and those of control. We have seen earlier in this study, that so far as mere activities are concerned, the administration in making an administrative decision often performs almost exactly the same functions as are performed by an administrative tribunal or by a court. It finds facts; it interprets the law; it applies the law to the facts; it makes a decision. One great difference between the activities of the administrative and the judicial authorities is the purpose which each has in performing such actions. The administration wishes to execute the law, to carry out a function, to accomplish a definite result under the law. The administrative tribunal or the court, on the other hand, is (or should be) interested in no other function than that of controlling the administration for the purpose of keeping it within the bounds of legality and of seeing that it does not injure the rights of citizens. The court, whether judicial or administrative, should neither determine upon policy nor administer, under the guise of passing upon cases arising from administrative acts. It should merely hold the administration to legal action and thereby protect individuals.

3. The function of control. The only condition under which the administrative tribunals or the courts can exercise the controlling function in absolute purity is the existence of an adequate legal basis for administrative action and hence for judicial control. When the legislative and executive authorities have laid down a complete, clear, positive foundation of laws and regulations, the

administration can know its duty and the tribunals can compel it to do its duty. When this legal basis has not been established, and the administrative authority is enforcing such vague norms as "unfair methods of competition" or "undesirable alien," the administrator perforce becomes a legislator, and the court or the administrative tribunal to whom decisions and acts of the administration are appealed must either refuse to exercise control over these, or must itself do legislative work in either endorsing or superseding that done previously by the administrator. The tribunals thus review not merely quasi-judicial decisions, but review or even make legislative decisions fixing public policy.

Here we are confronted by the question, what is the purpose of control over administrative action, and how far is it necessary? In a broad way the purpose of control is to keep administrative action within the bounds of legality. In a more detailed way, the purpose of control is to compel the administration to respect its contractual obligations; to force it to perform those actions which it is legally required to perform; to see that it does not exceed its jurisdiction; to see that it follows the rules, procedures, and regulations that have been established by the legislature or by superior authority; to see that it does not abuse its power for political, religious, or personal reasons; to see that its actions do not violate rights already established by law; and to make it responsible, to whatever extent the law permits, for injuries and wrongs which have been caused by its operations.

On the negative side, control should not be exercised in order that the court may do those things which the legislature has determined shall be done by itself, the executive authority, or the administrative authority; such as the laying down of norms, standards, methods, and procedures, the finding of facts, or the exercise of requisite discretion.

4. Methods of control. By what methods shall the necessary control be exercised? We have spoken of control by quasi-judicial or judicial courts, but other authorities exercise control in various fields. In both England and the federal government of the United States, direct suit for damages caused by or attributable to the functioning of the administration is not allowed, except in regard to matters as to which the legislature has given special permission to bring suit, such as contracts, expropriation, or injuries falling under the employers' liability laws. In other matters the legislature itself may act as the controlling agency, by voting special grants as compensation for particular injuries. The uncertainty and obvious injustice of such a situation must be ended. The authors hold very strongly that all injuries of the type under discussion should be redressed through direct suits in administrative courts, brought as of right by the persons affected. Such a system, properly worked out in detail, would both "establish justice" and control the administration.

Earlier in this study we made a brief examination of the principal remedies through which an individual injured by administrative or administrative judicial action may seek redress: a suit as to the constitutionality of an action under the due process of law clause of the Constitution; the mandamus; the injunction; the writ of habeas corpus; the writ of prohibition; appeals; certified questions, and the writ of certiorari. By one or the other of these means, the courts may take jurisdiction to control various types of action. We have found, however, that these remedies are effective neither in protecting individual rights in respect to administrative or administrative judicial action, nor in properly controlling the administration. The due process of law clause is not always applicable; the discretionary nature of many of the writs and the limitations upon their use prevent them from meeting the needs of either private rights or administrative efficiency.

Since Congress has complete power in respect to remedies, we suggest that it shall abolish by statute all the remedies just mentioned against administrative and administrative judicial action, and substitute therefor a simple appeal as of right, instead of a discretionary writ. It cannot, of course, abolish the right to bring suit on constitutional questions; but it can establish administrative and administrative judicial authorities and procedures which will give due process, and hence minimize the number of such suits.

The law should state definitely what pleas the individual or the government might make against administrative or administrative judicial action. These pleas should correspond precisely to the type of control which should be exercised over administration, and to the type of redress which the individual might desire. In substance, the following pleas are needed:

a) That the government has injured the individual or interfered with his property rights or other rights in such a way that compensation should be made.

b) That an administrative or administrative judicial agency has exceeded its jurisdiction.

c) That such an agency has abused its powers.

d) That the agency has violated its contractural obligations.

e) That it has violated the forms, procedures, or

methods which law or superior regulations prescribe.

f) That the authority has violated established legal rights.

g) That the authority refuses to take action required of it by law.

5. The results of control. What results does the individual hope and seek by means of such control as has just been described? If he has the right to seek for control over the administrative adjudicatory agency by means of definite pleas, what action does he wish to have taken by the controlling authority? Or, from another viewpoint, what action should the controlling authority take?

In respect to injuries for which the individual seeks compensation, there will generally be a request for monetary payment; occasionally a request for restoration of confiscated goods, and so on. In respect to contracts made with administrative agencies, the individual wishes to have his rights enforced just as they would be in respect to any other contracts. Where legal rights are concerned the individual merely wishes to have them enforced against the administration. He wishes a judgment rendered which enforces these rights, whatever they may be.

In a surprisingly large number of administrative actions, the individual is merely anxious to have the action of the administrative or administrative judicial authority annulled. This is particularly likely when the authority has exceeded its jurisdiction, has abused its powers, or has not followed the forms, procedures, or methods that it is required to follow. Here what is required is as a rule a simple annulment of the act, and at times a remanding of the case to the administrative authority for proper action.

What effects of a general nature may be anticipated in respect to control? By the method of establishing a definite right to a review based upon specific pleas, not only could the elaborate set of remedies now in use be done away with, but with them would automatically go those numerous criteria as to when the courts will or will not take jurisdiction—criteria which have done so much to confuse and confound federal administrative law and to prevent the individual from securing his rights. On the other hand, this change would largely prevent the use of that vague remedy, if remedy it can be called, the due process of law clause, which is now invoked as a means of securing every sort of exemption from adequate administrative action.

6. Special recommendations as to control. (a) There should be a statutory right of appeal from the decisions of every administrative tribunal of first instance to a higher administrative tribunal. Because of the very great number of administrative judicial decisions that are continually being made, however, the right of appeal should be exercised only in respect to a mere fraction of such decisions. This means that the lower tribunals must be manned by persons of such ability, experience, and independence, working under such careful rules of procedure and of evidence, that their decisions would relatively seldom be subjected to appeal.

b) The necessary remedies and controls could be enforced by means of two main types of suits: (1) Those in which the injured person seeks to have his claims adjudicated and to have a binding decision thereon made by a tribunal; and (2) those in which he merely wishes to have an administrative or administrative judicial act annulled, suspended, set aside, or amended in whole or in part.

The first type of suit evidently demands procedures and rules of evidence which will guarantee an adequate trial of the case. The parties should be represented by attorneys, and a careful record should be kept of the proceedings, as a basis for appeal.

In the second type, the cost of bringing the suit should be negligible, and the procedure should be as simple as possible. The administrative authority, before acting, should notify the individual of its intentions, by means of what the French call an executory decision. This notice should specify the laws and regulations under which the authority is acting, the reasons for taking action, and the time within which the individual may seek protection from the tribunals before final action will be taken. Such preliminary notice, which closely resembles forms already in use in connection with tax administration and certain other federal functions, would generally furnish a sufficient documentary basis for the purpose of review. All administrative judicial decisions should be in writing and should contain an explanation of the legal points involved and a statement of the relevant facts. The reasons why the administrative judicial authority has reached the decision should be stated clearly. A record of the hearing, and the decision in proper form, should be a basis for action by the higher administrative court.

A system of administrative judicial control along these lines should bring about not only a larger measure of justice to the individual, and a more efficient control over administrative and administrative judicial authorities, but also a great simplification of enforcement methods. Much of the present confusion in enforcement methods is a result of the attempt to enforce orders, the legal basis of which is complex and uncertain. If the orders and decisions of the administrative and administrative judicial

agencies are issued merely to enforce existing laws, orders, and regulations governing the subject matter, and
if the controlling authority is merely keeping the administration within the bounds of legality, then, as a rule,
the decision of the controlling authority (whether regular court or administrative court) becomes the law which
the administrative authority is to follow in the case
before it.

Thus, if the Customs Court or the Court of Customs
and Patent Appeals says that an article on which the
customs authorities levied a duty as a toy, is, in fact,
under the intent of the statute, a decoration or a con-
tainer, this decision, unless overruled by a higher court,
is law by which the action of the administration is bound.
When the controlling authority remands a case to the
administrative authority for action along indicated lines,
the directions of the court bind the administration.

No special problems of enforcement are likely to arise
under these conditions, since the decisions of the controlling authorities are enforced administratively. In
cases where they cannot be so enforced, the decisions of
the administrative reviewing authority should be executed by its own agents, as the decisions of judicial courts
are executed. There should be no call upon the ordinary
courts to enforce the decisions of administrative tribunals.
We have seen that in nearly every instance the decisions
of the now existing special administrative courts are executed by mere administrative action on the part of the
authority concerned.

7. The controlling authorities. Our next question of
fundamental importance is, what shall be the nature of
the authorities which exercise control over administrative
action in both first and later instances? Shall these au-

thorities be only judicial courts? Shall they be only administrative courts? Shall there be a mixed system, such as exists today in respect to several functions, where in the first, the second, or less frequently, even the third instance, cases are passed upon by administrative courts (as, for example, in tax, customs, and patent cases) with the possibility of some sort of final review by the ordinary judicial courts? In the opinion of the present writers, it should be an established principle that all cases involving the control of administrative or administrative judicial action must be heard by administrative tribunals. Only for cases in which a constitutional question is involved should there be an departure from this principle; but, as we remark elsewhere, the number of these cases could be reduced to a minimum if the administrative court system were properly organized, regulated, and controlled. Several reasons may be advanced for requiring that all administrative cases shall come before the administrative courts.

a) The first reason undoubtedly is the fact that there are such a multitude of cases of an administrative nature. For example, in the Veterans' Administration there are from 10,000 to 15,000 appeal cases alone within a year. From the organization of the Board of Tax Appeals in July 1924, until February 1, 1933, there have been 69,635 appeals filed with this Board, or an average of nearly 8,000 a year.[1] The Board of Appeals and Review of the Civil Service Commission received during the fiscal year ending June 30, 1932, a total of 10,820 appeals. Of these "appeals from the ratings and other actions taken by the Commission were made in 1,255

---

[1] J. Emmett Sebree, "The United States Board of Tax Appeals," 7 *Temple Law Quarterly* 9.

instances."[2] In the fiscal year ending June 30, 1932, there were presented for consideration before the deputy commissioners of the Employees' Compensation Commission 30,807 cases involving compensation orders under the Longshoremen's and Harbor Workers' Compensation Act.[3] It is obviously impossible for our regular courts, already overburdened with work, to handle these great numbers of administrative cases.

b) The second reason why such cases should be handled by administrative courts is the technical nature of many judicial controversies. Thus, veterans' cases involve not only the application of law, but the determination of complex medical facts. It is for this reason that a medical man is on each regional review board. Medical men as well as lawyers are on the Board of Appeals. The Board of Tax Appeals, the Board of Appeals in the Patent Office, and the Court of Customs and Patent Appeals are dealing with extremely technical subjects. It is impossible for an ordinary court, deciding cases in civil, criminal, and public law, to become an expert in all these fields and in highly specialized fields of administration as well.

c) In the third place, although there are an extremely great number of administrative cases, in many instances they do not involve important questions of law. As we have already pointed out, frequently all that is wished by the individual is the annulment of an action, on the ground that the authority which took the action has exceeded its jurisdiction, has abused its discretion, or has violated forms, rules, and procedures by which it is sup-

---

[2] *Annual Report of Civil Service Commission* for fiscal year ended June 30, 1932.

[3] See *Sixteenth Annual Report of the Employees' Compensation Commission*, p. 40.

posed to act. The individual wishes the easiest, most expeditious, and least costly method of having the act annulled, and does not desire, or need, elaborate and costly procedure, or the comparatively slow and formal action of a regular judicial court.

d) It is important that there shall be a break from the old court methods, procedures, rules of evidence, remedies, criteria, and so on, in favor of simplicity and speed. This can best be brought about by the establishment of a unified administrative court system which has its own principles governing such matters.

e) Another manifest advantage of administrative courts is the fact that they can take cases which do not fall strictly within the category of "cases and controversies" as provided for in the Constitution and defined by the courts, for the reason that the action attacked is held to be legislative or administrative in nature.[4] Superior administrative courts can review cases which are not final judgments according to the Supreme Court.

f) The administrative courts can be organized so that they include persons who are experts in administration as well as those who are trained in law. It is highly important to the control over administration that those familiar with the methods, viewpoints, and feelings of administrators should assist in the process of control; for any real and effective control over administration must partake to a certain extent of superior administrative control as well as control over strict legality.

g) The same reasons which demand that original suits shall come before administrative courts demand likewise that appeals shall lie to higher administrative courts. If such higher administrative courts are divided into sec-

---

[4] *Keller* v. *Potomac Co.*, 261 U.S. 428; Ex parte *Bakelite Corporation*, 279 U.S. 438; *Williams* v. *United States*, 289 U.S. 553, 577, 578, 579.

tions, each section can become expert in respect to certain types of cases.

A supreme administrative court, better than any other type of agency, could act as an authority to unify and develop the present chaotic and incomplete administrative law of the federal government. Its work could be largely freed from those entanglements of constitutional law which have so complicated and confused our administrative jurisprudence while the ordinary courts have controlled it.

8. The administrative tribunals. What type of administrative tribunals shall be established? How shall these tribunals be organized? Before trying to answer the foregoing questions, let us glance at the existing tribunals. We have seen that within the federal government there are at least nine different general types of authorities carrying on administrative adjudication, as well as three types of related agencies, which by slight changes in set-up or in function might well be classified as administrative tribunals. It is true that several of these types of authorities are primarily exercising other functions, and are only incidentally administrative tribunals. Nevertheless, we are forced to admit that there is a good deal of variety in federal administrative courts.

Can there not be a great simplification of these different types of authorities? Is it necessary that we retain, in any system, some administrative tribunals which carry on special administrative functions, some which carry on regulatory functions, some whose functions are largely investigatory, some which are really judicial courts but which serve incidentally as administrative courts, some which in theory are advisory bodies but in practice are adjudicating agencies, some which are licensing authorities, some which are primarily conciliatory and mediating authorities, and some which are executive and administrative authorities?

If our distinctions between administration and administrative adjudication, and our analysis of the differences that should exist between the function of administration and the function of control, are correct, there is no necessity for these numerous types of administrative judicial agencies. The administrative authority should have a wide power of making decisions which are recognized as being fundamentally administrative in nature even though such decisions involve the interpretation of law, the finding of facts, and the application of the law to the facts. Only when objection is made to such decisions should administrative adjudication take place.

a) It is entirely possible to establish administrative courts solely and exclusively for the purpose of controlling administrative action by deciding the controversies arising therefrom. Since the function of these tribunals is that of control, they should be organized outside of the active administration, and not, as is the case with some administrative tribunals already discussed, inside some department or agency.

The number of such administrative tribunals, and the particular functions which they are to perform, would depend almost entirely upon the practical consideration whether a sufficient number of cases may be expected to arise in connection with a given function to require the establishment of a special lower tribunal for such cases. From this viewpoint, several kinds of special tribunals, already in existence, would be needed under any system; especially tribunals for customs cases, tax cases, patent cases, veterans' cases, civil service cases, longshoremen's and harbor workers' cases, and perhaps other types of cases which arise in very large numbers.

b) It might be advisable, also, to establish a special lower tribunal for cases arising in connection with the regulatory functions of the government, such as the regulation of interstate commerce, the regulation of securities and stock exchanges, the regulation of banks, stockyards, and so on. It may be that, if the NRA is given more powerful and direct administrative functions, the number of quasi-judicial controversies resulting from its actions will be sufficient to warrant the establishment of a special lower tribunal to handle such cases.

c) In addition to these special lower tribunals, there should be a general lower administrative court to hear in first instance the miscellaneous cases that arise from the functioning of all government services for which no special administrative tribunal is provided.

9. Certain factors should be safeguarded in all instances. (a) Thus, the various administrative courts, if they are to perform their function of control fairly, impartially, and efficiently, should be composed of persons of great ability who are placed in as independent a position as possible. These persons should have a long or permanent tenure of office, should not be removable except for cause, and should have adequate salaries. It would be highly desirable if a certain number of the administrative judges were selected from among persons in the higher administrative service. All these tribunals should be collegial bodies, although one judge might act under special conditions.

b) The procedure and the rules of evidence in such tribunals should be simple, but they should be sufficiently definite to guarantee a fair and impartial trial. An intelligent effort should be made to work out rules of evidence that would be applicable to all such tribunals. The better these tribunals are made as to personnel, procedures, and rules of evidence, the fewer will be the cases that will come up for review.

c) Is it necessary or desirable to have appeals from all decisions of each and every one of these tribunals, or should their decisions in certain classes of cases be final? We have precedent for such finality in respect to the decisions of several existing authorities, such as the Board of Appeals in the Veterans' Administration, and the Board of Labor Review in the emergency Public Works Administration. It is the opinion of the authors, nevertheless, that in all types of cases there should be a possibility of appeal to a higher administrative court. Such right of appeal would do much to unify and develop administrative adjudication. The argument against such an appeal, that the sums involved may be small, or that no large interests are affected, does not seem valid; for small sums may be more important to the poor than large sums are to the wealthy. An individual's claim to a fair examination, a fair rating for promotion, a fair compensation for injury, or a restoration of invaded rights, may be of great significance to him; and justice demands that he be protected in these matters.

d) Whether or not the administrative tribunals should hear both questions of fact and questions of law would seem to depend upon the nature of the investigation made by the administrative authority, and especially upon the possession or non-possession, by such authority, of a competent staff to make investigations. If the facts are properly established, the administrative tribunals should pass only upon questions of law.

e) Should there be more than one review from the decisions of the lower administrative tribunal, such as we now find in respect to the decisions of several authorities? For instance, a controversy may be taken from the

Chief Examiners in the Patent Office to the Board of Appeals in the Patent Office, thence to the Court of Customs and Patent Appeals, and ultimately to the Supreme Court by way of certiorari. In case the lower and superior administrative courts are properly organized and manned, there would seem to be no reason for more than two appeals, always excepting constitutional questions.

f) The problem of administrative areas for such tribunals is not one of great difficulty. Where the original administrative action is that of a local authority, as in customs administration and tax administration, the court may be organized into divisions which go on circuit and hold hearings locally. As in the case of the Veterans' Administration, local boards of review may be established; or, as in the case of controversies under the Longshoremen's and Harbor Workers' Act, deputy commissioners located in several districts may serve as administrative tribunals of first instance. Another example of the present settlement of cases locally is the matter of land claims; in controversies concerning public lands, the first decision is made by the local register of the Land Office.

Some services have no local administration. Thus, the decisions regarding patents, copyrights, and trade marks are all made at Washington. The same is true in respect to most of the great regulatory functions. Undoubtedly, some sort of decentralized system of adjudication will be needed for the regulation of business under the NRA if such regulation is to continue permanently.

For services which have nothing but central administration, obviously no district administrative tribunals are necessary. In most instances where there is a large amount of local administration, the problem of areas can be solved either by having the administrative tribunal of first instance organized into divisions, the members of which go on circuit for the hearing of cases, or by having several first instance tribunals located in different places in the United States. The number of cases would seem to be an important factor in the choice between these two possible arrangements. No doubt the work of several of these administrative tribunals could be greatly improved by providing them, like the present Board of Tax Appeals, with an assisting staff.

g) In all cases, the decisions of these lower administrative tribunals should be published. They should contain in each instance sufficient information to constitute the basis for an appeal. Such tribunals should decide finally, except for the possibility of appeal; and their decisions should control the action of the administrative authorities. In some instances undoubtedly the tribunals should order a remanding of the case to the administrative authority for further action along lines indicated by the order.

10. The appellate administrative courts. The problem of the organization of the appellate authority must now be considered. As has been said before, appeals should lie to an administrative court rather than to the ordinary courts. This superior administrative court should probably be organized into several divisions, some of which would hear only particular types of cases. The number and the special functions of the divisions would have to be determined according to the number and the nature of the cases.

a) Such an administrative tribunal should be composed of persons of great ability and training. At least half of its membership should be recruited from the higher branches of the administrative service. It might prove a great stimulus to the lower administrative tribunals if a part of its membership were selected from among the members of the lower administrative courts. All administrative courts should be provided with assisting staffs, the members of which should be especially well qualified and should rank as persons in the higher administrative service, with eligibility to appointment as administrative judges after a certain number of years of experience. The procedure and the rules of evidence for such a tribunal should be very carefully formulated.

b) The superior administrative court should have power either to settle a case finally and conclusively; to remand a case to the lower administrative tribunal for a rehearing; or to refer the controversy back to the administrative agency which made the original administrative decision, for such further action as might be indicated by the court. No appeal would lie from the decisions of this tribunal to the ordinary courts; except an appeal to the Supreme Court in regard to questions of constitutionality.

III. SUMMARY

The chief features of the suggested system of administrative legislation and administrative adjudication may be summarized as follows:

A. The legislature should fix the main outlines of organization, and lay down the most important norms, standards, and methods for carrying on the various functions of government.

B. The President, assisted by a special board and by the executive authorities, should be given wide regulatory and rule-making powers, so supplementing and implementing legislative action as to furnish a complete and satisfactory basis for proper administration and adequate control over administration. This would do away to a very large extent with the need for sub-legislation by other administrative and regulatory agencies.

C. The administrative and regulatory agencies should receive broad powers of discretion, as well as authority to find facts and to make detailed rules for the administration of their own functions. They should have no general sub-legislative or quasi-judicial powers.

D. Control over the actions of the administrative and regulatory agencies should be exercised by administrative courts acting in first and in second instance. There should be no control over administrative action by the ordinary courts, except in respect to questions of constitutionality.

E. Control by the administrative courts should be exercised only to keep administrative action within the bounds of legality definitely established by statute and superior rules and regulations. It should consist only in correcting illegal acts or compelling the performance of required acts. Private parties would thus be made secure in their legal rights, in so far as such rights might be affected adversely by administrative action. The administrative courts should not control public policy or the discretion vested in administrative bodies by the legislature. Yet their power should be fully adequate to its purpose, and they should be able to annul even the sublegislative acts of the highest executive authorities if these acts pass beyond the boundaries set by statute, or otherwise lack a legal basis.

F. The various ordinary and extraordinary legal remedies now in use should be done away with, so far as application to administrative action is concerned; and there should be substituted a definite right of appeal to a lower administrative tribunal. The bases for making the appeal should be clearly defined by law.

G. Hearings before the administrative courts should be made as simple and inexpensive as possible. The procedure and rules of evidence should be simple, yet effective in protecting the individual. In general, they should be much the same before all lower administrative tribunals.

H. In all cases an appeal should lie to a higher administrative court, on questions of law alone.

I. So far as possible, the decisions of administrative courts should be enforced by further administrative action. If necessary, the administrative tribunals should have the power of enforcing their own decisions. There should be no appeal to the judicial courts for enforcement.

J. The decisions of administrative authorities should be made in executory form, thus laying the basis for proper action by the lower administrative courts. The decisions of the lower administrative courts should not only be published, but should contain reasons and arguments showing how each conclusion was reached. This not only gives the parties concerned the satisfaction of knowing the basis of the decisions, but also accomplishes two other desirable objects: it helps to develop a comprehensive system of administrative law and jurisprudence, and it assists the higher administrative courts in making their decisions.

No feature of the system here outlined is altogether new. Each has been tested long and successfully in several modern governments; and practically all, though in no systematic pattern, have been used in some government agency or other in this country. The changes which are suggested have all been considered from the standpoint of their suitability to our own institutions, and of the possibility of avoiding legal and constitutional difficulties in introducing them. It is the firm conviction of the authors that if administrative legislation, regular administrative action, and administrative adjudication were organized along the lines of the system explained above, the present confusion could be almost entirely abolished, and both the government and the individual citizen would receive great and definite benefits.

INDEX

291

only adjudicating and controlling authorities,
concurrent jurisdiction of ordinary courts, 251
faulty constitutional position, 251
final review by writs of certiorari, 251, 252
Disadvantages of regular authorities acting as administrative tribunals,
blindness to individual rights, 243, 244
combination of fact-finding, prosecuting, and judging, 241, 242
combination of quasi-legislative and quasi-judicial functions prevents adequate control, 238-41
complex and questionable criteria, 249, 250
decisions may contain provisions legislative in nature, 237, 238
different type of thinking in administration from that in adjudication, 244, 245
lack of check upon sub-legislative activities, 247, 249
public may not know real basis for decisions, 246, 247
regulatory authorities may not act as unified body, 245, 246
remedies and controls inadequate, 250
uncertainty and inconsistency, 242, 243
Discretion, 36 ff.
Distinctions between administrative and ordinary adjudication, according to,
formality, 103-04
nature of action taken after fact-finding, 102-03
nature of authority, 101-02
subject matter, 100-01

Effect of administrative adjudication upon remedies, 15
Effect of administrative legislation and adjudication upon,
government organization, 12, 13
legal system, 12
procedures and rules of evidence, 14-15
relationship between the administration and the courts, 13, 14
relationship between various government authorities, 13
Effect of increase of government business upon judicial and quasi-judicial functions, 4
Effect of increase of government functions upon administration, 3
Effect of type of control upon administrative legislation and adjudication, 7
Enforcement methods,
administrative enforcement, 168, 169
application to court, 172
boycott, 174
dependent upon the making of an appropriation, 170
making decisions final with right of appeal, 174
placing the burden of enforcement on authority, 170 ff.
placing penalties on those who disregard orders, 173, 174
self-executing, 168-69
through aid of public prosecuting authorities, 172, 173
use of mandamus, 174
Examples of administrative adjudication, 93 ff.
Executive as a sub-legislative authority, 66 ff., 71
Extent of administrative legislation and adjudication, 9 ff.

Faults of existing administrative adjudication. *See under* Disadvantages

PUBLICATIONS OF THE BROOKINGS INSTITUTION*

INSTITUTE FOR GOVERNMENT RESEARCH SERIES

Studies in Administration

(1.) THE SYSTEM OF FINANCIAL ADMINISTRATION OF GREAT BRITAIN.
> By W. F. Willoughby, W. W. Willoughby, and S. M. Lindsay. 362 pp. 1917. $3.

(2.) THE BUDGET: A TRANSLATION.
> By René Stourm. 619 pp. 1917. $4.

(3.) THE PROBLEM OF A NATIONAL BUDGET.
> By W. F. Willoughby. Out of print.

(4.) THE MOVEMENT FOR BUDGETARY REFORM IN THE STATES.
> By W. F. Willoughby. 254 pp. 1918. $3.

(5.) THE CANADIAN BUDGETARY SYSTEM.
> By H. C. Villard and W. W. Willoughby. 379 pp. 1918. $3.

(6.) ORGANIZED EFFORTS FOR THE IMPROVEMENT OF METHODS OF ADMINISTRATION IN THE UNITED STATES.
> By Gustavus A. Weber. 391 pp. 1919. $3.

(7.) TEACHERS' PENSION SYSTEMS IN THE UNITED STATES.
> By Paul Studensky. 460 pp. 1920. $3.

(8.) THE FEDERAL SERVICE: A STUDY OF THE SYSTEM OF PERSONNEL ADMINISTRATION OF THE UNITED STATES GOVERNMENT.
> By Lewis Mayers. 607 pp. 1922. $5.

(9.) THE REORGANIZATION OF THE ADMINISTRATIVE BRANCH OF THE NATIONAL GOVERNMENT.
> By W. F. Willoughby. Out of print.

(10.) THE DEVELOPMENT OF NATIONAL ADMINISTRATIVE ORGANIZATION IN THE UNITED STATES.
> By Lloyd M. Short. 514 pp. 1923. $5.

(11.) THE STATISTICAL WORK OF THE NATIONAL GOVERNMENT.
> By Laurence F. Schmeckebier. 574 pp. 1925. $5.

* The parentheses indicate that the volume itself does not carry the number since it was given subsequent to publication.

LIST OF PUBLICATIONS

(12.) MANUAL OF ACCOUNTING AND REPORTING FOR THE OPERATING SERVICES OF THE NATIONAL GOVERNMENT.
By Henry P. Seidemann. 399 pp. 1926. $5.

(13.) THE NATIONAL GOVERNMENT AND PUBLIC HEALTH.
By James A. Tobey. 423 pp. 1926. $3.

(14.) THE NATIONAL BUDGET SYSTEM, WITH SUGGESTIONS FOR ITS IMPROVEMENT.
By W. F. Willoughby. 343 pp. 1927. $3.

(15.) THE DEPARTMENT OF JUSTICE OF THE UNITED STATES.
By Albert Langeluttig. 318 pp. 1927. $3.

(16.) THE LEGAL STATUS AND FUNCTIONS OF THE GENERAL ACCOUNTING OFFICE.
By W. F. Willoughby. 720 pp. 1927. $.

(17.) THE PROBLEM OF INDIAN ADMINISTRATION.
By Lewis Meriam and Associates. 872 pp. 1928. $5.

(18.) THE DISTRICT OF COLUMBIA: ITS GOVERNMENT AND ADMINISTRATION.
By Laurence F. Schmeckebier. 943 pp. 1928. $5.

(19.) THE DEVELOPMENT OF GOVERNMENTAL FOREST CONTROL IN THE UNITED STATES.
By Jenks Cameron. 471 pp. 1928. $3.

(20.) MANUAL OF ACCOUNTING, REPORTING, AND BUSINESS PROCEDURE FOR THE TERRITORIAL GOVERNMENT OF HAWAII.
By Henry P. Seidemann. 570 pp. 1928. $5.

(21.) THE GOVERNMENT AND ADMINISTRATION OF GERMANY.
By Frederick F. Blachly and Miriam E. Oatman. 770 pp. 1928. $5.

(22.) GROUP REPRESENTATION BEFORE CONGRESS.
By E. Pendleton Herring. Out of print.

(23.) REGISTRATION OF VOTERS IN THE UNITED STATES.
By Joseph P. Harris. 390 pp. 1929. $3.

(24.) THE GOVERNMENT AND ADMINISTRATION OF THE DISTRICT OF COLUMBIA: SUGGESTIONS FOR CHANGE.
By Laurence F. Schmeckebier and W. F. Willoughby. 187 pp. 1929. $2.

LIST OF PUBLICATIONS

8. Steamboat-Inspection Service. 130 pp. 1922. $1.
9. Weather Bureau. 87 pp. 1922. $1.
10. Public Health Service. 298 pp. 1923. $2.
11. National Park Service. 172 pp. 1922. $1.
12. Employees' Compensation Commission. 86 pp. 1922. $1.
13. General Land Office. 224 pp. 1923. $1.50.
14. Bureau of Education. 157 pp. 1923. $1.
15. Bureau of Navigation. 124 pp. 1923. $1.
16. Coast and Geodetic Survey. 107 pp. 1923. $1.
17. Federal Power Commission. 126 pp. 1923. Out of print.
18. Interstate Commerce Commission. 169 pp. 1923. Out of print.
19. Railroad Labor Board. 83 pp. 1923. $1.
20. Division of Conciliation. 37 pp. 1923. $1.
21. Children's Bureau. 83 pp. 1925. $1.
22. Women's Bureau. 31 pp. 1923. $1.
23. Office of the Supervising Architect. 138 pp. 1923. $1.
24. Bureau of Pensions. 111 pp. 1923. $1.
25. Bureau of Internal Revenue. 270 pp. 1923. $1.50.
26. Bureau of Public Roads. 123 pp. 1923. $1.
27. Office of the Chief of Engineers. 166 pp. 1923. $1.
28. United States Employment Service. 130 pp. 1923. $1.
29. Bureau of Foreign and Domestic Commerce. 180 pp. 1924. $1.
30. Bureau of Immigration. 247 pp. 1924. $1.50.
31. Patent Office. 127 pp. 1924. Out of print.
32. Office of Experiment Stations. 178 pp. 1924. $1.
33. Customs Service. 191 pp. 1924. Out of print.
34. Federal Farm Loan Bureau. 160 pp. 1924. $1.
35. Bureau of Standards. 299 pp. 1925. $2.
36. Government Printing Office. 143 pp. 1925. $1.
37. Bureau of the Mint. 90 pp. 1926. $1.
38. Office of the Comptroller of the Currency. 84 pp. 1926. $1.
39. Naval Observatory. 101 pp. 1926. $1.
40. Lighthouse Service. 158 pp. 1926. $1.
41. Bureau of Animal Industry. 190 pp. 1927. $1.50.
42. Hydrographic Office. 112 pp. 1926. $1.
43. Bureau of Naturalization. 108 pp. 1926. $1.
44. Panama Canal. 413 pp. 1927. $2.50.
45. Medical Department of the Army. 161 pp. 1927. $1.50.

LIST OF PUBLICATIONS

46. General Accounting Office. 215 pp. 1927. $1.50.
47. Bureau of Plant Industry. 121 pp. 1927. $1.
48. Office of Indian Affairs. 591 pp. 1927. $3.
49. United States Civil Service Commission. 153 pp. 1928. $1.50.
50. Food, Drug and Insecticide Administration. 134 pp. 1928. $1.50.
51. Coast Guard. 265 pp. 1929. $1.50.
52. Bureau of Chemistry and Soils. 218 pp. 1928. $1.50.
53. Bureau of the Census. 224 pp. 1929. $1.50.
54. Bureau of Biological Survey. 339 pp. 1929. $2.
55. Bureau of Dairy Industry. 74 pp. 1929. $1.50.
56. Bureau of Engraving and Printing. 111 pp. 1929. $1.50.
57. Bureau of Prohibition. 333 pp. 1929. $2.
58. Forest Service. 268 pp. 1930. $2.
59. Plant Quarantine and Control Administration. 198 pp. 1930. $1.50.
60. Bureau of Entomology. 177 pp. 1930. $1.50.
61. Aeronautics Branch: Department of Commerce. 147 pp. 1930. $1.50.
62. Bureau of Home Economics. 95 pp. 1930. $1.50.
63. United States Shipping Board. 338 pp. 1931. $2.50.
64. The Personnel Classification Board. 160 pp. 1931. $1.50.
65. The Federal Radio Commission. 159 pp. 1932. $1.50.
66. The Veterans' Administration, 490 pp. 1934. $2.50.

INSTITUTE OF ECONOMIC SERIES

(1.) GERMANY'S CAPACITY TO PAY.
By Harold G. Moulton and Constantine E. McGuire. 384 pp. 1923. $2.50.
(2.) RUSSIAN DEBTS AND RUSSIAN RECONSTRUCTION.
By Leo Pasvolsky and Harold G. Moulton. 247 pp. 1924. $2.50.
(3.) MAKING THE TARIFF IN THE UNITED STATES.
By Thomas Walker Page. 281 pp. 1924. $3.
(4.) AMERICAN AGRICULTURE AND THE EUROPEAN MARKET.
By Edwin G. Nourse. 333 pp. 1924. $2.50.

LIST OF PUBLICATIONS

LIST OF PUBLICATIONS

LIST OF PUBLICATIONS

LIST OF PUBLICATIONS

51. THE BRITISH ATTACK ON UNEMPLOYMENT.
   By Isador Lubin and A. C. C. Hill, Jr. (In press.)
52. CURRENT MONETARY ISSUES.
   By Leo Pasvolsky. 192 pp. 1933. $1.50.
53. THE ECONOMICS OF FREE DEALS: WITH SUGGESTIONS
   FOR CODE-MAKING UNDER THE NRA.
   By Leverett S. Lyon. 228 pp. 1933. $1.50.
54. THE ABC OF THE NRA.
   By Charles L. Dearing, Paul T. Homan, Lewis L.
   Lorwin, and Leverett S. Lyon. 185 pp. 1934.
   $1.50.
55. AMERICA'S CAPACITY TO PRODUCE.
   By Edwin G. Nourse and Associates. 618 pp. 1934.
   $3.50.
56. AMERICA'S CAPACITY TO CONSUME.
   By Maurice Leven, Harold G. Moulton, and Clark
   Warburton. 272 pp. 1934. $3.
57. THE HOUSING PROGRAM OF THE CITY OF VIENNA.
   By Charles O. Hardy and Robert R. Kuczynski. 143
   pp. 1934. $2.

MISCELLANEOUS SERIES

PORTO RICO AND ITS PROBLEMS.
   By Victor S. Clark and Associates. Out of print.
STEPHEN J. FIELD: CRAFTSMAN OF THE LAW.
   By Carl Brent Swisher. 473 pp. 1930. $4.
THE SPIRIT OF '76 AND OTHER ESSAYS.
   By Carl Becker, J. M. Clark, and William E. Dodd. 135 pp.
   1927. $1.50.
ESSAYS ON RESEARCH IN THE SOCIAL SCIENCES.
   By W. F. G. Swann and others. 194 pp. 1931. $2.
THE SOCIETY OF NATIONS: ITS ORGANIZATION AND CONSTI-
   TUTIONAL DEVELOPMENT.
   By Felix Morley. 678 pp. 1932. $3.50.
THE AMERICAN TRANSPORTATION PROBLEM.
   By Harold G. Moulton and Associates. 895 pp. 1933. $3.
THE ECONOMICS OF AIR MAIL TRANSPORTATION.
   By Paul T. David. 235 pp. 1934. $2.
TREND ANALYSIS OF STATISTICS: THEORY AND TECHNIQUE.
   By Max Sasuly. (In press.)

LIST OF PUBLICATIONS

PAMPHLETS

No. 1. RECENT GROWTH OF THE ELECTRIC LIGHT AND POWER INDUSTRY.
By Charles O. Hardy. 53 pp. 1929. 50 cents.

No. 2. FIRST MORTGAGES IN URBAN REAL ESTATE FINANCE.
By John H. Gray and George W. Terborgh. 69 pp. 1929. 50 cents.

No. 3. THE ABSORPTION OF THE UNEMPLOYED BY AMERICAN INDUSTRY.
By Isador Lubin. 36 pp. 1929. 50 cents.

No. 4. SOME TRENDS IN THE MARKETING OF CANNED FOODS.
By Leverett S. Lyon. 57 pp. 1929. 50 cents.

No. 5. THE FECUNDITY OF NATIVE AND FOREIGN-BORN WOMEN IN NEW ENGLAND.
By Joseph J. Spengler. 63 pp. 1930. 50 cents.

No. 6. SOURCES OF COAL AND TYPES OF STOKERS AND BURNERS USED BY ELECTRIC UTILITY POWER PLANTS.
By William H. Young. 83 pp. 1930. 50 cents.

No. 7. FEDERAL SERVICES TO MUNICIPAL GOVERNMENTS.
By Paul V. Betters. 100 pp. 1931. 50 cents.

No. 8. REORGANIZATION OF THE FINANCIAL ADMINISTRATION OF THE DOMINICAN REPUBLIC.
By Taylor G. Addison. 105 pp. 1931. 50 cents.

No. 9. ADVISORY ECONOMIC COUNCILS.
By Lewis L. Lorwin. 84 pp. 1931. 50 cents.

No. 10. UNEMPLOYMENT INSURANCE IN AUSTRIA.
By Mollie Ray Carroll. 52 pp. 1932. 50 cents.

No. 11. PRICE-CONTROL DEVICES IN NRA CODES.
By George Terborgh. 45 pp. 1934. 50 cents.

No. 12. CORN AND HOGS UNDER THE AGRICULTURAL ADJUSTMENT ACT: DEVELOPMENTS UP TO MARCH 1934.
By D. A. FitzGerald. 107 pp. 1934. 50 cents.

No. 13. DAIRY PRODUCTS UNDER THE AGRICULTURAL ADJUSTMENT ACT: DEVELOPMENTS UP TO MARCH 1934.
By F. F. Lininger. 99 pp. 1934. 50 cents.

No. 14. WHEAT UNDER THE AGRICULTURAL ADJUSTMENT ACT: DEVELOPMENTS UP TO JUNE 1934.
By Sherman Johnson. 103 pp. 1934. 50 cents.

No. 15. COTTON UNDER THE AGRICULTURAL ADJUSTMENT ACT: DEVELOPMENTS UP TO JULY 1934.
By Henry I. Richards. 133 pp. 1934. 50 cents.